TRAVELERS' TALES

TUSCANY

TRUE STORIES

TRAVELERS' TALES

TUSCANY

TRUE STORIES

Edited by

JAMES O'REILLY AND

TARA AUSTEN WEAVER

TRAVELERS' TALES

SAN FRANCISCO

Cover design: Michele Wetherbee
Interior design: Kathryn Heflin and Susan Bailey
Cover photograph: © FPG International
Illustrations: courtesy of San Francisco Public Library archives
Maps: Keith Granger
Page layout: Cynthia Lamb, using the fonts Bembo and Remedy

Distributed by: Publishers Group West, 1700 Fourth Street, Berkeley, California
94710.

Library of Congress Cataloguing-in-Publication Data

Travelers' Tales Tuscany: true stories / edited by James O'Reilly and Tara
Austen Weaver.
    p. cm.
  Includes bibliographical references and index.
  ISBN 1-885211-68-6
    1. Tuscany (Italy)—Description and travel. I. O'Reilly, James, 1953– II.
Weaver, Tara Austen.

DG734.23.T73 2001
945'.5—dc21   2001034699

First Edition
Printed in the United States
10 9 8 7 6 5 4 3 2 1

The sunshine had the density of gold-leaf; we seemed to be driving through the landscape of a missal.

—EDITH WHARTON, in Tuscany

Table of Contents

Part Two
SOME THINGS TO DO

Part Three
GOING YOUR OWN WAY

Part Four
IN THE SHADOWS

Part Five
THE LAST WORD

Tuscany: An Introduction

WHEN YOU HAVE GROWN UP IN ITALY, HER LANDSCAPE IS THE map of your heart, a geography that is at once history and event. That stalwart and rocky boot, daring in its poise, has for millennia been encroached from every side, yet each time Italy stamped an indelible print on her invaders. Both brazen and vulnerable, Italy penetrates. Region by region, though, the shape of that mark differs. Italy is never one.

The part of Italy you have sprung from—or have made your home—tells the story of your passions and forbearance. Italians are fierce regionalists, unwilling to discount their differences. It is the foreigner who coalesces Italy into a continuous entity. Italy herself could not manage to unite until 1861—making her one of the last European countries to unify. The Italian is likely to know (and name) himself differently if his childhood summer days were drawn on Tuscany's Tyrrhenian coast or the Emilian north Adriatic. The former, a cliff- struck coast, plunging and rocky; the latter, a ruler-flat, sea-lake of calm, horizonless sand. One, a lesson in beauty born of tectonic struggle; the other, erosion's final offering of endless ease. These territories are lessons in life, lessons in one's dreams and designs within a landscape—that has become oneself.

So what is this region—of the heart, in the heart of Italy—of Tuscany? It is the one region Tuscans *and* travelers single out. Ask anyone about Italy; he can usually name cities and Roman monuments with alacrity, but regions? You must mean Tuscany.

The writers in this volume awaken in us the discovery that Tuscany herself is multiple. In fact, her geographic compilation—somehow everything in one—is of great pride to Tuscans. Tuscany is the sculpted Tyrrhenian coastline and a sprinkling forth of sun-swept islands: Elba, Giglio, Gorgona, Capraia. She is mountain-sides of Carrara, home to the purest white marble in the world; choose Michelangelo as testimony. South, however, her Maremma—old haunt of the enigmatic Etruscans—festered with unapproach-able malarial swamps well into the 1950s. Not far away, in opti-mistic opposition, thermal springs bubble. Since the Roman Empire, they have misted hill and vale with the call of their healing. Not only a landscape, Tuscany raised the cities of Pisa, Siena, and Florence. Their competitive patronages caused an artistic furor, spawning a Renaissance that changed the face of the Western world. Lucca, San Gimignano, and Viareggio are also hers. Surrounding these, rise the rolling hills of chestnut and oak woods, inhabited by wild boars (*chinghiale*) and buried truffles (*tartufi*). Where this wilderness ends, Tuscany's agriculture unfolds in a production of wine, olive oil, mustard, sunflower, and barley as glorious to the eye as it is fecund. A silver olive grove is shot through with vermilion fodder. Magenta poppies shake their un-ruly heads at the insistent, articulate, patterns of vintners.

This landscape of agriculture is what I awoke to the summer I turned fifteen. We were driving across Italy, east to west, taking in Tuscany. It was July and hot, in an *epoca* when air-conditioned cars were unheard of, and I, a teenager, practiced in the art of boredom, counted every minute of being stuck, sweating, in a car with adults. I lived in Italy, which meant Italy was no big deal. Except that Tus-cany sprung me out of my posed malaise; I never intended to be willing. The hills were a roiling of blue-green, switching to fields of ochre, rising to gold leaves. Vineyards and orchards marched in columns that faded downhill, and rose again kilometers away. I stuck my face out the window and stayed in position for hours. As the Australian Gary Topping says of his encounter with Tuscany: "Even after years of traveling the world, I never knew...that scenery could make me cry."

It is Tuscany's scenery, her feast for the eyes which becomes an equivalent feast for the body, that is most reported in the travel media, thus perhaps most familiar. Open *Travel & Leisure* or *Condé Nast Traveler* to glorious pictures of restored stone farmhouses with pools. Tuscany *is* a laden table set before a terraced view. Tuscany is silence amidst an infinity of sage hills. Here you may learn the art of making chicken *involtini* or spinach *gnocchi* from a modern daughter of the venerable deMedici, as Stephen Hall did. Here you could lose your way on the unmarked web of countryside *strade bianche*, as did Susan Storm—frightened until she stopped for directions and found herself joining a local Tuscan meal. In fair or foul weather, there's nothing wrong with falling in love with the land that feeds you. After all, history teaches us that no less than Pythagoras, Cicero, Plutarch and Pliny celebrated Tuscany's truffles. David Yeadon reminds us that Julius Caesar favored his retreat near Lucca. What nourished him here as he labored to formalize the Empire's structure? The Tuscan stone? The russet earth? The violet grapes? What lives here must harken to something central or dearly hopeful in us. Frances Mayes' book *Under the Tuscan Sun*, about restoring her villa outside Cortona, became an international bestseller, as has her sequel *Bella Tuscany*. Why do we find ourselves here?

There are historical roots. Since Renaissance times, Tuscany has been an area of solid landowners, small and large. The local stone and brick farmhouses, known as *case coloniche*, have a staple structure: stables and food stores on the ground floor and lodgings overhead on the second floor. Standard are their large inelegant ceiling beams, wide functional marble sinks, and narrow bathrooms. These farms and fields were handed down and subdivided or expanded for over six hundred years. It was primarily World War II, with its wake of industrialization, that dramatically changed the face of a country that had always been largely agricultural. As work, and even capital investment opportunities, grew many Tuscans abandoned their old farmhouses, leaving them to the ravages of the seasons.

The scene was ripe. For centuries now, British and American readers had been savoring Tuscany through literature and the visual arts. From John Milton, Lord Byron, Percy Shelley, the Trollopes, John Ruskin, Henry James, George Eliot, Elizabeth Barrett Browning, Nathaniel Hawthorne, Edith Wharton, Virginia Woolf, Elizabeth von Armin, E. M Forster, and D. H. Lawrence (this being the *short* list), Tuscany was an inherited image, the territory of the cultured mind. When, on hilltops and hillsides, disregarded farm properties went up for sale—with olive orchards, vineyards, and plum trees tossed in—the low asking prices far underestimated the vast dreams they would enclose. Decades later—and for those who cannot or do not want to buy—the dream can be rented. Those who savor it, still find it fresh.

And few stay tucked solely in Tuscany's homes in the hills. "There's something about entering a city for the first time through the pages of a book. The experience...becomes magnified—" writes Lucy McCauley about exploring Florence with Forster's *A Room With a View* in hand. Linda Watanabe McFerrin plunges into Florence, instead, by absorbing lines from Dante's *Paradise Lost*. And why not? Dante Alighieri (1265-1321) was schooled by the gentlemen-poets of the nearby Tuscan towns before he rose to become Italy's most famous poet. It is an updated version of his vernacular Italian that has earned Tuscan Italian the title of "purest" Italian. Of course, in other regions, this qualification is proudly disputed. The Tuscans wink, safe in their claim.

Whether the art leads to experience, or the experience of Tuscany awakens us to new art, in her cities one contends with the force of creativity. For centuries, Tuscany was an assembly of city-states warring for land, commercial power, *and* artists. Woolen textiles, the growth of banking, fine printing, tooled leather, necessary and luxury foodstuffs; these fueled the economies of Siena, Pisa, Florence and Lucca, but emergent capitalism is the least of what we remember. In her book *Landscape in Italy*, Lisa St Aubin de Teran bemuses: "Christ may have stopped at Eboli...but he was born in Tuscany and lived and died there. Most...great Renaissance paintings, the pictorial Bible of the world, were painted there, either on the spot, or by Tuscan painters who remembered their own homeland." Vibrant guilds and visionary leaders, religious or worldly, spawned an artistic fervor that clasped, not only Christ, but his mother, Mary, the saints, angels, patrons, and biblical cohorts, creating a spiritual history, almost entirely Tuscan. Those who think God is Tuscan have some justification.

What a pictorial legacy. The burgeoning of perspective, soft tonalities and shades of color, the humanity to be found in face, limb and fabric—these glowed, shifted, transformed, in the hands of Giotto, Fra Lippi, Duccio, Botticelli, Fra Angelico, Ghiberti, Brunelleschi, Donatello, Piero della Francesca, Uccello and others. In these pages, we too stand before their classic works, listening to Jason Epstein, Barbara Grizzuti-Harrison, Jan Morris or William Weaver remind us of what it is to enter life through a painting or a bronze, transfixed. The journey into Tuscany is a journey into and out of time; it *is* the past, it *is* the present.

For some writers in this collection, this landscape is neither a territory to be acquired, nor an art drawn by human hand; it is, instead, a bodily journey. Much as for St. Francis of Assisi, it is the pilgrimage that counts, and the small creatures that may harken to one on his way. Hikers, trekkers, and bikers uncover the roads least traveled in Tuscany. In fact, here Heidi Schuessler unveils a venerable history of Tuscan cowboys, or *butteri*. Is this why horse-riding trips through Tuscany are growing in number? And what about Siena's Palio? That mad, nearly one thousand-year-old horse race, in the center of this modern city. The horses, representing *contrade*, almost *are* the city. Manfredi Piccolomini describes this with passion.

There are venerable travel writers' names here and new ones, not all of whom am I able to reference in this introduction. There are luscious wine estates, tending Sangiovese, Malvasia, Canaiolo, and Trebbiano grapes, which I leave unmentioned. Though, within these pages, you will find accounts of their *vendemmie*. I might have told you about my experience harvesting olives; wherein, one person to a gnarled tree, you clamber up to hand-strip limbs, knocking olives into red nets below. Standing back, the scene is like the line-up of a cast in a musical, or the display of characters from Italo Calvino's *Baron of the Trees*. In addition, some contend it is the quality of Tuscan light that contributed to the art of the Renaissance. Certainly poets have named it. Though I have not begun to exhaust the number of artists, Tuscan and foreign, who have laid claim to this landscape or its white-gold light.

Lastly, I am never able to forget, as is true for many an Allied soldier who, like William Zinsser, found himself here, got out alive, and lived to write about it—that these hills were raided and bombed, both when Italy was the enemy and when she had fallen away from the Axis triumvirate. Some ruins are attributable to those painful years. Hillside cemeteries columned in cypress trees record Italy's war losses. Too, some farmhouses rashly, bravely, hid and saved partisans and Jews. When Tuscany is not the landscape of man-made bloodshed, it is sometimes the land ravaged by floods. Still, to a traveler, this layering, tragic and victorious, is symphonic. Tuscany is resonant and complex. Grievous/resplendent, verdant/chalky, pure/invaded, invigorating/lucullan, stern/delectable, wild/cultivated, ancient/renovated.

To this Rome-grown girl, "Tuscany" was one of many Italian exports, each one unequal, or incomparable, to the other. In William Weaver's words; "...my Italian friends thought I was crazy.... Only a crazy American...would want to spend good money bringing water and electricity and a telephone to a near-ruin...." Tuscany's geography, of ruin and possibility, timeless and redemptive, is most specific. Her qualities are not true of all of Italy, though Tuscany lies at Italy's center. My Italian friends argue that there are subtle differences in the shape of Tuscan hills, immediately discernible when crossing to the next region. Perhaps. Tuscans are known for their pride, a slightly arrogant sense of entitlement that they represent the highest status of linguistic and scenic "Italian-ness." If the increasing numbers that flock to Tuscany means anything, they are right. But that's okay because the Romans know there is only one Rome, the Milanese mistrust what isn't Lombardian, and the Neapolitans are sure no one is cleverer than they.

My beloved *zia* used to say; *Tutto il mondo e' paese,* All the world is a town. This book reports that we have arrived from our cities and towns, from different spots on the globe, to travel down rivers, up hills, into the museums, out into the countryside to become transformed, ready to hang the memory and the flesh of Tuscany in our hearts.

—ANNE CALCAGNO
Chicago, Illinois

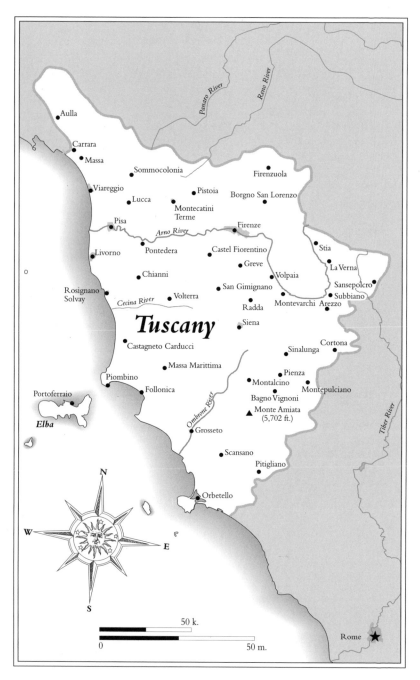

Aulla

Carrara
Massa

Sommocolonia

Viareggio
Lucca

Pistoia

Firenzuola

Borgno San Lorenzo

Montecatini
Terme

Pisa

Arno River

Firenze

Livorno

Pontedera

Castel Fiorentino

Stia

Chianni

Greve

La Verna

Rosignano
Solvay

Cecina River

Volterra

San Gimignano

Volpaia

Sansepolcro
Subbiano

Montevarchi Arezzo

Radda

Tuscany

Siena

Castagneto Carducci

Cortona

Sinalunga

Massa Marittima

Pienza

Piombino

Follonica

Ombrone River

Montalcino

Montepulciano

Bagno Vignoni

Portoferraio

▲ Monte Amiata
(5,702 ft.)

Elba

Grosseto

Scansano

Pitigliano

Orbetello

N

W

E

Tiber River

S

50 k.

0   50 m.

Rome ★

PART ONE

ESSENCE OF TUSCANY

FRANCES MAYES

* * *

Yearning for the Sun

Home is where the heart opens.

MY HOUSE FACES SOUTHEAST, TOWARD A ROAD LINED WITH cypress trees, toward the foothills of the Apennines, and toward Lake Trasimeno, where Hannibal defeated the Romans in 217 B.C. I am amazed at how often Hannibal comes up in daily conversations around here; previously I had not heard him mentioned since World History in eighth grade. Now I know the weather conditions the morning of the battle (foggy), the route and the number of elephants Hannibal took over the Alps on the way to Rome, even what the Roman soldiers wore as they were driven into the misty lake and drowned.

Because I grew up in the American South, where hardly a day goes by that the War Between the States is not mentioned, I am used to the past intruding on the present. But the past in Tuscany goes back far beyond the reach of my most indefatigable Georgia aunts: I am driving with a friend and she points out the villa of someone she knows, saying, "That's where Luca Signorelli died when he stepped backward on the scaffolding to get a better look at the fresco he was painting." She speaks as though recalling an unfortunate accident last year, not the fate of the Signorelli, who died in 1523.

I wonder if this is why I came here, why I instantly felt so at home in Tuscany when I have not a drop of Mediterranean blood. In the South of my childhood, every house contained a story; those who lived earlier seemed about to walk in the door at any moment. It is the same here, only the people of the Tuscan past stand against a mighty background of art, philosophy, history, and religion.

Since 1993 I have been a part-time resident of Cortona, which remains an essentially medieval hill town with layers and layers that peel back to pre-Etruscan times. Farmers still plow up in their furrows small bronze horses that Etruscan artisans made in the sixth century B.C. At the same time, the Tracy Chapman rock concert on a summer evening draws thousands to the parking area in front of the church where the incorruptible body of Saint Margaret of Cortona (folk rock pulsating in her bones?) has lain since the thirteenth century. The one-day photo service thrives in a dark twelfth century rabbit warren of a shop with a new glass front, and there I receive faxes from faraway California.

For me, buying a house in a foreign country was an audacious act. The end of my long marriage seemed to return me to the adventurer I was in my youth. When the smoke from the divorce cleared, I found myself with a full-time job, a daughter in college, a stash of stocks and bonds, and a new life to invent. I was in no hurry, but I had a clear desire to transform those static blue chips into something pleasurable—a house with land. I could hear the echo of my grandfather's voice, "Buy land, they aren't making it anymore."

In my (scary) freedom, I began to vacation in Italy. Since I teach in a university, I have three months off. For five summers I rented farmhouses all over Tuscany. I tried Cortona, then Montisi, Florence, Quercegrossa, Rignano sull'Arno, Volterra, Siena, Vicchio—two weeks here, a month there. Always I was drawn back to Cortona, to my first impressions of old houses tawny as loaves of bread and the bells of thirty-odd churches ringing over the fields. I thought that here I would begin to write poems, not in the usual way, on a legal pad or a laptop, but with a pen and real ink in one of those handmade, marbled-paperbound books, a big one, with thick, creamy pages.

That fifth summer I began to look seriously for a place to buy. I was no longer amused by the caprices of rented houses, however charming: sagging beds, no hot water, bats roosting in the fireplace, a caretaker who, uninvited, flies through the rooms shrieking and banging shutters whenever it rains. Because I was by then establishing a relationship that seemed permanent, the quest for a house was linked to whatever patterns Ed [my husband-to-be] and I would create in the future. He shares my passion for Italy and also the university boon of free summers.

My daughter, Ed, and friends who came to visit drove with the agent and me over back roads that turned into paths, participated in discussions about how cow mangers could be turned into banquettes, cooled my enthusiasm for one enchanting place that had no access road at all and a family of blacksnakes guarding the threshold. We found several houses I wanted, but Tuscans hate to part with property so owners often changed their minds. One ancient contessa

---

Dreaming through the noble Tuscan landscape, the terraced hills crowned by churches and towers and blessed by vineyards, and everything—stone houses, silver-green olive trees, blue-green undulating fields, triangles and bowls of wheat-green land bordered by dark exclamatory cypresses and shaded by beneficent umbrella pines—everything bathed in the austere, uncompromising Tuscan light, I feel that life is altogether bounteous and good, lovable, manageable, sweet.

This landscape is unchanged since the nineteenth century, one of my trainmates remarks (and indeed it is a landscape Victorians loved); but because so many Florentine painters set Christ among the cypress groves, Mary among the olive trees, it seems centuries older; a dream of Bethlehem.

—Barbara Grizzuti Harrison,
Italian Days

cried to think of selling, doubled her price, and seemed cheered when we walked away.

By the time I saw my house, I had given up. I was leaving in two days, had thanked the local agent, and said good-bye. The next morning I ran into him in the piazza. "I just saw someone who might be interested in selling a house," he greeted me.

Outside town, he took the winding road that climbs around to the other side of the hill Cortona is built on. He turned onto a *strada bianca,* a road white with pebbles, and after a kilometer pulled into a sloping driveway. I caught a glimpse of a shrine with a ceramic saint and then looked up at a tall apricot-colored house with green shutters and tumbles of overgrown bushes and briars. I was silent as we drove up. There was a lovely wrought-iron fanlight over the door. The walls were as thick as my arm is long. Old glass in the windows wavered. I scuffed through silty dust and saw smooth terra-cotta floors in perfect condition. He showed me two bathrooms, rough but functioning bathrooms—after all the houses I had seen with no water, much less plumbing. No one had lived in the house for thirty years, and its five acres seemed like an enchanted garden rampant with roses and blackberries. Ivy twisted into trees and ran over fallen stone walls.

The agent shielded his eyes and surveyed the land. *"Molto lavoro,"* he pronounced, much work.

"It's unbelievably romantic," I answered. I already envisioned myself snipping sun-warmed herbs into a basket, setting a long table with a checked cloth under the linden trees, Ed roasting boar in the big fireplace. I wanted to hang my summer clothes in an armoire and arrange my books under a window with a view of the winding row of cypresses beside the road, each one planted for a boy who died in World War I. After weeks of looking at ruins with collapsed roofs or at tasteless modernizations, after miles of dusty roads, this house seemed to have been waiting all along.

The Tuscan sunlight pouring into every room warmed me. There is something especially beneficent about the Italian sun; it seems to seep farther in, clarifying the mind. I felt renewed, excited, and calmly right, and I suppose this is part of what it feels like to be at home.

In America I have bought and sold a few houses—loading up the car with the blue-and-white Wedgwood, the cat, and the ficus for the drive across town or across the country to the next doorway where a new key would fit. Choices were always practical, bound to graduate schools or jobs. But this time the new door's iron key weighed half a pound and the doorway was 7,000 miles from home. The legal language and the baroque arrangements of buying baffled me. Currency rates were falling. My broker was selling my life savings and chiding me about *la dolce vita*. But years later I still feel stunned by my good luck, although I can also wake up thinking, *What on earth have you done and why, when you could have had a cottage right here on the California coast where you would buzz up for the weekend?*

One San Francisco August, I had looked for idyllic cottages and had even made an offer on a log house on the foggy Mendocino coast. I was instructed by how relieved I felt when the offer was turned down. I already knew what to expect from California, and from my home state of Georgia, which I also considered. I was running on instinct, and instinct said time for a new kind of home. Time for the unknown. Time to answer the question Dante faced in *The Divine Comedy*: What now to do in order to grow?

My little villa made of enormous stones perches on a terraced hillside covered with olive trees. Close to the house some intelligent soul planted fruit and nut trees—apricot, fig, plum, apple, hazelnut, almond, and many kinds of pears that bear in sequence. From summer through late fall I find pears to pick and a reason to stock the kitchen with the local Gorgonzola, the perfect accompaniment.

A neighbor said, "Your house is only a couple of hundred years old—mine is a thousand." He's right, the house is not old by local standards. It is not the classic stone farmhouse called *casa colonica*, nor is it a real villa. Although there are fourteen rooms, none have the ample proportions of a house of the nobility. It might have been the country place of some genial Cortona *parvenu* who brought his family here when July heat struck the stones of the town. The symmetrical house rises three stories with a fanciful iron balcony on the second floor above a double front door. From it I train hanging nasturtiums, but I can imagine someone, sometime stepping out to hear a lover sing "Ecco Maggio," or some equally corny popular song.

I bought the place from a doctor, who had recently bought it from five ancient sisters of Perugia. The doctor thought to make it a summer house, then changed his mind (turning a great profit, no doubt). I never think of him because he never lived here, but I often think of the five sisters. They must have been girls here; I can see them simultaneously pushing open the shutters of their five bedrooms and leaning out in their white nightgowns. This is the kind of fancy the house inspires. Why? Because it is a dream house. Not a dream house that has a perfect kitchen and ideal floor plan—I don't think dream houses have albino scorpions in the bidet—but it resembles a house from a dream, one where you discover a room you did not know existed and in it a dry plant bursts into full bloom. Oddly, everyone who visits comes downstairs to breakfast the first morning and says, "I had the strangest dream." Here I have a recurrent dream of swimming without effort in a clear green river, totally at home in the water, buoyantly carried downstream.

Reality is just as remarkable. I am dazzled by the remains of a Roman road at the edge of my property. I follow that stony path through the poppies into Cortona for espresso. I am dazzled by the cistern near the well. When I shine a flashlight into it, I see a brick archway underground. The caretaker at the Medici fortress on top of the hill claims that an underground escape route runs from the fortress all the way down to the lake. He shrugs. "Possibly your cistern was part of the passageway." How casual the Italians are about such things; that one is allowed to own something so ancient amazes me.

I am still learning to be casual about far more everyday experiences. Even the roof is extraordinary. I climb up the terraced hill and look down on the old tiles, formed over someone's knee and now alive with lacy gray moss. What else? The deeply satisfying tilt of the demijohn as I draw off some of my own olive oil for tonight's salad, oil from olives we picked and had pressed at a local mill. Also the thick, cool marble kitchen counters where the pizza dough never sticks, the small owl that lights on a windowsill and looks in, the straight stone stairs with a wrought-iron railing that kept some smith busy an entire winter.

Ed stripped and waxed each room's chestnut beams—some genius had slathered all of them with a sticky mud-colored varnish—and all the rooms are newly whitewashed. In one bedroom, a friend painted blue domes over the windows and filled them with Giotto-like gold stars. Walls are bare, except for a few of my daughter's paintings; tabletops are bare; casement windows are bare except for their sets of solid and louvered shutters. This house is now ready for long afternoons of reading or baking or putting up plum preserves—once we prune the olives and reset the stone terrace walls.

At least once a day I go out on the second-floor terrace and

It isn't necessarily the great and famous beauty spots we fall in love with. As with people, so with places: Love is unforeseen, and we can all find ourselves affectionately attached to the minor and the less obvious. I do not have an art historian's response to places. I can discern and admire a late-Renaissance gate, a medieval street, a Romanesque church or an Etruscan wall, but my first thoughts are for the warmth of the stone or for the clouds, when they look like a fifteenth-century painting with a chariot or a saint zooming up into them. I notice the light and shade on buildings grouped on a hilltop, the rich skin colors and the shapes of the people around me. I love to watch people, to sit in a *trattoria* listening in to their talk, imagining the rest.

—Muriel Spark, "Side Roads of Tuscany"

look up the hill. I can see a section of Etruscan wall that has the exact orientation of the house. If the wall had not securely kept vigil over this land for twenty-six centuries, I would be afraid it might tumble down on us: blocks of stone as big as the flat I rent, blocks on blocks. Etruscan walls form part of Cortona's town wall, and a couple of Etruscan gates and tombs remain scattered about.

From its position, historians think this wall is a remnant of a sun temple. The name of my house is Bramasole, from *bramare*, to yearn for, and *sole*, sun: something that yearns for the sun. I used to be surprised that everyone knew this house. *"Ah, Bramasole, si, una bella casa,"* they say. Delivery people, even from miles away, do not need a map. *"Si, si, la villa Bramasole,"* they say. They have picked cherries or nuts here during the thirty years of abandonment, or even earlier. They have gathered mistletoe from the almond trees at Christmas. Their grandmother picked figs every September.

One day in town, I spotted a postcard of the Etruscan wall said to be "in the locality of Bramasole." The owner of the shop, a life-long resident and neighbor who lives just under the wall, explained that our whole section of the hillside was once known as Bramasole, not just my house, and long before my house existed. Perhaps the name goes back to the ancient purpose of this site, to the lost temple where people like me came when they were yearning for the sun.

Frances Mayes has written for The New York Times, House Beautiful, *and* Food and Wine. *She is also a widely published poet and food and travel writer. She divides her time between Cortona, Italy, and San Francisco, where she teaches creative writing at San Francisco State University. Her books include* Under the Tuscan Sun *and* Bella Tuscany.

FERENC MÁTÉ

* * *

The Crush

He participates in the timeless dance
of the harvest.

WE LOOKED FORWARD TO OUR FIRST *VENDEMMIA* LIKE CHILDREN
look forward to Christmas. Old Italian movies flashed before our
eyes; the young picking grapes, brawny laughing men hauling
grapes in *bigonce* strapped over their shoulders, barefooted women
stomping grapes in great vats, the must running, and at day's end
the great meal—the long table under the arbor, laden with food
and wine, surrounded by happy, boisterous people.

Halfway through September the grapes had fully blushed, looking as dark as they could possibly get. When Paolucci and I sam-
pled his most southerly vineyard, the grapes tasted flavorful and
sweet to me, but he crushed a grape between his finger, rubbed
away the juice, then touched them against each other and said,
"Not enough sugar yet. My fingers don't stick." So the date for the
vendemmia was set for the first weekend in October.

We rose early. The low autumn sun slanted across the hills,
ground fog still huddled below us in the valley, and the crisp air
against our faces told us that summer was over. High on the ridge,
Paolucci's old orange tractor swung out of his yard, pulling the
battered metal cart, and behind him in a straggling line, already
talking at the top of their voices, directing, arguing, advising,

bantering, was the *vendemmia* party, of the entire Paolucci family plus in-laws. There was Franco's sister Anna, big voice, round face, either admonishing or laughing; and her husband, rotund Pasquino, who loved all women madly; and Rosanna's dad, gaunt with a constant cigarette; and Rosanna's quiet brother; and noisy Bazzotti.

The tractor slowed and the crowd bunched up on the ridge and argued about where to begin. It was astounding that with only three small vineyards, everyone had thought of a different place— high, low, flat or hill, shade or sun, this end or that—and they all talked at once. Then Candace said quietly but firmly that we better get started because I think it's going to rain. "How can it rain from a clear blue sky?" Bazzotti shrilled, and Nonna mumbled glaring at him, *"Più ignorante d'una gallina,"* Dumber than a hen, and Pasquino laughed in utter approval and scratched himself joyfully between his legs.

Then we began. Each of us took a *paniere*, the shape of the basket Little Red Riding Hood carried to grandmother's house, and we fanned out along two rows of vines, some of us on one side and some on the other, and finally, the *vendemmia* began.

The clusters of grapes were enormous and dense, peeking out from under fading leaves. I groped around for the stem of one near me, found it, and pulled. Nothing happened. I pulled again. The vine shook. Then I noticed Nonna standing beside me, holding out a pair of pruning shears, smiling kindly and saying, *"Sono più forte di noi."* They're stronger than us. It was only then that I heard the subtle clicking of everyone's pruning shears as they clipped the thick, woody stems of the grapes.

Paolicci swung his tractor and cart between the narrow rows, and everyone scrambled for his life. Once past us, he switched off the motor, clambered back into his cart, and stood among the pile of tall containers, the *bigonce*, which yawned empty awaiting the grapes. We snipped and cut and chatted away, kidding, bantering, yelling, and laughing—just like the movies—calling for someone to come and take away the loaded *paniere* and bring empty ones— *Madonna benedetta*—because where can we put the grapes, in our pockets? And Pasquino, waiting for his basket, dangled an enormous compact clump of grapes before his pants and called to his wife Anna, "What does this remind you of?"

She laughed loudly and shook her head. "Your dreams."

The vineyard rang with laughter.

We lugged the full baskets to the cart and hoisted them up to Paolucci who emptied them into the *bigonce,* scraping the last crushed grapes from the bottom with his fingers. The sticky nectar was dripping everywhere. It ran down our shears, and ran down the baskets and into our shoes. Bees buzzed. The wind rose; the sky to the south had darkened with clouds. By mid-morning the *bigonce* were full and tightly packed against each other, and we lashed them all together with a rope. The tractor lurched and we followed it up to the cantina.

Paolucci backed the tractor under the old roof that covered the brick *forno* and the cantina door, and we

I met a man from Tuscany some time ago.

"You are an artist?" I asked.

"Of course!" was his unequivocal reply.

"To what do you attribute all of this art—all of the great and wonderful talent that has come from Tuscany for hundreds and thousands of years?"

"I am Etruscan," he commented wryly, again as if I should know.

"Then that's it! It's an Etruscan legacy!"

"No," he said, head tilted slightly upward as he sauntered away. "It's in the soil—it's all in the soil." I grinned, imagining boxes of Florentine soil sold to tourists in the way packages of *"terra sancta"* are sold in the Holy Land.

Then last year I returned to Italy and again walked in wonder through the streets of Florence. Pausing at a souvenir stand, there among the t-shirts, I saw brightly packaged flower pots under a sign which read: "Pots of Tuscan soil, pre-seeded with Italian herbs." I bought a case.

—Jeanne Conte,
"Art and Those Etruscans"

lifted the beastly heavy *bigonce* to the ground. Then we crushed.
We didn't crush with our feet, but used great carved wooden
pestles. The grapes turned to must—unfermented wine. Then, to
reduce the weight, we poured half of the must into an empty
bigoncia, lugged the now half-full ones inside, and shoved them up
the old wooden ladder to Paolucci with cries of "Oh my back,"
"Oh my God," "Oh my hernia," and "How can you have a hernia when you have no balls?" Then we poured the crushed grapes
into the vats.

When the cart and the *bigonce* were all empty, we headed back
to the vineyard again. The black clouds had edged nearer and a
cold breeze blew that smelled and felt of rain.

"What do you say now, *meteorologo*?" Pasquino joshed Bazzotti.

"Not a drop of rain," Bazzotti snapped.

"At least hens lay eggs," Nonna said.

We began picking again. With a great satisfaction to pick those
grapes, great bursting clusters, many of which weighed well over a
kilo—a whole bottle of wine right there in my hands. Time
seemed to slow, and I was reminded of simpler days centuries past.
It was a labor that bound us to ancient tradition and to each other,
if for only a moment.

As we neared noon, the wind brought the fragrance of roast
meat and garlic, and onions stewing, from the direction of the
house. We accelerated the pace like horses that smelled the stable.
We felt the weights of the *bigonce* less as we wrestled them up the
ladder, just rushed those last loads, then went into the house to eat.
The church bells tolled midday. Dark clouds were sweeping toward
the San Biagio.

We feasted. Loudly. The bottles of wine seldom stopping, and
no one noticing that outside, the day had turned to night, until the
dreaded sound of hail clattered on the windows. Everyone fell
silent. The forks stopped, faces turned weary. A minute of pounding could turn the grapes to mush and they could mildew within
hours. We went to the door and windows. The hail sputtered then
stopped, but the day was darker than twilight. Across the valley a
great gray curtain obscured the hill and town.

"Cannetto's getting *martellato*," Paolucci said. Hammered.

"What do they care," Il Suocero said, "they have hail insurance."

"And you don't?" Candace asked.

"Ha. Us?" Rosanna said.

"We better go then," Candace said. "I think it's going to rain."

And even Bazzotti laughed in grudging admiration.

We picked like ones possessed. The shears flashed and Paolucci loaded like a demon. Across the valley you could hear the hail hiss, riddling the air. We threw grapes, we threw *paniere*, we ran from vine to vine, and the cart was almost loaded when the sky fell upon us. Rain. We threw a tarp over the *bigonce* to stop the rain from watering down the wine, put the *paniere* over our heads, and ran for the protection of the cantina. We huddled with the chickens and the pigeons and watched the rain make rivers in the barnyard.

The rain moved quickly on. A hard wind whipped the black clouds past the towers of the town. The wind blew through the night and dried the vines. In the morning, under a bright sun, we loaded up and waded out for the second day of the *vendemmia*, slipping and sinking in the mud. New reinforcements came, Carla's husband-to-be, and some cousins from out of town, and we picked and griped about the mud.

That night, after the last *bigoncia* was poured into the vat, and all the baskets and *bigonce* were washed and rinsed and turned upside down to dry, and the mud was hosed from the cart and our boots, we sat down in the long entry hall with all the tables end to end. We ate and laughed and drank—just like in the movies—stuffed ourselves with *crostini*, and then the pastas—*gnocchi*, potato dumplings with mushrooms and *pici* with chicken liver—then stuffed veal, and stewed tripe, and all kinds of roast birds and pork and rabbit, and Anna's specialty, snails—that she gathered in some secret woods—cooked in tomatoes, garlic, oil, and a bit of wine, and roast potatoes and finely chopped salad drenched in olive oil, then cheeses and then so many *dolci* that I couldn't count them all, with sparkling wine and *vinsanto*, until Pasquino, in his leather cap, leaned back against the wall, put his head down on his chest and began an uproarious, window-rattling snore. Bazzotti was so drunk he slurred; I was so drunk I spoke flawless Italian; and Paolucci was so drunk he went and got more wine.

That was our first *vendemmia*.

God bless the grape.

Ferenc Máté spent years roaming from Central America to Canada with his wife, Candace. He has now settled down in Tuscany, living in a stone farmhouse they call La Marinaia. He is the author of a number of sailboat-related books, as well as A Reasonable Life, *and* The Hills of Tuscany: A New Life in an Old Land, *from which this piece was excerpted.*

JAN MORRIS

✦ ✦ ✦

Dreaming Florence

Special places dwell within us
long after we've left.

THIS IS THE TIME OF YEAR, IN THE MELLOW OF THE FALL, WHEN WISE travelers go to Florence; but I don't need to make the journey myself because I see the city two or three times a month, whenever I drive out of England to my home in Wales.

It happens when I cross the low hills of the Herefordshire border and find before me a sheltered green bowl of meadowland, perfectly proportioned around the little river Cynon. In a trice, Florence appears there, like a hologram. Across the stream an ancient covered bridge swarms with people. A great dome rises above the fields, with a campanile beside it, and there are lines of palaces along the riverbanks, and clumps of dark poplars, and squares with statues in them. Everything is bustle and color, smoke curling from medieval chimneys, echoing cries of hawkers and boatmen, strains of monkly chanting. All too soon the road leaves the valley and the lovely illusion is gone. Twelve miles to Rhayader, says the signpost.

The truth is that to me Florence is more than just a city: It is the idea of a city. No place on earth offers me an image more concentrated and more exact—the look of it, its history, its style and reputation all bundled into one intoxicating fancy. I think of

Florence not as a municipality, with the usual problems of sewage, traffic and petty crime, infighting among city councilors and shady practices concerning planning permissions. Those citizens I see swarming over my mirage-bridge are artists and poets every one— or if not, master craftsmen, philosophers, or cultivated merchants of ancient lineage. Princes live in those insubstantial palaces, and masterpieces adorn all their drawing rooms. Magnificent prelates preach beneath that dome. Immemorial bells sound from the campanile. If there is crime, it is gorgeous crime, all daggers and secret poisons. If there are squabbles about civic development, they concern the best place to erect a figure by some genius sculptor, or a dispute over who is to carve the baptistery doors.

In short, I am dreaming as I drive, and all my notions of Florence are misty and golden, like that transient vision on the road to Rhayader.

Misty, yet decidedly precise. I have always particularly admired buildings that look as though you could pick them up, so functionally compact do they seem, so absolute. The Palace of Westminster strikes me as one such structure, also the Doge's Palace in Venice and the Chrysler skyscraper in Manhattan. So it is with my conceptual Florence. It is like a model for me, everything complete and compact and crystal clear.

It is of course true that when we think of most cities in the world we think only of their centers, disregarding the sprawling suburbs all around. New York is just Manhattan to most of us, give

---

F lorence is beautiful, as I have said before and must say again and again, most beautiful. The river rushes through the midst of its palaces like a crystal arrow, and it is hard to tell, when you see all by the clear sunset, whether those churches, and houses, and windows, and bridges, and people walking, in the water or out of the water, are the real walls and windows, and bridges, and people, and churches.

—Elizabeth Barrett Browning,
Letter to Mr. Boyd (1847)

or take a bit of Brooklyn; how many people include Crouch End in their mental image of London, or see Parramatta behind the Sydney Harbor Bridge? My feelings about Florence, though, are different. It is not that I willfully ignore its suburbs; it is that in my mind's eye, it has no suburbs, has no ring roads or railway sidings or supermarkets, but is simply a shapely medieval cluster of buildings glorious with art and history beside its river.

This is not all mere romanticism. Florence really is snugly couched, like my holographic version of it, between low and gentle hills upon the River Arno in Tuscany. Generations of artists have painted it from the high ground around and given the impression that it is a small, idyllic settlement clustered around the covered Ponte Vecchio, surveyed by the grand dome and campanile of the Cathedral, and by the castellated tower of the Palazzo Vecchio. Generally, the painters bind their views with blue hills so that the city seems to lie there serenely in a contoured embrace, waiting for you to touch it, or stroke it—or pick it up. Even the oldest depictions of Florence indulge this fancy. The earliest realistic picture of them all, engraved in the late fifteenth century, is actually enclosed within an engraved chain, complete with engraved padlock, as if to demonstrate the levitable nature of the place.

So my vision of Florence owes much to the artists who have always made it seem a privileged enclave, separate from everywhere else. But it derives too from my first genuine, wide-awake experience of the city, at the end of the Second World War. My introduction to Florence was a helter-skelter, free-wheeling ride into town, more or less out of control down the hill of Fiesole, in an armored scout-car whose engine had given up; and no impression could have been more lasting than the blissful sensation, as we skidded at last into the venerable downtown streets, that we had arrived at some blessed haven of consolation.

Then again, in my consciousness—or subconsciousness—Florence occupies its own cultural capsule: detached, separate, and unmistakable. Its name triggers a Pavlovian response in me, as in nearly everyone else. Say Florence and I will cry, "Civilization!"

My mind's eye, which has already seen the city stylized physically into that glorious little clump of towers and rooftops beside its single bridge, imagines it populated too by all the geniuses of the Middle Ages and the Renaissance. Dante hobnobs there with Petrarch and Boccaccio. Raphael chats with Botticelli. There stands Michelangelo, supervising the dragging of his great statue of David into the piazza, inch by inch on greased beams. Brunelleschi is round the corner, watching the construction of his cathedral dome, and Ghiberti inspects his marvelous baptistery doors. Donatello walks over the bridge to supper, Fra Angelico returns to his monastic cell after painting another lovely angel. Leonardo, Uccello, Giotto, Fra Filippo Lippi—all are there in my Florence, all apparently at the same time, all in harmony. No matter that many of them lived and worked in other cities, too. It is to Florence that reputation has assigned them, and with them throng all their followers down the centuries—the scholars, the connoisseurs, the dilettantes of the Grand Tour, the international art dealers and the auctioneers and the groups of t-shirted students shepherded awe-struck from gallery to gallery.

Anyone interested in Florence and the history of architecture will enjoy Ross King's *Brunelleschi's Dome: How a Renaissance Genius Reinvented Architecture*. It is replete with insight not only into early fifteenth century Florence, but into the eternal struggle between artists and the status quo. King's description of the famous goldsmith and clock maker from the book: "Now in middle age, Filippo was short, bald, and pugnacious looking, with an aquiline nose, thin lips, and a weak chin. His appearance was not helped by his dirty and disheveled clothing. Yet in Florence such an unsightly display was almost a badge of genius, and Filippo was simply the latest in a long and illustrious line of ugly or unkempt artists."

—JO'R & TAW

And what about political history? Florence is always and only a city-state in my imagination, and its consequence is all embodied in one glittering family of rulers: the Medicis. I can see them clear as life in my imagination, with their bright wide eyes and patrician noses, leaning elegantly against pillars or smiling benevolently from thrones. Did they not make Florence the humanist capital of Europe? Did not Galileo name the moons of Jupiter after them? In my fantasy of Florence I dismiss all its lesser rulers, ignore the old feuds between the political factions of Guelphs and Ghibellines,

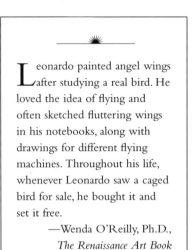

Leonardo painted angel wings after studying a real bird. He loved the idea of flying and often sketched fluttering wings in his notebooks, along with drawings for different flying machines. Throughout his life, whenever Leonardo saw a caged bird for sale, he bought it and set it free.
—Wenda O'Reilly, Ph.D.,
The Renaissance Art Book

turn a blind eye to Savonarola, the fanatic who held the Florentines in thrall, pretend that the Florentine Machiavelli never lived. It is the Medicis for me, as it probably is for most of us; and most vividly of all, when I think of Florence, I see Lorenzo de Medici, the lordliest of them all, duke of dukes, scholar, musician, poet, architect, and lover. Everything that is civilized and worldly and elegant and splendid boils down in my fantasy to Lorenzo the Magnificent of Florence.

This blend of images, together with many more subliminal ones, gives my idea of Florence a mellow aura. It summons in me sensations deliciously autumnal. Others, I know, have seen the place as emblematic of spring, or harvest time—"flowers and grapes and olive leaves" was Mendelssohn's metaphor, and Byron wrote of the city's corn, wine, oil, and plenty "leaping to laughing life." But mellow is my word for it. Its buildings seem to me matured by time, molded into each others' presences, accustomed to one another; the colors of its great pictures, recalled collectively in my memory, are never lurid or dazzling, but reverently noble; and I always seem to see dim blue wood smoke rising from its elaborate chimneys, casting fragrances of pine or oak all across the city. Surely no vulgar rivalries or sleaze ever disturbed the serenity of this glorious place (say I to myself, as I meander dreamily on to Rhayader)...

Is it only a dream? Well, Florence has suburbs and a railway station and cinemas and supermarkets and armies of tourists and rubbish and quarrelsome civic councilors like everywhere else. Eight bridges, not one, cross its river. It was always as much a center of moneymaking as of art. Its history began long before the Renaissance, in Roman times, and Mussolini called it *Firenze facistissima*. Its great artists often quarreled. Its rulers, far from being just enlightened art lovers, went in for every kind of political skullduggery. It has not been an independent state since 1737. Lorenzo the Magnificent was extremely ugly. What's more, Florence was never, as I have loved to imagine it, a single bright prodigy burning there beside the Arno, but was only one of several such city-states, frequently rivals. It was not always mellow, by any means, but often very brash.

Only a dream? Yes and no. As a matter of fact, in that Welsh valley where I see my mirage-Florence so vividly, the thirteenth century English conquerors of Wales did try to create a city. It never came to anything, though, and all that remains of it now is a line of cottages, a church, a country mansion, and some grandly named village lanes. No Ponte Vecchio crosses the river Cynon. No Dantes or Verrochios stroll those lanes. No curled *magnifico* looks down upon his people from the windows of the big house. The real Florence could exist nowhere else than where it is, below the sweet hills of Fiesole, beside the river where the poets sang; but there, to this day, its reality remains dream enough.

Welsh essayist Jan Morris is the author of more than forty books, including Hong Kong: Epilogue to an Empire, The World of Venice, Fifty Years of Europe, *and* Trieste and the Meaning of Nowhere.

JASON EPSTEIN

* * *

This Side of *Paradiso*

A compatriot in the kitchen
is a beautiful thing.

IT MUST HAVE BEEN THE TUSCAN HILLS ON A SEPTEMBER MORN-
ing that inspired Dante's *Paradiso*: the pure and boundless light; the
planted hillsides, with their rows of vines and silver olive trees,
looking as if they had been painted; the valleys, with their fields of
sunflowers, the walled towns in a blue haze cresting the hills. To
see all this from the hilltop farmhouse that some friends and I
rented for a few weeks is to know what Dante meant when he said
that he had found, at last, all the leaves of the universe bound into
one volume.

Our farmhouse, pale yellow trimmed in tan, with a classical
façade, a Palladian roof, and symmetrical windows framed by shutters, turned out to be a much larger and more splendid place than
we needed or had expected. It came complete with servants: Silvia,
the cook; her husband, Francesco, who looked after the garden;
and Ivana, the maid, who helped in the kitchen and waited on
table, and who believed that if she spoke in a lilting cadence, as if
addressing an infant or a cat, and shaped each word carefully with
her hands, we would surely understand her fine Tuscan speech.

Some weeks earlier, I had written to the agent from whom we
rented the farmhouse to say that I would like to cook some of our

meals myself, and she replied that Silvia would be delighted. This turned out to be true; Silvia proved a joy to cook with and, unlike many cooks in her situation, soon found my meddling in her kitchen entertaining rather than a threat or a nuisance. By the time our stay was over, she had taught me more than I could ever have learned by deconstructing the dandified tourist dishes we were served in the half-dozen expensive Tuscan restaurants that we visited. Yet the beginning of our collaboration was difficult, for on the day of our arrival, when I accepted Silvia's invitation to come down to her spotless kitchen, with its floor of red tiles, and ran my hand along her white marble counters and admired her eight-burner stove, with its electronic pilots and enough oven space for a half-dozen pies, she could see at once that I was disappointed.

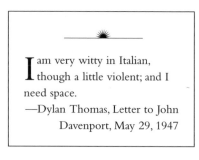

I am very witty in Italian, though a little violent; and I need space.
—Dylan Thomas, Letter to John Davenport, May 29, 1947

In those first, stiff moments, as we groped toward a mixture of English and Italian that would suit us both, I asked, more brusquely than I meant to, whether we couldn't buy in the market something better than the cottony, unsalted bread with the spongy crust that I found on the counter. *"Insipido"* was the tactless word I used. She said, with an apologetic shrug, "No. No one has time to bake bread at home now, and the old village bakeries are gone. This is what they sell here now." And when I asked if she had some good ripe tomatoes—round ones rather than the pale plum tomatoes in her basket—she said, "Not in the market, but maybe Franco can find a few in his garden." But why, her puzzled expression implied, would I want red, ripe tomatoes? Then she laid a few scrawny, factory-raised chickens from Livorno on the counter for our first dinner, and I asked whether there wasn't a farmer in the neighborhood who sold plump, farm-grown chickens. "No," she said. "The *contadini* raise their chickens for themselves. Everyone else goes to the Superal and buys these." But then, sensing my disappointment had gone too far, she said, "Look at this," and, with a confident smile, opened a big stainless-steel freezer and removed a pale-pink haunch of what looked like veal. *"Bellissimo!"* she said.

"Vitello!" I replied, relieved to find at last something to praise.

"Vitello no," she said, holding the haunch up to the light and patting it. *"Cinghiale.* Maybe for tomorrow, if you like, or *lunedì,* if you'd rather. Wild pig. The best part." She thrust her hip out and rubbed the top of her rump to show where the meat had come from. "Shot in the forest. The best part."

"Fine," I told her. "Anytime you like." I was charmed by her good nature and by the way her face reacted instantly to each passing emotion, mine as well as her own. At that moment, it became plain that Silvia and I were going to get along. She handed me a piece of pecorino—the straw-colored cheese made from sheep's milk—that Franco, she said, had bought from a farmer on a back road to Florence. The cheese had a slight sharpness tucked beneath its gentle surface, and it was better, I told Silvia, than the pecorino I buy on Grand Street in Manhattan. She answered not in words but with an uplifted right shoulder, as if to say, "What else would you expect?"

But why were Silvia's bread and chickens such miserable imitations of what could be found on Grand Street and in countless other postmodern culinary enclaves in the United States? At first I was puzzled, but soon the answer became obvious. America's appetite for what might be called retro food—authentic reproductions of classic staples, such as crusty, firm-textured bread baked in brick ovens, and well-fed poultry raised not in cramped factory cages but in airy outdoor yards—was a reaction to the mechanized American diet that accompanied the hegemony of the supermarket after the Second World War. Except for a few items, like Silvia's bread and chickens, the Tuscans had yet to suffer the full assault of this modernization, and so they felt no urgency to re-create the old forms of production. It occurred to me that this might change as the E.C. imposed its uniform agricultural standards throughout Europe and forced the Tuscans to restore their old village bakeries and poultry yards in self-defense. But this wasn't about to happen during our Tuscan holiday, and it didn't matter. The rest of Silvia's ingredients, to say nothing of her technique, were as authentic as the Tuscan hills where her family had lived, as far as she knew, forever.

Silvia was in her forties, though she seemed younger, and she had two grown sons—one in the *carabinieri*, the other still at school. She was no longer slim, but with her dyed yellow hair, her enthusiasm, and her agility in the kitchen, she seemed girlish to me. I would have been happy spending all my time with her at the farmhouse or exploring the markets at Castelfiorentino at the base of our hill, and at Gambassi Terine, in the hills on the road to San Gimignano, some twenty kilometers to the south. But the others wanted to visit churches and look at pictures, so every morning, despite unusually hot September weather, we would set out for Volterra or Siena or Arezzo or Florence or Lucca. None of these cities were more than an hour away on roads that twisted through the beautiful Tuscan hills, their slopes covered with neat rows of vines bearing the Sangiovese grapes from which the local Chianti gets its flavor.

Each day, after we had visited the churches and had seen the pictures, we would find a place for lunch. Before lunch, I would look in the shops for some good bread, always in vain, and a ripe tomato or some good ham and local cheese. One day, in a small shop in a town called Radda, where a number of English and American vacationers rent villas for the summer, I was lucky enough to find two farm-raised chickens. As I was paying for them, it struck me that I was as eager to surprise Silvia with my discoveries as I was to provide for our own meal.

In Siena, nothing seemed to have changed. The fan-shaped Piazza del Campo, its lovely brick pavement sloping down toward the seven-hundred-year-old Palazzo Pubblico, was no different from what I remembered from my last visit to Siena, thirty years ago. Except for a few Sienese on motor scooters, and the café, with its San Pellegrino umbrellas, very little had changed—at least out-wardly—since the time of Cosimo de' Medici.

To judge by the expensive shops along the narrow Gothic

streets that surround the piazza, Siena's sixty thousand inhabitants were evidently prospering despite Italy's widely proclaimed economic mess, including a national debt that is said to be 120 percent of last year's G.D.P. The lira was very low, and the extravagant Italian pension system still took 40 percent of the national budget. There is no telling how much had been stolen by corrupt businessmen and politicians of all parties, thousands of whom, under Italy's peculiar criminal code, were now imprisoned and denied bail as they awaited trial. Though the shops selling good antique furniture, expensive hams, and the confection called *panforte*, which the Sienese have been making since the Middle Ages, were evidently aimed at the tourist trade, this could not be true of the shops selling rare wines, wild game, and fish—the fish lit theatrically from above and arranged, like jewels, upon beds of ice. These shops obviously catered to the Sienese themselves, some of whom apparently didn't mind paying the equivalent of fifteen dollars a kilo for fresh sardines and even more for red mullet.

But on our two visits to Siena we saw very few Sienese. Except for groups of tourists, with their green *Michelins* and their video cameras, the streets in September were almost empty—a phenomenon that we noticed wherever we went in Tuscany. In some of the smaller cities and towns, it was as if a neutron bomb had landed. "Everyone is still at the seashore," I was told, or people were in their houses having lunch, but these explanations seemed inadequate. I knew that Italy had the lowest birth rate in the world and was losing population, especially in the north, but this could hardly account for the empty streets. I never did find the answer, but I was grateful that in Siena the churches and the museums weren't crowded and there weren't many customers in the shops that sold autumn's first plump porcini—the apotheosis of edible mushrooms. Moreover, the price was only about twenty thousand lire a kilo—twelve dollars for nearly two and a quarter pounds, or less than a quarter of the price of porcini in New York, if they could be found there at all. Greedily, I bought the entire basket. I also bought some Treviso radicchio—the kind you toss in olive oil and grill lightly over a wood fire.

That morning, on the way to the piazza we had passed a *macelleria* that displayed in its window one side of a short loin of beef. When I crossed the narrow Via della Sapienza with my sack of porcini and stepped through the beaded curtain into the *macelleria*—it was called Cetoloni Alberto—I could see that the loin was about two-thirds the size of its American equivalent. That meant that it came from the white Chianina steers that produce the famous *fiorentina* T-bones—a local specialty that is never found outside Italy and that is now increasingly rare even in Italian restaurants. Certainly those T-bones can't often be found three inches thick, which is how I asked Signor Cetoloni to cut them for our dinner that night.

"These are the best," he told me when the steaks were wrapped and tied in a neat bundle. *"Autentico,"* he added, pointing to a medallion on the wall behind him which displayed the slogan *"Cinque Erre,"* meaning "Five 'R's," for the five *razze*, or breeds, of cattle raised in the region. The Chianini are descended from the white oxen that have been bred here since Etruscan times. They are traditionally butchered before they reach full growth, when they are relatively lean and their meat is tender but Chianini don't lend themselves to large-scale industrial production, and as less expensive beef produced elsewhere in the E.C. enters the Italian market, the Chianina breeders are gradually going out of business.

As I was leaving, Signor Cetoloni asked me to wait and took from the counter behind him a large roulade of piglet, which he called a *porchetta*. *"Un tantino di questo?"* he asked, offering me a bit that he held out on the end of his knife. It was still warm from the oven and was filled with a mixture of herbs and spices, in which I could detect black pepper, rosemary, sage, nutmeg, and probably some juniper and thyme. I bought a kilo, though I had no idea what we would do with it since it hardly belonged with a dinner of steak and porcini and would cool off and become greasy by the time we got home. In the shop, however, it was glorious. It would have been insane not to buy some. When we got home, we gave the *porchetta* to Silvia, who took it away with her, holding it in its wrapper against her shoulder as if it were an infant. She said she would warm it later in the oven in the apartment that she and Franco share in a wing of the farmhouse.

Since two more of our fellow tenants had arrived, and there were now six of us living in the farmhouse, which nevertheless still felt as underpopulated as Italy itself, I had bought three of the T-bones and expected some leftovers for the next day's lunch or for Silvia, Ivana, and Franco if the *porchetta* wasn't enough. As it turned out, there were no leftovers.

By now, Silvia and I had been cooking together for several days, and she had grown used to having me in her kitchen. At first, she would stand, hands on hips, watching me work at her counter as if I were a potentially dangerous eccentric, likely to ruin the meal and possibly even the kitchen. But soon she relaxed. At dinner on the night we arrived, I had peeled some garlic in the familiar way—by smashing the clove with a flat of a knife, so that the skin can be slipped off easily. Silvia had never seen this done before. With a quizzical look, she picked up her paring knife and began to peel a clove in her own style—by holding it close to her eye and loosing the skin with the knife, then peeling it off bit by bit. Suddenly, she tossed her head slightly, as if to say "Let's see who wins," and began to race me. I was unaware at first that a contest had begun, but, nevertheless, I won easily. *"Bravissimo,"* she whispered and bowed slightly. Thereafter I felt that she had begun to trust me. I noticed, too, that as her trust increased so did our fluency in the pidgin Italian that she and I had concocted. It was by means of this odd language that I managed one afternoon to understand why Tuscans prefer their tomatoes underripe. In the south, where tomatoes are abundant, they are allowed to ripen for the table, and they are also canned and used for sauce. But in Tuscany, where the weather is cooler, tomatoes are grown mainly for the table and are used sparingly, if at all, in sauces. For this purpose, one wants them just this side of ripe, still with a tinge of yellow, so that they will be both sharp and sweet, with a firm, almost crisp texture. In America, she said, we probably eat our tomatoes the way the Neapolitans do, soft and ripe, and in this way we miss their true flavor. She said this sympathetically, as if my American taste in tomatoes were the result of a handicap, for which I could not be held responsible.

While we were away in Siena that day, Silvia must have gone to Francesco's garden, because now on her counter were a dozen or more tomatoes ripe and plump, as red as blood. Francesco, she said, had been thinking of using them for sauce or giving them to his goats, but if I wanted them for our dinner I could have them.

The radicchio, the porcini, and the T-bones were stacked on the counter beside the tomatoes and some basil from the garden. While Silvia cut the porcini in thin slices from top to bottom, so that each slice resembled a tiny two-dimensional umbrella, I went out to the herb garden beside the kitchen door to cut some parsley. When I returned, I found that she had already tossed the porcini in a large kettle with some chopped garlic, olive oil, and a dash of salt and pepper, and had left them to sweat over a low flame until they absorbed most of the oil. Then she added a little more water and half covered the kettle until the porcini, with their aroma of earth and heaven, were simmering. Ten minutes later, she spooned them out of the pot. They were silky and tender, having absorbed almost all the liquid in which they had simmered, leaving only enough for a fine *jus*.

On the terrace the others were seated in semi-darkness around the table. The evening was still warm, and the candles that lit the table heated the air around them like tiny furnaces. Ivana had put the steaks on an iron grill over an olivewood fire; Silvia had brushed a few embers to one side, putting them under a smaller grill, upon which she had spread the radicchio. I had sliced half a dozen of Francesco's tomatoes and let them sit for half an hour in oil, a little pepper and sea salt, and a touch of vinegar, and I asked Ivana to serve them as our first course, with some leaves of fresh basil on each plate. Except for a band of red turning purple behind the hills, the sun had set. I made a martini for myself and joined our friends, confident that this would be our best meal so far in Tuscany.

My collaborations with Silvia had by this time acquired their own rhythm, and the dinners we produced harmonized her Tuscan orthodoxy with the improvisations that I had learned in my culinary wandering. I saw that we had formed one of those late marriages, devoid of illusions, in which one values the other's distinctiveness and does not attempt to impose one's will.

A few nights after our dinner of porcini and Chianina steaks, a well-known Italian politician drove up from Rome to join us for dinner. That morning, the others had driven over to San Gimignano to buy some of the good grappa that is sold there and to look at Gozzoli's seventeen frescoes of the life of Saint Augustine. I had seen the Gozzolis the day before, so I went with Silvia to Castelfiorentino, the market town in the valley beneath our farmhouse. There was a large Superal in Castelfiorentino, and on the day of our visit the traveling market, which comes to each of the neighboring towns once a week, had also arrived. Silvia suggested that we get to this market early, before the best things were gone. But even here all the poultry I saw was factory-raised, and the bread was poor. We did, however, find some good ham and local cheese, which kept us going through the morning. We also bought some whitebait at one of the fish stalls and then set out for the Superal.

When I go to the market, I usually go without a list, and even when I have one I ignore it and fall instead into a sort of trance, waiting for the menu to create itself, so to speak, from what happens to be for sale. My inspiration that morning in the Superal came from a display of pink and black octopuses, their heads the size of softballs and their glistening tentacles like oiled bullwhips. The supermarket itself was dreamlike. Opposite the checkout counter was a hairdresser's shop, with half a dozen clients draped in long yellow clothes and staring like Medusas through fringes of wet hair. Infants were sitting on the hairdresser's floor, playing with a large, odd-shaped objects made of red and yellow plastic. Expensive espresso machines were stacked in their cartons next to a display of computer programs. At the fish counter, I imagined the octopuses, cleaned and cut into segments, stewing with garlic and

onions in white wine, to which I would add tomato and bay leaf
and peppercorns just before tossing in some clams and mussels.
Then I would add rosemary and a few lemon slices, peel and all,
and just before the stew was ready for the table I would put in
some cubes of blackfish, or the local equivalent, and more garlic
and wine to roughen the broth a bit, and I would serve it in deep
bowls with thick slices of good bread, toasted and rubbed with still
more garlic. But where, I wondered, would I find the bread?

It was the bread problem that brought me out of this reverie.
"Pasta," I said to myself. "That's what I'll use instead." I asked the
clerk for some mussels and clams, and instead of octopus, which
now seemed too coarse for what I had in mind, I asked for a kilo
of the smallest squid he had. Then I went to look for Silvia. I
found her at the poultry display, her chin resting on a bent index
finger as she gazed warily, I thought, at the chickens in their plastic wrappers.

"Perchè non dei piccioni?" I suggested, holding up a plump pigeon
that fitted neatly into my hand. Unlike chickens, pigeons aren't
mass-produced; they're raised on farms or in coops and are fed real
corn, the way chickens used to be raised. We bought a dozen and
headed for home. We agreed that the whitebait, dusted in flour and
tossed quickly in very hot oil, would be the hors d'oeuvre. The
clams, mussels, and squid we would make into a stew with a little
white wine, garlic, and hot peppers, and serve over pasta, and the
pigeons we would bone, marinate in muscatel, and grill on the fire.
To go with them, we could braise some fennel from the garden,
and then we could slowly bake some underripe tomatoes and mix
them with a touch of grilled eggplant. For dessert, there were figs
from the tree near the pool, ricotta *salata* that I had bought the day
before in Volterra, and biscotti left over from the night before. The
politician, I told myself as I boned the pigeons that afternoon and
made a stock of their ribs and breastbones and necks, would have
a good dinner. He was a man of some amplitude, and I was eager
to feed him well.

As it turned out, he had so much to say that night that he hardly
noticed what he had been served. The pasta, under its sauce of

clams, squid, and mussels, with a sprinkling of diced tomato and a
shower of parsley, looked like an Italian flag that had been abandoned on his plate by a fleeing army. Like so many of his
colleagues from the previous government, he was in legal difficul-
ties. Unlike so many of the others, however, he was not being held
without bail, so perhaps the allegations in his case were not serious. Even so, it would have been outrageous to ask where he stood
with the law. By the time Ivana had removed our pasta bowls and
returned with the grilled pigeons—glinting in the candlelight
under a sheen of reduced stock flavored with rosemary—and
poured some Poggio Rosso into our glasses, the conversation had
become entirely his. The rest of us had faded silently into the darkness of the terrace while his large, pale face and fluttering hands
bobbed in the candlelight to the rhythm of his monologue.

On the following day, we drove over to San Gimignano for a
final visit. By now, I understood why this town had made such an
erotic impression upon E.M. Forster when he visited it as a young
Cambridge graduate and chose it as the setting for *Where Angels
Fear to Tread,* the novel of sexual discovery that launched his
career and also a procession of imitators. San Gimignano is, of
course, famous for its slab-sided towers, which when they are seen
from a distance resemble the towers of lower Manhattan. These
stone towers were probably erected by feuding groups of Guelphs
and Ghibellines—the former owing allegiance to the Popes in
Rome, and the latter to the Holy Roman Emperors, on the far side
of the Alps. Their quarrel was complex and has puzzled generations of historians, but perhaps it is not entirely unlike the disputes
today between advocates of a strong central government and those
Italians who prefer regional autonomy.

The towers and the violent legends attached to them give San
Gimignano a forbidding aspect at first, but this is soon dispelled by
the unmistakable erotic intensity of the place—suggested, for instance, by the twelfth-century frescoes in the Museo Civico, which
show a young man and woman quite naked except for the man's
hat and the woman's headband. They are sharing a bath. The

woman's hand rests upon the man's shoulder, and his hand, hidden by the tub's rim, rests, perhaps, on her upper thigh. In the adjacent panel, the woman is in bed, her back to the man, who, still naked, is climbing in after her. San Gimignano's patron saint is a young woman named Fina, whose martyrdom began when a young man of the town offered her an orange. So intense was her revulsion that she took to her bed and never ate again. Some years after her anorexic martyrdom, Ghirlandaio painted for Fina's chapel the scene of her transfiguration, using as his model a pink-cheeked young beauty in excellent health, reclining on her couch, her eyes shut, her palms pressed together in a gesture whose piety seems, if not actually coy, then certainly hesitant.

> In 1990 the historic center of San Gimignano was declared a World Heritage Site by the United Nations Educational Scientific and Cultural Organization. It joins other UNESCO World Heritage Sites in Tuscany such as the Piazza del Duomo in Pisa and the historic city centers of Siena, Florence, and Pienza.
>
> —JO'R & TAW

On that last visit to San Gimignano, as I was standing beneath the great Ghirlandaio fresco of the Annunciation outside the Duomo, which houses Santa Fina's chapel, and was trying to imagine how this young woman's story must have struck the young Forster, I became aware of a melody coming from the grassy courtyard behind me. I turned and saw that the source of the music was a handsome young flutist wearing a burgundy cape over a pair of jeans. His hair rose and fell as he swung his head in time with the music. He was playing, of all things, one of Grieg's Norwegian folk songs, and was creating from this grammar school chestnut a tune so vivid that a group of tourists had put down their video cameras and gathered silently around him.

A few minutes later, under the flutist's spell, I walked back into the square to rejoin my friends, and there I glimpsed what Forster might have seen when he conceived his novel's hero. Reclining on a balustrade, his back against a pillar, his head turned to one side, a book unread in his hand, and his expression distracted or irritable, was a young man of such forbidding beauty that he dispelled any inclination to possess it, even if one were so inclined. He might have been a Della Robbia if he were not so clearly human. Forster's young English suburbanites flung themselves incautiously at such a Tuscan beauty and never recovered their native aplomb. This was a blessing in Forster's estimation, though not nearly as great a blessing, of course, as the divine enlightenment bestowed upon Dante by Beatrice. Yet the transformation that was undergone by Forster's suburbanites was not entirely incompatible with Dante's, either. In Tuscany, you approach heaven by way of the senses. Beauty is all.

I was eager to return to the farmhouse and Silvia's kitchen. Tonight was our last dinner in Tuscany. Silvia was going to make wild boar, and she said that for our farewell meal she would prefer to cook alone. The meal was sublime, but our imminent departure inspired that melancholy premonition of death typical of all leave-taking.

The following morning it rained. As we were getting ready to drive down to Rome, Silvia handed me a jar of spices that she had ground into powder, and a handwritten recipe for wild boar: three kilos of *cinghiale* rubbed with her ground spices, two chopped onions, three branches of rosemary, some parsley, a little white wine, salt, pepper. Though the chances of finding wild boar in New York City are slim, I carried Silvia's recipe in my pocket for weeks after I returned and eventually tucked it into my copy of Forster's novel.

Jason Epstein has been the editor-publisher to some of the twentieth-century's greatest writers (Edmund Wilson, Vladimir Nabokov, Jane Jacobs) as well as the virtual inventor of the trade paperback. He has spent forty years at Random House, founded, along with wife Barbara, The New York Review of Books, *and is an author himself, most recently of* Book Business: Publishing Past, Present, and Future.

BARBARA   GRIZZUTI   HARRISON

✦ ✦ ✦

In San Gimignano

Tourism, that terrible thief, hasn't been able
to rob this lovely place of wonder.

THERE ARE PLACES ONE COMES HOME TO THAT ONE HAS NEVER
been to: San Gimignano.

An English spinster, almost deaf, attaches herself to me on the
bus to San Gimignano. She tells me of her adventures and mis-
adventures in Spain, Portugal, Italy—all having to do with trains
nearly missed, roads not taken, the kindness of strangers. I am not
feeling particularly generous or kindly, except toward the green
hills and fields of yellow flowers in which I wish to lose my
thoughts. "Rape, I think those flowers are," she says, "horrible
name. I think they make oil of it." I think it is saffron, perhaps
crocus....

Butter-yellow flowers bloom from the medieval towers for
which San Gimignano is famous. They are variously called wallflowers and violets (and said by townspeople to grow nowhere else
on Earth). The small and fragrant flowers sprang up on the coffin
of Saint Fina (among whose gifts was the ability to extinguish
house fires) and on the towns' towers on the day of her death. (On
that day bells tolled; they were rung by angels.) Saint Fina is sometimes called the Saint of the Wallflowers. (Wallflower, in addition
to its botanical meaning, in colloquial Italian means, as it does in

36

English, a "girl who is not invited to dance"—*ragazza che fa de tappezzeria*.) She died when she was fifteen. She was loved for her goodness and beauty; she had butter-yellow hair, she once accepted an orange from a young man at a well, and she died on an oak plank in penance for what seems to have been an entirely blameless life. In paintings by Ghirlandaio in San Gimignano's cathedral, she is so slender and delicate, so attenuated, as to cause one pain.

Modest Saint Fina, a silent slip of a girl, might seem an odd choice for veneration in a walled city of military architecture— proud ramparts and aggressive towers built by suspicious patrician families to hide treasures and to assert the will for power. (Alberti railed against towers, regarding them as antisocial; in the sixteenth century Cosimo de' Medici ordered a halt to the expansion of San Gimignano, forbidding the commune of Florence to allocate to it "even the slightest amount for any need, be it sacred or profane.")

There is a wrinkle in time in San Gimignano. There is no such thing as a mellow or lovable skyscraper, but the towers of San Gimignano, glibly called the skyscrapers of Tuscany, seem to have been born old...or at least to have anticipated the day when gentle Saint Fina would, like Rapunzel, who also lived in a tower and whose hair was also gold, seem the perfect anointing presence. One imagines her—one imagines both Rapunzel and Saint Fina—at the top of a steep, narrow, spiraling stone stairway, breathing silently in a slender shaft of brief light from a narrow window...everything military has retreated from this fairy tale place.

There are fourteen tall towers in San Gimignano; there were once seventy-two. They are surrounded, on the narrow city streets, by *palazzi*, and modest houses, all higgledy-piggledy, with projecting Tuscan roofs. They stretch from earth to sky and are built on shifting soil; and they speak, as Georges Duby says, two languages: "on the one hand the unreal space of courtly myth, the vertical flight of mystic ascension, the linear curve carrying composition in to the scrolls of poetic reverie. And on the other, a rigorous marquetry offering the view of a compact universe, profound and solid." They have one peculiar property: Their stones remain the same color—a gray-gold with a suggestion, a faint *pentimento*, of black—whether wet with rain or hot with sun. The little guide-book I bought in San Gimignano is quite lyrical and accurate about the walls and towers of San Gimignano, which embody, as its author says, the contradictions of the medieval mind, a mind "reserved and hospitable, bold and fearful. Fearful of enemies, of strangers, of nighttime, of treasons." The walls kept enemies out; they also kept people in; they imparted, to those within, a "sense of community, of common interests and ideals never denied." San Gimignano is formidable in its beauty; every description of it I have ever read makes it sound both forbidding and delightful. Forbidding it once was, in the days of fratricidal warfare, when families threw collapsible wooden bridges from the window of one tower-fortress to that of another (the days when it traded with Egypt, Syria, and Tunisia and men vied for great wealth); now it is simply delightful. And sheltering. The walls cup and cradle (as in Niccolò de Pietro Gerini's painting of Saint Fina, she cradles the walled city in her slender young arms). The towers exist not to keep enemies—the Other—out, but to house the soul warmly; one has a sense of great bodily integrity in these spaces, one feels safe. When Saint Fina drove the Devil out of San Gimignano with a gesture of her long and lovely hand, she did it for us.

Because one yields, in San Gimignano, to the fancy that the world is created anew each day, that time does not, in the way we ordinarily understand it, exist, it is exactly right, and so lovely, to find in a deserted piazza a small thirteenth-century church dedicated to Saint Augustine, whose reflections on the nature and mea-surement of time so profoundly informed his love of God (and an-ticipated the existentialists):

> But if the present were always present, and would not pass into the past, it would no longer be time, but eternity. Therefore, if the present, so as to be time, must be so con-stituted that it passes into the past, how can we say that it is, since the cause of its being is the fact that it will cease to be? Does it not follow that we can truly say that it is time,

only because it tends towards non-being?.... How then
can...the past and the future be, when the past no longer is
and the future as yet does not be?

On the chancel wall of the church are lively fifteenth-century
frescoes by Benozzo Gozzoli of the life of the great theologian. I
am surprised to see Saint Monica plump, peasant-sturdy, and care-
worn; I always imagined that one who prayed unceasingly, as she
did, for the salvation of her son, would find one's flesh melting in
the process. (I think of a life of prayer as inimical to fat.) Of all the
charming frescoes, the most charming is that of Augustine chatting
with the infant Jesus about the Mystery of the Trinity (that which
might be remote and austere Gozzoli rendered immediate and
intimate); the Child attempts to empty the sea into a puddle—
much as any child might at the seashore, with a pail, or a shell—
the impossibility of which convinces Augustine that the Trinity
cannot be comprehended by reason alone.

Everything You have made beautiful, Augustine said to his
God, but You are more beautiful than anything You have made.
In the cloister of the Church of St. Augustine, that beauty is pal-
pable; one feels one has entered the light and peace of God. The
cloister is divided by box hedges into four quadrangular plots of
land in which grow irises and tulips and palm trees and white and
yellow dandelions and pink and blue wandering flowers.... How
sweet, these enclosures within an enclosed opening: open/close,
close/open; a cypress punctuates each of four corners. A loggia—
with pots of yellow flowers and geraniums—looks out over a
central cistern; the scent of lilacs is pervasive, the lilacs swarm with
bees. The fragrance of lilacs mingles with the fragrance of wood
smoke. I walk beneath a tree, the leaves of which are the color of
China tea; a cobweb brushes across my forehead. A jet plane streaks
across the fragrance of lilacs; an orange-and-black cat mews
piteously in the garden.

(Were mazes an outgrowth and elaboration of these enclosures
within enclosures? Why would anyone wish to complicate and
convolute so simple, satisfying, and sweet a design?)

The sacristan plucks tenacious thorns from my coat. He is listening to a popular love song on his transistor radio in the sacristy. I light a candle and the sacristan extinguishes the flame. Even God has a *riposo* in Italy at lunch hour.

My hotel, once a *palazzo*, is the Piazza della Cisterna, in the middle of which is a thirteenth-century cistern. From this piazza, through the battlemented archway, I can reach the square of the cathedral with its seven towers. I like the feel of the herringbone-patterned bricks under my thick sandals. I wander up and down steep hills and arched alleys, passing old men and women with canes. I never want to leave. My terraced-hilltop room looks out over roofs and towers and blessed hills to the Colle Val d'Elsa. I am beginning to believe the Annunciation did take place here. Art plagiarizes nature. I want to fly, as Cellini wanted to fly, "on a pair of wings made of waxed linen." And I want to stay here, rooted, forever.

At dinner a baby boy crawls through the tunneled legs of diners, to the cooing delight of waiters. A woman lights a cigarette, over which a British man and woman make a great disapproving fuss. "There is no remedy for death," the smoker says, coolly addressing the room at large. She says this in English and then in Italian.

After dinner, in a dim lounge, I watch *Two Women*, a movie with Sophia Loren. I am joined by the Italian woman who smokes. Out of an abundance of feeling I cry, not so much because this is the story of a rape, not because of the girl's loss of innocence and the mother's rage and grief, but because the injured girl is singing, her voice frail, a song my grandmother used to sing: *"Vieni, c'è una strada nel bosco…*I want you to know it, too…*c'è una strada nel cuore…*there's a road in my heart…" That woman who smokes is crying, too. I am thinking of my daughter. When she leaves, the woman kisses the crown of my head. We have exchanged no words. Men have stood on the threshold and not come in. I never see her again.

I cross the piazza to sit in a brightly lit outdoor café. It is late. I am the only woman in the café. I fend off three approaches. I won't be denied the pleasure of seeing the light and shadows of the lovely square, the purple night sky. Inside, male voices are raised in a sentimental love song; they sing to the strings of a mandolin. Their singing is saccharine, their laughter is boisterous, and there are no women here. I wonder, with some little anger, what it would be like to be part of their sentimental, prideful, tough, and tender world. I put on dark glasses. A little boy eating a *gelato* plays hide-and-seek, covering his eyes with sticky fingers (hide), waiting for me to smile (seek). A policeman strolls by apparently without purpose. I am an anomaly. I remove my glasses, thinking that if I can't see men's faces, they can't see mine.

What pleasure does it give men to sing of the beauty of women when there are no women in the café?

I find myself thinking of the handsome guide at the Davanzati who held the elevator for me.

I shared an apartment with Georgina, a young archeology student who worked at the pizzeria across the cobbled square. One of the village's few public phones was located in a dark corner and when it rang, every Latin ear would tune in to the nuances of the conversation. If it was a lover's quarrel, there'd be calls of encouragement; if a deal was being concluded, advice would fly thick and fast. Then the men would resume their draughts game, returning late to their wives who'd been up to their elbows rolling dough or picking olives.

—Susan Storm, "Carrying on in Chianti"

The bed linen smells of lilacs. The air vibrates with the after-sound of bells.

In San Gimignano the birds sing all night long.

In the morning I drink my coffee from a mug bearing the words OLD TIME TEA.

In the Piazza della Cisterna there is a *sala di giochi*—video games. Is it possible that the children who grow up here—young men with studied, languid poses—think they are living in a hick town?

On the Via San Martino, away from the cathedral and the Cisterna, there is a café peopled entirely by old men. The café is part billiard parlor; newspapers are bought and read in common. I am accepted here in the morning light of day; I would not have been accepted here last night. I am served my morning coffee with old-fashioned gallantry by a man in a shiny black suit. With great difficulty he recites something he has been taught by an English-speaking cousin: "'We shall sit upon the ground and tell sad stories of the death of Kings.' Is sad?" he asks.

To leave a walled city is to feel evicted, cast out—cast out of paradise; no matter that the countryside outside the walls is paradisiacal.

The bus, full of high-spirited schoolchildren, that stopped at Porta San Giovanni was the wrong bus, but the driver took me on anyway, avuncularly advised the children to be more calm in the presence of *la bella signora*, and deposited me at the right bus stop. We went by back roads, and I had the sensation, for the first time in Tuscany, not of passing but of being in the countryside, part of (not merely an observer of) a gorgeous (and calm) crazy quilt of silver-green olive trees and flowering peach and cherry trees; the yellow and red bus wound its way through the intricate sensual folds of hills dignified by cypress trees: "And you, O God, saw all the things that you had made, and behold, 'they were very good.' For we also see them and behold, they are all very good."

The bus went slowly, like a swimmer who loves the water too much to race and challenge it, and the world unfolded like a child's picture book: gardeners turning over soil with gnarled, patient hands; bronzed youths of Etruscan beauty casually strolling by the roadside as if here were just anywhere and everywhere was beautiful; showers of wisteria framing old women shelling peas in doorways; lovers picnicking in a vineyard; laughing nuns pushing children on orange swings, their heavy habits floating on magnolia-scented air: "Your works praise you."

Barbara Grizzuti Harrison is the author of one novel, Foreign Bodies, *as well as nonfiction books:* Unlearning the Lies: Sexism in School; Visions of Glory: A History and a Memory of Jehovah's Witnesses; Off Center; *and* Italian Days, *from which this story was excerpted. Her work has also appeared in* The New York Times, Harper's, GQ, Traveler, *and* Vanity Fair. *She lives in Manhattan, on the East River.*

WILLIAM ZINSSER

✦ ✦ ✦

Siena Revisited

An old soldier touches the past.

IN EARLY MAY OF 1945 MY ARMY UNIT WAS STATIONED IN AN
Italian seaside town south of Leghorn. World War II was ebbing to
a close, and talk of Germany's surrender was in the air. For GIs like
us, far behind the lines, there was nothing to do. I remember that
we played a lot of baseball. I also remember that I kept hearing
about a town called Siena, two or three hours' drive away. It was
one of those names that travelers listen for, like Kyoto or Fez, and
I persuaded three of my friends—we were all sergeants—that we
should try to go see it. We got permission to take a company jeep
for one day, and on the morning of May 7 we set out.

The gravel road left the coast and climbed across a landscape of
hills and farms and brought us to Volterra, an old Etruscan town,
hunched like a fortress on a hilltop. It was famous for its alabaster,
and with the fervor of all tourists coming upon a local specialty of
unsuspected beauty, we bought alabaster cigarette boxes and ash-
trays for our unsuspecting families back home. The ancient city
held us with its power, and it was midday before we pushed on.
Later, far off to the left, we saw a sight so fanciful, an illustration
from a child's fairy tale, that I thought if I blinked it would go
away. It was a cluster of stone towers rising out of a village on a

hill. After the war I would learn that it was San Gimignano, a relic of the many Tuscan towns that once had such towers, built for defense and long since fallen down. But on that afternoon it was only a teasing apparition; there was no time to go chasing mirages.

If San Gimignano was the perfect miniature, Siena was the master painting. Announcing itself to us from a distance, it looked both proud and playful, arrayed across three hills and sprawling down the sides, all contained within a medieval wall. Bestriding the city from its highest ridge was an immense white cathedral. Inside the wall, I was struck by the city's harmony. The prevailing color was pale red brick, the prevailing architecture was Gothic, and the geometry was uniformly random: all curves and inclines. Yet such was Siena's gravitational logic that the streets from all three hills funneled down into one large public square, the Piazza del Campo.

It was the most beautiful square I had ever seen, partly

Very early one morning I ventured through the rolling hills of Tuscany to take a balloon ride. As the balloon slowly rose up, I gained a much greater appreciation for the architecture of the charming sixteenth-century church, Madonna di San Biagio, erected just outside the medieval walled city of Montepulciano. When we drifted higher yet, above herds of scurrying sheep and fields of brilliant sunflowers, I could see other walled cities in the distance sprawling across the ridges of the hills. Recalling the museum paintings of medieval battles I had seen in Florence, the view illuminated in my mind the historical importance of these fortifications. For centuries they had been a bastion from many invasions, and even today they were the hub of life for the surrounding area.

—Maryanne Hamilton, "A Different Point of View"

---

because it wasn't square; it was shaped like an open fan. Anchoring the Campo was the handsome Palazzo Pubblico, or city hall, built around 1300, which had a bell tower so slender and audacious, so much taller than anyone would expect, that it set a tone of high civic enjoyment. The square sloped upward, and all the buildings around its rim were consistent in their height and sensibility. It was a collective work of art, and we sat at an outdoor café and had lunch, our goal achieved, hardly believing our good luck.

The square had the serenity of well-proportioned space, but it was also alive with people; obviously it had always been the emotional center of Sienese life. At that time I hadn't even heard of its most famous event, the horse race called the Palio, held every summer since 1659 amid much medieval pageantry and hysteria. The nags that clomp around the perimeter of the Campo represent Siena's contentious political districts, and the event takes its passion from the fact that it's much more than a horse race. It's a ritual acting out of an arcane system of municipal governance by seventeen highly territorial tribes.

After lunch we walked up to the cathedral which, along with a striped campanile, regally occupied the city's high ground. But nothing about the exterior of the church prepared me for its interior. All I could think when I stepped inside was "How wonderful!" I was amazed that an isolated Italian town in the early 1200s had found the energy to raise such an exuberant house of God. The nave was a fantasia of zebra stripes—alternating bands of black and white marble that formed not only the walls of the church but two rows of massive columns, which supported two rows of Romanesque arches, which supported two higher rows of Gothic arches and windows, which in turn supported a blue ceiling with gold stars and a vaulted dome. Other wonders gradually revealed themselves: a mosaic floor that covered the entire area of the church, a superb marble pulpit by Nicola Pisano, a Saint John the Baptist by Donatello, and a profusion of other works tucked into every niche. From there we went next door to a small museum, where Siena sprang its final marvel on us: Duccio's group of small paintings of the life of Christ that had been part of the duomo's original altarpiece.

All those Duccios completed our crash course in Sienese art,

and we began to think about heading back. Just then we noticed a
stone stairway that a guard said would take us to a panoramic view.
The museum, it turned out, was housed within the walls of a new
nave that the city started adding to the cathedral in 1339 but had
to abandon, and our stairs, spiraling up and up, deposited us on top
of its unfinished façade. From that catwalk we could look down on
the entire city. The time was around 4:20. I remember that it
wasn't on the hour or the half-hour because we were startled
when the bells in the campanile began to ring. It was a jubilant,
spread-the-news kind of ringing, and suddenly it dawned on us
what news was being spread. The war was over!

Below us the city exploded into life. Men and women and children came running from every direction down the streets that
emptied into the Campo. We scrambled down to join them. The
square was a sea of happy people, and it already had an air of
pageantry—heraldic banners were hanging from the windows of
the Palazzo Pubblico. We seemed to be the only Allied soldiers
there; Siena had been skirted by the retreating and pursuing
armies, and whatever troops may have once been stationed in the
city were gone. Later it occurred to me that all four of us had
German names: Helmuth Gerbich, Herbert Myers, William
Schramm, and William Zinsser.

Now, seeing four GIs, the people of Siena hugged us and
shouted "*Viva America!*" and lifted us onto their shoulders and carried us around the square. We didn't feel like conquering heroes—
none of us had seen combat. But we had lived with the smashed
towns and smashed lives that were the residue of that bloody cam-
paign up the Italian peninsula, and on behalf of its real heroes we
acted as happy as we felt, bobbing above the crowd. Darkness had
fallen by the time we got back to our jeep. But we weren't allowed
to leave; little bands of musicians and revelers kept falling in ahead
of us and behind us as we inched our way through the crowded
streets. Finally we broke away, reached a gate through the wall, and
found our road to the coast.

The night was black and the countryside was asleep. But the villages were awake, and when the people heard our jeep they ran out

to shout "*Viva la pace!*" One old man handed a bottle of Chianti into our jeep and we all joined him in a drink. At one point we saw a bonfire on a hill far ahead. Eventually our road took us past that bonfire, which was being tended by some farmers, and from there we could see another bonfire on another hill, and when we reached that bonfire we saw still another one, far away. Only after three or four bonfires did we make the connection: the country people were spreading the news. Many hills later, around midnight, we got back to our base. The next morning we learned that nobody else had been allowed off the base. When the end of the war was announced on Armed Forces Radio, all passes were suspended.

But that wasn't the end of Siena in my life. After V-E Day the army faced the problem of keeping its men occupied, not having enough troopships to bring us home. As one solution, it started a college in Florence, recruiting its faculty from officers and enlisted men who had been teachers in civilian life. My unit had moved back to a dismal region of southern Italy; months of tedium stretched ahead of us. One day I saw in *The Stars and Stripes* an item announcing the new college. It said that only one man per unit would be admitted. Being whisked off to Florence was the ultimate fairy godmother's intervention, and I ran to the adjutant to be the first to apply. My lifelong newspaper reading habit was rewarded, and on the first of July I went off to college.

Our campus was a former Italian air corps academy just outside Florence. My dormitory window had a perfectly framed view across the red tile roofs to Brunelleschi's cathedral dome and Giotto's campanile. I decided to sign up for art history courses, never having taken any, and they became my passport into the Renaissance. In the morning I could look at slides of Ghiberti's baptistery doors and then go see the doors on my own; our afternoons were free, and we were the only tourists in town. The city had just begun to bring its masterpieces out of hiding, and sometimes I caught one of them being hauled through the streets or hoisted back onto its pedestal—I looked Cellini's Perseus in the eye. That summer was a re-Renaissance—art again belonged to the Florentine people, as it had when the statues were first put up. By September the city was in my bones. I found myself dropping in on statues and paintings that had become old friends, or hiking across the Ponte Vecchio—every other bridge across the Arno had been blown up—and climbing up to my favorite church, San Miniato, and my favorite view of Florence, lying below me in the palm of my hand.

When the summer was over I reported to an embarkation depot at Naples to wait for a troopship to take me home. There I had plenty of time to think about returning to civilian life. Everything depended on whether I would have to go back to college. When I left Princeton to enlist in the army I had a grab-bag of accelerated wartime credits that almost added up to a B.A. degree. Now I had three more credits, which Princeton granted just for serving in the armed forces, plus some certificates for the courses I took at Florence. Originally I had thought I would want to go back to Princeton to round out my fragmented college years. Now I only wanted to get on with whatever I was going to do next.

In November a troopship finally brought me home, and I went to Princeton for an interview. I was nervous as I walked toward Nassau Hall, its walls clothed in 200 years of historic ivy; the army certificates I was clutching suddenly looked crude. Worst of all, I learned that my interview would be with Dean Root. Robert K. Root, dean of Princeton's faculty and guardian of its academic honor, was then in his late sixties, the prototype old professor: stern and dry and dour. I had taken his lecture course in eighteenth-century English literature and had listened, week after week, as he rained on our unappreciative heads the pearls of his scholarship, excavating with dry precision the buried ironies of Jonathan Swift and the unsuspected jests of Alexander Pope, which even then we continued not to suspect. It never occurred to me that he and I would ever meet, and I was dismayed to be meeting him now. He looked just as stern up close.

Dean Root studied my Princeton transcript and then looked at my army certificates. He said he had never seen anything like them; my impression was that he didn't think I had spent the summer at Oxford. He examined my Princeton transcript again and took another look at the certificates and made some notes. I could see that he was adding up my credits and that they weren't coming out right. Finally he shook his head and mumbled that I seemed to be a little short. I told myself I was a dead duck.

Then, abruptly, I was no longer being interviewed by a dean. A real person was sitting across from me, his features not unkindly, and he was asking me what I had done during the war. I found myself telling him about my year in North Africa and how it had opened my eyes to the Arab world. I told him about my trips to Rome, and about seeing *La Bohême* in the Naples opera house, and about my Renaissance summer in Florence, and about the weekend jaunts I made to Pisa and Lucca and Siena. A clouded look came over Dean Root's face.

"Tell me," he said, "I suppose Siena was mostly destroyed during the war." I realized that I was the first returning veteran to bring him news of the city. Suddenly I understood what Siena would mean to this quintessential humanist; probably he had first visited Siena as a young man himself. Suddenly it was possible to understand that Dean Root had once been a young man. I told him that Siena hadn't been touched by the war and that the great duomo was still there on the crest of the hill.

Dean Root smiled fleetingly and saw me to the door. He said Princeton would inform me of its decision soon. Two weeks later he wrote to say that I had met Princeton's requirements for a B.A. degree and that I would receive my diploma at a special winter graduation for returning servicemen. I was quite sure he had waived one or two credits to make the total add up. I think that in the middle of my interview he decided to stop counting. Numbers weren't as important to him as learning, and he freed me to get on with my life. But I also think that if Siena had been destroyed I would have had to go back for one more term.

In the fall of 1992 I watched the steady approach of my seventieth birthday and wondered how to contend with it when it arrived. Then one day I knew what I wanted to do. "Let's go to Siena for my birthday," I said to Caroline. I would celebrate the day by going back to the place where I spent the most celebratory day of my life. I didn't want to relive that moment; I just wanted to make a connection with its emotions—to borrow its essential joy. Whether such emotions were transferable across the decades I wouldn't know until I made the journey.

Over the years I had been back to Tuscany several times, but always as part of a longer trip, not as a destination, and always in summer. Florence was then so swollen with tourists that I could hardly find the city I remembered. But now it was fall, and I made a one-week itinerary that would take Caroline and me to Siena by way of Florence, starting in Rome. There was no question of starting anywhere else. My Italy begins and ends in Rome, and has since I was a schoolboy, when my Latin teacher kept plaster statues of the Roman gods on his desk. He knew that the icons that inhabit the classrooms of our youth can exert a lifelong spell, and in my case he was right. As soon as the war landed me in Italy I fidgeted to see Rome, though I was stationed in far-off Brindisi, in Italy's heel. When I finally wangled a five-day pass, I hitchhiked to Rome in a truck, over the Apennines in midwinter, taking two days to get there and two to get back. But the day in between was one I've never forgotten.

Since then I've stopped off in Rome whenever I could. I go to Rome the way other people go to the Bahamas and lie in the sun—to be renewed. Friends try to warn me; the traffic, they say, is "impossible." But it's never any more impossible than it was the last time, and it wasn't impossible when Caroline and I arrived there on a Friday morning in October of 1992. After twenty-four hours of walking all over the city, I felt young again.

On Saturday afternoon we took a train to Florence and headed out into the streets to get reacquainted. I was wary, recalling my earlier sense of loss. But the summer hordes were gone, and Florence was no longer their captive. The city had a mercantile bustle, going about its old business. Money was still its lubricant— the shops were elegant and expensive—and the Medicis were still around every corner. I had forgotten what a serious face Florence presents to the world, its color relentlessly brown, its grid flat and rectilinear, its buildings massive in their stonework—just the opposite of gay, red, undulating Siena. No wonder the two medieval city-states, so unalike in temperament, were enemies for so many centuries.

Now, rediscovering Florence, I felt fresh respect for the city. If it was serious, as many serious people are admirable without necessarily being much fun, it insisted that I take it seriously, and I did. It had the earnest familiarity of an old college roommate. So did the other guests at our hotel: professorial men and tweed-skirted women ensconced under reading lamps. They looked as if they had been coming there every year since the 1920s—sent by, or perhaps invented by, E. M. Forster.

On Sunday my feet took me all over Florence; they still knew the way. Ghiberti's baptistry doors were still "worthy to be the gates of paradise," as Michelangelo described them. His own statue of David in the Galleria dell'Accademia and Giotto's frescoes in the church of Santa Croce were no less worthy, and Fra Angelico's frescoes in the convent of San Marco had lost none of their unassailable purity. Caroline let me follow my inner compass, and when it pointed to San Miniato I warned her that we were in for a climb. Walking across the Ponte Vecchio, I was back in my army boots: left along the Arno, then a right turn, then through the old wall, then up the long penitential steps. San Miniato was waiting for me at the top. I remembered the church as being so likeable, almost toy-like in its gaiety and in the daring of its split-level nave—it was begun in 1013—that I was afraid my older self would find it too likeable, too ingratiating; my naïve soldier self had

> Caeser decided to call the... city Florence (Fiorenza), as it was a very beautiful name and very apposite, and it seemed, with its suggestion of flowers, to make a good omen.
> —Benvenuto Cellini
> (1500–1571)

undoubtedly been seduced by it. But that fear evaporated as soon as I walked in, and when my art-wise wife pronounced it a gem and my guidebook pronounced it "one of the finest Romanesque churches in Italy," I felt that my pilgrimage to Florence was complete, the circle full.

On Monday we rented a car and headed south for Siena, first stopping in San Gimignano whose phantom towers had hailed me so long ago. It turned out to be real, a medieval jewel. Beyond it I found the country road my friends and I had taken on the day the war ended, and I followed it toward the coast. But the road hadn't improved much since 1945, and I decided to turn south to Siena.

"I thought this was a return trip," Caroline said. "Keep going to Volterra." I told her that Volterra was quite a push. "I want to see it," she said, and after quite a push we sighted it in the distance, silhouetted on a hill behind its armament of walls. The brooding city held me again, and I was glad I had come—another memory nailed down. When at last we did head for Siena we ran out of daylight and ended up driving in the dark. No bonfires kept us company; in 1992 any news worth spreading would be spread by television. But otherwise I imagined life on those Tuscan farms to be not much different. For the grandchildren of the villagers who cheered our jeep through the night with bottles of Chianti, it was probably still 1945.

At Siena our hotel was outside the wall, as most of Siena's hotels are, and we spent Tuesday visiting some of the distinctive hill towns of that region, like Pienza and Montepulciano. I was saving Siena for my birthday, and the next morning Caroline and I went into town. We entered by the Porta Romana and walked up a meandering street that I had no doubt would bring us to the Campo. When it did, the square looked exactly as I remembered it; nothing had changed. I felt a surge of gratitude that such a place existed in my life, always available, no appointment necessary. I strolled over to the restaurant where I wanted to have lunch and reserved an outdoor table for four. Just before leaving New York I had run into old friends, Rosa and Al Silverman. They happened to mention that they would be vacationing in Perugia, and I asked

if they would drive over to Siena on October 7 to help us celebrate. They said they would, and we set a rendezvous for 1:30 at
the restaurant.

Caroline and I lingered in the Campo, but I could feel the
cathedral pulling me up the hill, and I didn't resist. As soon as I
stepped inside I thought "How wonderful!" It, too, was unchanged.
We spent an hour marveling and then went to the museum next
door to see the Duccios. But I also kept an eye out for my stairway,
and when I found it I knew what I had to do. At the summit my
view was intact—no postwar buildings, as in London or Paris,
impinged on a remembered skyline. Far below, the Campo spread
its fan, and I mentally filled it with crowds hurrying from every
direction. Except for the vertigo, I felt terrific.

By then it was almost 1:30, and we made our way back down
to the Campo. Rosa and Al were there, and the four of us settled
down to lunch. As the October sun moved across the sky, the
buildings around the Campo turned in subtle gradations from red
to rose to pink. In the square, people came and went, meeting and
separating. Toddlers played, mothers watched, teenagers lounged,
old men and women gossiped. Watching them, I was struck by
how much it meant to me to be with good friends from my own
real life. None of us talked about tourist things—where we had
been or what sights we had seen. We talked about the same things
everyone in the square was talking about: children and grandchildren, food and drink, work and play. Things got said that we
hadn't known about each other.

Ordinarily I seek change—it has always been a tonic to me. But
on that October 7th in Siena I was at ease, slipping over into my
next decade without regret. The connection I had hoped to make
was made; the joyful emotions of May 7, 1945 did turn out to be
transferable. But mainly I was contented because I was in a place
where values that are important to me had endured for a thousand
years: the humanity of urban space, the integrity of architecture,
the magnificence of Christian art.

Dean Root's rueful question came back to me. The thought
that Siena might have been destroyed seemed unthinkable now, as

it hadn't when the dean was old and I was young, home from the war that destroyed so much. Now the continuity of the city mattered just as deeply to me. Siena had survived, and so had I.

William Zinsser, a writer, editor, and teacher, is the author of sixteen books, including the classic On Writing Well, *now it its sixth edition, and, most recently,* Easy to Remember: The Great American Songwriters and Their Songs. *He began his career at the* New York Herald Tribune *and has since written regularly for leading magazines.*

SAUL BELLOW

* * *

A Tuscan Winter

This season has special rewards.

WINTER IN TUSCANY? WELL, WHY NOT. MILLIONS OF ITALIANS DO
it. The modern tourist takes his winter holidays either in the sun
or on the ski slopes. But business brought me to Florence in
December, and I had put it to my wife that, with two weeks free
when business was done, the Sienese countryside might be just the
place to restore the frazzled minds of two urban Americans. The
crowds of winter would be madding elsewhere—in the Caribbean
or on Alpine slopes—and we should have the whole of this ancient
region to ourselves, sharing the cold with the populace.

Anticipating severe weather, we had brought our winter-silks,
goosedowns, rabbit linings, mufflers, and Reeboks. Montalcino was
cold, all right, but the air was as clear as icicles. Autumn had just
ended, the new wine was in the barrels, the last of the olives in the
presses, the sheep were grazing, the pigs fattening, and the ancient
churches and monasteries were adding yet another winter to their
tally. From the heights near Montalcino we could see Siena. In
forty kilometers there was nothing to block the view—I have no
special weakness for views. It was the beauty of the visibility as
such, together with the absence of factories, refineries, and dumps,
that penetrated the twentieth-century landscape armor of my soul.

To admire views, however, you need to stand still, and you had to endure the cold. The *tramontana* was battering the town when we arrived. It forced open windows in the night and scoured our faces by day.

Generations of Americans brought up with central heating can endure the cold on skis, in snowmobiles, on the ice, but they lack the European ability to go about their business in cold kitchens and icy parlors. Europeans take pride in their endurance of winter hardships. It gives them a superiority which to us seems less Spartan than masochistic.

I can remember cursing the management in grim English hotel rooms while going through my pockets for a shilling to drop in the gas meter, and as a guest in a Cambridge college I was driven once to the porter's lodge to ask for a little warmth. The gentleman porter said, "If you will look under the bed, sir, you will discover a heating device."

Under the bedspring, when I lifted the coverlet, I found a wire fixture holding a naked forty-watt bulb. The heat this bulb threw was supposed to penetrate the mattress and restore you to life. This austerity went with the dusty ragged academic gowns of the dons, held together, literally, with Scotch tape and staples. It pleased these scholars to be dowdy, indifferent to blue fingers and red noses, and heedless of freezing toilet seats. For the mind was its own place and made a heaven of hell. The door to this mental heaven stood open, but I was freezing.

Once freed from dependency on heating, you don't mind the cold. The Tuscan winter didn't affect your appreciation of Tuscan cheeses, soups, and wines. On your hummocky mattress you slept well enough, and after breakfast you went to visit a Romanesque church, a papal summer residence; you walked in the fields. You can sit comfortably in sheltered sunny corners and watch the sheep grazing.

The people you meet are happy to have you here; they take your off-season visit as a mark of admiration for the long and splendid history of their duchy and like to reward you with bits of information. In passing, one tells you about the deforestation of hilltops during the Dark Ages; another mentions the ravages of malaria and the Black Death of 1348; a third fills you in about exports to England from medieval Tuscany. The soils of all these fields seem to have passed through millions of human hands, generation after generation. Our American surroundings will never be so fully humanized. But the landscape carries the centuries lightly, and ancient buildings and ruins do not produce gloomy feelings. Romanesque interiors in fact are a good cure for heaviness.

The region is as famous for its products—oil, wine, and cheeses—as for castles, fortresses, and churches. A disastrous freeze killed the olive groves some winters ago—the ancient trees now furnish farms with winter fuel. The new plantings do not as yet yield much oil, but the wine reserves are as full as ever.

In the Fattoria dei Barbi, belonging to the Colombini Cinelli family, the vats, some of them made of Slovenia oak, resemble the engines of 747 jets in size. On walls and beams there are thermometers and gauges. We are conducted here by Angela, a young woman whose pretty face rivals the wine display in interest. Clean quiet cellars, level after level—the only living creature we meet below is a cat who seems to know the tour by heart. During World War II false partitions were put up to hide old vintages from the Germans. The almost sacred bottles are dimly, somewhat reverentially lighted. You feel called upon to pay your respects to this rare Brunello di Montalcino. With a banner tail, the cat is an auxiliary guide and leads the party up and down, in and out, from cellar to cellar. We take to this tomcat, who has all the charm of a veteran of the sex wars.

When we return to ground level the cat leaves the building between our legs. We enter next an enormous room where white pecorino cheeses, regularly spaced on racks, are biding their time. After the cheeses come the meat-curing rooms. In spiced air the hams hang like the boxing gloves of heavyweights. To see so much meat takes away the desire for food, so that when we go into the excellent Taverna dei Barbi I am more inclined to admire the pasta than to eat it. But you can never lose your desire for the Brunello wine. Your susceptibility returns at the same rate as the glass fills.

Once again it makes sense to be a multimillionaire. The Brunello fragrance is an immediate Q.E.D. of the advantages of the pursuit of riches. (I never joined up.)

"Don't miss Pienza," we were many times advised, so we recruit Angela to drive us there on a sunny but very sharp morning. Pienza was the birthplace, in 1405, of Aeneas Silvius Piccolomini, later Pope Pius II. He was responsible for the handsome group of Renaissance buildings at the center of the town. It is the finest of these buildings, the Palazzo Piccolomini, that we have come to inspect.

From our parking place we ascend to the main street. The first impression is one of stony Renaissance elegance combined with the modern plate glass of shops. The temperature is a bar or two below freezing. A fine group of old gents standing outside the open door of a café acknowledge us with dignity as we move down the all-stone pavement to the palazzo. As cultural duty requires, we look into the church of Pop Pio, where we see long fissures running through the stone nave. (How to keep up with the maintenance of monuments!) Continuing to the palazzo we are overtaken in the courtyard by the custodian. He spots us from the café *en face*, his warm hideout. Thickly dressed in wool and leather, he comes with his ring of silver-glinting keys to lead us up the stairs. We pass through the small living quarters used until not very recently by surviving members of the family. A Piccolomini Count Silvio lived in the three front rooms until 1960. We understand from our guide that a picture of an aviator atop the piano in the music room represented the last of his line. Perhaps he was Count Silvio's son and heir—exact information is hard to come by.

In the living quarters there is a framed genealogical tree weighed down by hundreds of names. We pass through the noble library and the armor room. We circle rugs so ancient, so thin, so pale that a step might shatter them. On bookshelves are huge leather-bound volumes of the classics. I note that fifteenth century popes were reading Thucydides and even Aristophanes, and as we enter the papal bedroom I think how difficult it would have been

to handle these folios in bed. In this freezing chamber the imposing bed is grandly made and formally covered in dark green, a dire
seaweed-colored fabric, and sinking, sinking, sinking into decay.
Perhaps it goes back to the last century. The mattress and bedding
may be no more than eighty or ninety years old, but the thing
carries a threat of eternity and you feel that if you were to lie
down and put your head on this seaweed-colored bolster you
would never rise again. There is a fireplace, or rather a Gothic
cavity in the wall big enough to accommodate eight-foot logs, but
you'd have to fire it up for a week to drive out such an accumu-
lation of cold.

We are happy to escape again into the great-windowed hall.
The guide has gone out on a balcony to sun himself. Joining him,
we return to Italy itself and latch on to the sun with gratitude.

We order cappuccino in an open-to-the-weather café. The
great espresso machine sizzles and spits, and the cups are served on
the enormous polished bar. They lose heat so quickly that you'd
better down them before ice forms.

Catering to tourists, the boutiques are nicely heated. We go to
a stationery shop and buy a mini-volume of Petrarch and other
Florentine general-issue items—classy clutter for the apartments of
the well-traveled. The one prize is a Venetian glass pen from
Murano, an iridescent spiral.

In Montalcino I am treated by a local herbal specialist for a
sprained shoulder. His nickname is "Il Barba" and he is an old man
of heroic stature, more stubbly than bearded. He became a local
hero by playing the part of the brigand Bruscone (popularly
known as "Il Barba") at a party celebrating the new Bruscone dei
Barbi wine. Evidently he fell in love with his own portrayal of the
legendary bandit. Himself a man of action, he was a Resistance
fighter, and the walls of the narrow front room of his apartment
are hung with medals and certificates of valor. There is also a display of fine guns, for he is a hunter. This giant and his small wife
conduct us to the long cupboard-like kitchen, where he sets me
on a high stool and, like any doctor, asks me solicitously how I

came by this sprain. I tell him I took a header over the handlebars of a bike last summer in Vermont. It doesn't make much sense to him that the likes of me should be an intrepid bike rider. He tells me to strip. I take off my shirt and he examines me. When we have between us located the painful places, he pours his mixture into a small saucepan and heats it on the stove. At all times, the old wife is close behind him with her arms folded and held tightly to her body. While she gossips hoarsely with our Italian friends, he rubs my shoulder with his herbal remedy dissolved in olive oil. He applies the hot mixture using his hand like a housepainter's brush. At a nod from her husband, the wife steps out to the porch to fetch a salve to follow the ointment. Enjoying the massage, I begin to feel that this Barba may cure me. I have a weakness anyway for secret herbal remedies, and the treatment in the kitchen has its occult side. (Special security measures are taken.) I pull on my shirt again, altogether pleased with the occasion. The exertion of getting into my pullover causes no pain, and I tell him he is a wonderful therapist. He bows as though he already knew this. In the parlor he reaches into a cupboard next to the guns and takes down a drawstring sack containing a large number of wild boar tusks. I should never have guessed that they were so light. Some of these trophies have been dipped with silver, and I suppose necklaces or bracelets can be made of them. Thieves would rather have these than the guns, he says.

The great bandit Barba towers over us, smiling, and holds the door open, refusing payment and telling me to come back tomorrow for another treatment. He is so tall that we don't have to duck under his arm. We go down the stairs into the night very happy.

Further outdoor sightseeing: Habituated to the cold, we no longer shun it. We now prefer outdoor excursions to the inspection of church interiors. There is a charcoal burners' camp nearby, and an elderly gentleman, Ilio Raffaelli, who was himself until his twenty-fifth year a *carbonaro*, shows us how the workers lived and how the charcoal was made. The camp, which he has reconstructed himself, is extremely primitive. The little dwelling of the burners reminds me of an American sod hut, with soil and grass stuffed into a wooden framework. The place is windowless. The workmen and their families slept on simple wooden frames, which occupied most of the space. One was for man and wife, the other for the children, as many as five or six. All worked in the woods, bringing up water from the spring or, in season, gathering berries and other edibles. There were no metal artifacts except axes and saws. The shovels were wooden, the rakes were skillfully whittled. The burners contracted with the landowners, and they camped for half a year or so till they had cut all the usable wood on the property. Then they moved to another estate, where they built a new sod house. The huts were warm enough at night, said our guide, heated by a small fire.

Raffaelli is a sturdy, short man in a cap and an open jacket. (The afternoon was not particularly warm: our noses and eyes were running; his were dry. He was evidently indurated against natural hardships.) A black thread that had worked loose from the cap hung over his face unnoticed while he gave his explanatory lecture. (With his large objectives he didn't notice trifles.) In his description of the charcoal-making process, he was exceptionally precise: the cutting of the wood into proper lengths, the layers of leaves and soil piled on the mound, the space at the center for the fire, which had to be stoked day and night. There were wooden ladders leaning on the cone, and screens against the wind, which might drive the blaze too high, endangering the work of months.

So *this* was how people for many centuries lived upon the land, right *on* the packed earth, so to speak, so adept in the management of their pots, spoons, axes, and handmade rakes, so resourceful—to see this was a lesson worth a whole shelf of history books. I understood even better what life had been like when our guide said, "When one of our boys in the army sent a letter we gathered inside the hut and sat on the beds to listen to the reading." He laughed and added that they had all been sent to the priest to learn their letters.

His little Italian car was parked just at the edge of the woods, and he would get into it at dusk and drive to Montalcino, where he lived. You felt, however, that his real life was here, in this cold clearing. He seemed unwilling to part with the old life and was perhaps not a thorough townsman. A self-taught scholar, he had written a book about the plants and small fauna. Schoolchildren were brought to him for lessons about the woods. He taught them the names of the trees and sang them the charcoal burners' ballads, and reminisced about this vanished trade. He was a modest person, without the legendary airs of Signor Barba the herbal doctor.

Finally we go into the woods near San Giovanni d'Asso with two truffle hunters, Ezio Dinetti and Fosco Lorenzetti, and their dogs, Lola, Fiamma, and Iori. On our arrival in San Giovanni we are received by the young, dark-haired mayor of the town, Roberto Cappelli, who makes us a little speech of welcome and presents us with a heavy bronze truffle medallion.

The season for truffles is almost over. It has been an unexceptional year—slim pickings. But the dogs are no less keen, rushing from the cars as soon as the doors are opened. There is no breed of truffle hounds. Lola, Fiamma, and Iori appear to be ordinary no-account mutts, but they are in fact highly trained specialists, officially listed, with their own photo-ID license cards and tattooed registration numbers. Turn them over and you can see the numerals under the pink skin. The novice Iori, a skinny dark brown adolescent, is hobbled with a length of chain to prevent his rushing off by himself in his enthusiasm. The added weight gives him a bowlegged gait.

We set out after the dogs on a path through the poplars, tramping over dry leaves. Hurrying after them, you find yourself breathing deeper, drawing in the pungent winter smells of vegetation and turned-up soil. The experienced hunters work the dogs earnestly, with urgent exclamations and commands: Lola, *dai* (Go), *Qui* (Here), *Vieni qui* (Come here), *Giù* (Down), *Dove*? (Where?), *Piglialo* (Take it). They cajole, huff, threaten, praise, caution, restrain, interrogate, and reward their dogs. The animals track a distant scent. Though the ground is frozen they will sniff out a truffle under a foot and a half of earth. Each man has an imple-

ment on a leather strap slung over the shoulder, a device about two
feet in length with a sharp rectangular blade for digging and sampling the earth. With this
vanghetta the hunters scoop
up a clod of beige-brown
mud and nose it with intensity. If the soil is saturated
with the truffle odor they
halloo the dogs to dig
deeper.

> ───────※───────
>
> All truffles must be hunted
> with animals, usually pigs,
> which can smell the fungus
> when, upon maturity and a foot
> deep in the soil, it releases its
> aroma. The Italians prefer dogs.
> For one, the Tuscan *fungi* favor
> overgrown areas, and pigs are
> too big to get under the
> scrub...nor can pigs cover as
> much land (a truffle hunt easily
> spans eight hours). And finally,
> Mario says that Italians prefer
> dogs because "you look ridicu-
> lous hunting with a pig."
> —Eugenia Bone, "Bella Fungi"
> *Forbes FYI*

Single file, we cross a thin
bridge, a couple of logs
strapped together over a
gully. Lola, the gifted matriarch, has found something,
and the dirt near the
streambed sprays behind her.
Ezio knows exactly where to
intervene and, paying her off
with a treat, himself unearths
a smallish truffle, a mere nub-
bin, and slips it into his
pocket.

The sun is going down, and we stop more often to chat under
the chilly poplars. The afternoon has not been a grand success, for
the dogs have turned up only three truffles. Ezio and Fosco insist
on our taking them. As we head back through the woods we hear
a dark story. Sporting honor among the hunters is not all that it
used to be, they tell us. Jealous competitors have taken to poison-
ing the more talented dogs, tossing out bits of sausage containing
strychnine when they leave the grounds, Ezio says with anger. A
promising pup of his was among the six dogs lost to the poisoners
last year. Months of training wasted. In the old days it took only a
year to break in a dog. Now that there are more hunters and fewer
truffles, you need as many as three years of training, so that when
a dog dies, the loss is considerable.

The ungloved hands of the hunters, when we shake them at parting, are warmer than ours, for all our leather and wool and Thinsulate. Driving back to Montalcino we consider the mystery of the truffle. Why is it so highly prized? We try to put a name to the musk that fills the car. It is digestive, it is sexual, it is a mortality odor. Having tasted it, I am willing to leave it to the connoisseurs. I shall go on sprinkling grated cheese on my pasta.

Saul Bellow is one of America's most prolific and acclaimed authors. He has won the Pulitzer Prize, the National Book Award (three times), and the Nobel Prize for Literature. He is the author of Seize the Day, Ravelstein, Herzog, *and* Humboldt's Gift, *among many other books.*

SUSAN STORM

⋆ ⋆ ⋆

Lost and Found on Monte Amiata

Travelers are cared for in the ancient manner.

I'D WANTED TO SEE THE CHANGING COLORS OF THE CHESTNUT trees on Monte Amiata before winter settled in. The day was as clear as the spring water gushing out of stone spouts, but close to the mountain the sky became a venomous gray and sheets of ice stung the windscreen. Finally, when the air was brittle with cold, it began to snow, and the white silence wrapped itself around us like a blanket. Birds stopped singing, frozen in fright. Insects were buried under the icy onslaught. All sound was swallowed by the curtain of white flakes.

Georgina cursed. I jumped out of the car, leaping like a child to catch frosty flakes on my tongue, my eyelashes, and my red-tipped nose.

The picture postcard chalets were sill-deep in snow, and in the monochromatic scene it was easy to be disoriented. We put chains on the wheels and crunched our way down under chestnut branches sagging with snow, passing snowplows whose drivers were a foggy blur behind the battling windshield wipers. When we finally reached the ski lodge at Monte Amiata's base, we sat around a fire and drank glasses of steaming mocha.

The night was dark with snow. We took a wrong turn and, with no idea of where we were, landed up in a lane hedged on both sides with savage-looking thorn bushes. When I got out of the car, the cold knocked the breath out of me. I crunched toward the lights that streamed from the small windows of a stone house as the snow started falling with serious intent.

"*Buona sera!*" smiled the man who opened the door to my heavy knocking. "Come inside from the cold!" he said in Italian. The room was enormous, and warmed by a roaring fire where pumpkins ripened on the wooden mantlepiece. We shook off the snow and were immediately intoxicated by the array of aromas emitting from the kitchen.

His name, he said, was Marcello, and his wife was Francine. Would we stay for dinner, seeing that the car wouldn't get us home in this weather? Their friends would be arriving shortly, they said, and they would be proud to introduce them to the lost strangers.

Soon the room was filled with people stomping off snow, exuberantly kissing each other on each cheek and one extra for luck, inquiring noisily about recent events, and applauding the steady stream of food emanating from the warm kitchen. Marcello opened several bottles of wine from the local vineyard and lovingly wiped cobwebby dust off with a silk scarf. He poured each of us a deep glass in absolution of the cold. All held its deep red hues to the light for admiration, tested its warm, briny aromas with each nostril, rolled its smoothness over their tongue.

We sat down to dinner, squashed shoulder to shoulder. If anyone had looked in, they would have thought it was the last supper. The large wooden table, that had celebrated many banquets, been the deciding factor around many family skirmishes, and had had enough loaves of bread kneaded on it to feed Hannibal's army, creaked under the abundant weight of smoked loins of clove-studded pork, glazed and golden chickens, crusty warm loaves, sweet potatoes, bowls of linguini annointed with olive oil, a boiling caldron of *osso buco* and mushroom soup, plump pumpkins, ropes of salami, and skeins of pasta.

We ate the wild boar that had crashed through the bushes onto the road, compliments of the irate shotgun-wielding farmer from next door, accompanied of course, and I lost count of how often my glass was refilled.

That everyone was speaking an assortment of European languages didn't matter to my English-trained ear: somehow in that environment I understood everything that was said. To my surprise, when asked questions in strange tongues, I replied in English. The room was warm and energetic with discussion— about the merits of the wines and the labor of the food, about the mysterious workings of politics and the new grandchildren; about the problems with wild *cinghiale* and fears of this early snow. This was hospitality extended as only the Italians know how. Georgina and I soon felt we'd known these people all our lives.

Marcello, with a film-star face and elegant clothes, tipped the last of his wine into his mouth and walked to the white baby grand piano in the corner of the room. He lifted the cover and still standing above the ivory keys, began to tinkle a few notes from an Italian opera. Candles burned around the room, and everyone's faces glowed warm with food and ambiance.

He sat at the tapestry stool, trilled his fingers, and launched into a full rendition of "La Traviata." Francine came and stood behind him, her hand resting gently on his shoulder. Then she began to sing in a voice that equaled nightingales, the notes rising and falling in practiced cadence.. The room was quiet except for the magic of her voice and the piano, quiet as the falling snow as we all became immersed in our own, satiated contemplation.

We occasionally refilled our glasses, or broke more bread, or stoked the fire while "La Traviata" was sung to life. When I looked at the handsome Marcello in his elegantly crumpled linen pants, and watched his fingers fly across the keys, I wished there was a way of encapsulating pleasure.

Susan Storm is a widely published photojournalist working for Australian and international magazines and newspapers. Born in Prague, she grew up in South Africa and now lives in Australia. She has won many literary and photographic competitions, and now runs travel writing workshops.

PART TWO

SOME THINGS TO DO

HEIDI SCHUESSLER

✳

Tuscany's Wild, Wild West

Where the deer and the antipasti play.

"NIENTE, NIENTE," SIGHS PAOLO. NO FISH. HAND OVER HAND, HE and his assistant Massimo pull in a mile of fishing net from the depths of the Tyrrhenian Sea. It yields only two dozen small fish and five octopuses. To prove this is just an off-season slump and has nothing to do with his skills as a fisherman, he pulls from a hatch a bulging photo album that relives the day last October when he caught 55,000 pounds of fish.

Blond, broad-shouldered, and with eyes as blue as the sea in which he fishes, Paolo Fanciulli has been trolling for almost all of his thirty-eight years. He docks his boat at the village of Talamone, in the heart of Tuscany's coast, where he's lived all his life. "I went to Amsterdam last year to visit a friend for two weeks, and after two days I was crying for Talamone," he says. "I thought, 'Why did I ever leave the Maremma?'"

To the people who live and work in the forgotten corner of Tuscany called the Maremma, ties to the land are as strong as the summer's punishing heat (the temperature frequently tops 100 degrees in July and August). This is not the romantic Tuscany seen in coffee-table books; this is where people set their calendars by the season and their days by the sun. This is Tuscany at its most exposed: unguarded and without pretense.

✳

If it seems as if time has forgotten the Maremma, and in a way it has. The region is at once the oldest and youngest part of Tuscany. Here, Etruscans fought to make a living from the water-logged land (the word *maremma* means "swamp"), but the Romans who conquered them could never maintain the complex irrigation system, and the land fell into disuse. Widespread malaria made it uninhabitable for centuries, save by the criminals and bandits who fled here to hide among the dense *macchia* scrub. Even the Renaissance bypassed the Maremma. One of the only lasting Medici influences seen here is the series of ancient towers rebuilt by Cosimo in the sixteenth century to protect Tuscany's coast from marauders.

Only in 1828, when Grand Duke Leopold II, a member of the Austrian imperial family that ruled Tuscany until the mid-1800s, began broad land reclamation projects did people start filtering back in from the protective hills. When the last swamps were drained in the 1950s and malaria was finally eradicated, the modern Maremma was born.

Today, the region stretches from Cecina in the north to Monte Argentario in the south, from the Tyrrhenian Sea to the edge of the hilly interior. Within its borders are reminders of the more familiar Tuscany: a rolling landscape of sunflowers, grapes, and olives. But there are also fields of corn and wheat, coastal plains home to hundreds of shorebirds, dense woods sheltering deer and wild boar, and long corridors of umbrella pines and cypress trees that stand as barriers against the wind.

"As a child I remember how salty the winds were," recalls Franca Spinola as we drive through a long alley of cypress trees planted by her mother as windbreaks. Spinola is the owner of La Parrina, a 1,100-acre farm near Orbetello that was a wedding present from her great-grandfather. At the heart of the property is a cluster of farmhouses, originally built close together for protection against roaming bandits. Now the buildings constitute a beautiful *agriturismo* where guests can experience life in the country. But

with the region on the periphery of Tuscany, both literally and fig-
uratively, Spinola cannot rely on guests alone, so she continues to
make the farm self-sustaining. La Parrina produces cheese, olive
oil, fruit, yogurt, and, of course, wine. By Tuscany's standards, the
farm is a small producer—only 150,000 bottles a year—but it's
drawing an international following. Its wine carries an earthy
essence of rosemary and sage. "That flavor is everywhere in the air
here," says Spinola, who grows seven varieties of rosemary. "It is a
true Maremman wine."

Walking through the extensive vineyards later that day, Spinola
stops at a hilltop near an old barn. Bending low, she brushes away
the grass from a slate of white stone flecked with red—evidence of
ancient Roman construction. "See there? You can see where
there's a foundation laid," she says. "The Maremma is a very rich
place, but you have to go find the history yourself."

You also have to know where to look. Near the coast, by the
town of Alberese, is the Maremma's richest treasure—not a cathedral or a painting, but a park. A masterpiece of preservation, the
Natural Park of Maremma spans forty square miles and encompasses everything from marshes and mountains to calcareous cliffs
and sandy seashore. It was designated a protected area in 1975 and
is understandably called one of the last earthly paradises in Italy.
The best way to see it is with the men who know it best: the cowboys known as the *butteri*.

Everyday for more than one hundred years, these men have ridden out on horseback to herd the rare white cattle that roam the
park. I meet three of the *butteri* early one morning by the stables.
They arrive together on foot, dressed alike in plaid cotton shirts,
green vests, tan pants, and leather gaiters. After a nodded "Good
morning," two of them, Davide and Stefano, walk into the corrals
to choose today's horses from the herd at the fence.

"Carmen, Adriatica, Corsica, Lima..." Sandro, the white-haired
butteri captain, takes the morning roll call of horses, all 130 of
whom he knows by name. Sandro's body is hardened from twenty-
one years in the saddle, but smiles break through as he talks about
the animals and the job that has been a way of life for men here

since the nineteenth century. The *butteri* remain among the region's most visible symbols, and stories of their prowess are legendary. When William Cody's Wild West Show came to Italy in 1905, the American cowboys challenged the *butteri* to a test of skills. The *butteri* won.

Halfway through the morning, we leave the ranch boundary and turn into the park wilderness. Under a corridor of pines, we ride through a narrow valley alongside chalky cliffs topped with the crumbling defensive towers. Herons and egrets take off and land on the Ombrone River which feeds the region's only surviving marshes. The horses' hoofbeats scare up three wild boars, which bolt into nearby caves for safety.

The Uccellina Mountains ("mountains of the little bird") cover two-thirds of the park, standing only 1,362 feet high at the highest point, though dramatic nonetheless when set against the neighboring pastureland. Among the hilltops is the abandoned twelfth-century abbey of the monks of San Rabano, who once made a brave attempt to cultivate the swampy and pine-shrouded land.

Our final destination is the beach and the azure water of the Tyrrhenian Sea. By the time we reach the sand, we've ridden more than six miles, and the horses are just as glad to splash in the water as the riders. However, Davide allows only a few minutes of play before he signals that we have to return. There are schedules to

---

The first day, Claudio, an Italian lad with a ponytail and a long, waxed jacket, took half of our group out to get a bead on our varied riding abilities....

Claudio guided us past backyards, vineyards, olive groves, woodlands and along narrow, picturesque roads. We were surrounded by wildflowers, apple, olive, orange and lemon trees and raspberry and rose hip bushes. As we ambled past, our horses snatched mouthfuls of leaves and we grabbed handfuls of grapes.

—Wendy Carlson, "Trotting Through Tuscany," *Spur*

keep and he has farmwork to do. Leaving the beach behind, we canter back into the trees.

Though the Maremma is only a two-hour drive from Florence, many guidebooks barely give it a reference; others don't mention it at all. The north-south Via Aurelia speeds right down the middle, but no signs announce when you enter the Maremma. True to its past, it remains the most overlooked part of Tuscany. Even at noon on a Saturday, the stone herringboned streets of the medieval town of Sovana are empty. There are no visitors at the stunning pre-Romanesque *duomo*, and I study in solitude the intricately carved ninth-century ciborium at the Church of Santa Maria. Just beyond town, I hike through ancient trenches cut sixty-five feet into the earth by the Etruscans. (Though their exact purpose remains a mystery, the *vie cave* were most likely a method of moving people or animals between towns without being detected by enemies.)

In Pitigliano, an imposing fortress built entirely on soft tufa rock, the remaining thirteen arches of a sixteenth-century aqueduct, is almost as impressive as the city itself. Pitigliano is a frenetic jumble of building blocks growing straight out of the cliff on which it's built; you can't tell where the rock ends and the city begins. Dark windows and caves puncture the weathered rock façade—a multitude of eyes watching as you approach.

My day ends with a pilgrimage to beautiful Feniglia Beach. It's three miles long and connects Monte Argentario with the coastal city of Orbetello. On one side is the sand, on the other a wild strip of tall umbrella pines shading stands of myrtle and juniper. All I can think is that this is the last thing Caravaggio saw before he died. The painter was renowned for his ability to render light with an almost theatrical intensity. He escaped to the Maremma fleeing a murder charge in Rome. On a hot day in July, 1610, he is said to have expired on the sand of heatstroke.

I step off the beach and back onto the wooded path. The sun drops below the treetops overhead, creating a dappled chiaroscuro. A startled hawk flies up from the edge of the trail, and white egrets drift in for a landing among the reeds. In the distance, the lights of Orbetello flicker on, a prelude to the stars that will soon reflect in water the texture of billowing silk. Reluctantly, I turn back to the city.

Heidi Schuessler is a freelance writer specializing in travel, the outdoors, and technology. She lives and works in Seattle.

ANN   REAVIS

⁺

At the Butcher's

*The master of meat awaits you
in Panzano.*

ONE LEG TUCKED BENEATH ME, I SIT IN THE CORNER OF A WICKER bench, listening to a Verdi aria waft from the speaker on top of the bookcase behind me and watching the customers come and go in the Tuscan shop. The shop is full of paintings, sculpture, and books on art, history, poetry, cooking, and travel; and then also, there is a lot of meat. It is a butcher shop after all.

Things have changed in my life since I moved to Tuscany three years ago. I no longer spend my weekends in the library of a large corporate law firm churning out pleadings and briefs. Instead, on Saturday or Sunday I escape the narrow winding stone streets of Florence to visit my favorite places in Chianti. On the top of my list is L'Antica Macelleria Cecchini, the butcher shop of Dario Cecchini.

I go to Dario's not just because of the butcher, although he is tall, broad-shouldered, with a classical Italian profile, dark curly hair, and sparkling blue eyes. I spend hours there not because it takes thirty minutes to an hour to be served, although it always does. No, what brings me back over and over is the movable feast of food, wine, music, art, celebrities, and friends that move through Dario's shop every weekend in Panzano, a small hill town just fifty minutes south of Florence, high on a ridge above Greve in Chianti.

Except for the sides of beef and pork hanging in the meat locker across from the front door and the long marble and glass case full of prepared cuts of meat and other produce, L'Antica Macelleria Cecchini could be an art gallery, a bookstore, or a restaurant. A few years ago Dario transformed an adjacent room into a gallery with constant change of shows, the most recent that of a Japanese watercolorist; and Dario hosted the book signing for Faith Heller Willinger's book *Eating in Italy,* at the shop and on a table in the corner there is a stack of yellow paperback books—an anthology of Tuscan detective stories—that Dario is selling for a friend; and in the back of the shop there is a professional kitchen where a chef toils, catering not only to the weekend crowd, but also to a few large private events each month.

L'Antica Macelleria Cecchini does a brisk business during the week, much of it by same-day delivery to top restaurants throughout Italy; but it is on the weekends that a visit to the butcher shop becomes an "event." The place fills with villagers, artists, writers, and childhood friends of Dario, as well as members of the "villa crowd," wealthy Americans and Brits who vacation in Tuscany, and passersby, who stop to see why the crowd in the butcher shop is overflowing into the dusty street. Everyone gets the chance to munch on bread baked in a wood-burning oven, sip rich red Chianti, made from grapes from Dario's vineyard and served from traditional large straw-encased wine flasks, and taste the spicy pork sausages, *veal sugo,* pecorino cheese with hot pepper jelly, and *peposo,* chunks of tender beef slow-cooked in an iron caldron, prepared in the kitchen in the back of the shop.

Dario holds court from a raised platform behind the counter, working with an assortment of knives and cleavers on a long block of oak, trading quips with his friends and providing the assembled crowd with a clear view of his work.

"A butcher is like a priest," he says, only partially joking as he cleaves through the bone of a two-inch thick *bistecca fiorentina,* the classic Tuscan beefsteak. "We represent blood, life, and carnality. We understand about the flesh, about sin, about good food, and beautiful women."

In front of him, a display case on an antique base of creamy-white marble contains roasts, chops, fillets, sausages, salami, a huge bowl of whipped *lardo* (herbed lard, aged in small Carrara marble "tombs"), another bowl of spicy jelly made from tiny red chili peppers, a platter of black olives accented with orange peel, and packets of various prepared *sugo di carne*, meat sauce for pasta.

In the corner on a marble-topped table, at the feet of the bronze sculpture of a zaftig nude peasant woman, there used to be a fax in a plastic frame that read: "*Caro Dario, L'America sta diventando sempre più un Paese di astemi vegetariani e puritani. Personalmente, continuo a preferire il vino rosso, le carni e le belle donne. Con affetto.* Jack Nicholson." ["Dear Dario, America is becoming more and more a country of teetotalers, vegetarians, and puritans. Personally, I continue to prefer red wine, meat, and beautiful women. With affection, Jack Nicholson."] Then the fax was gone, replaced by a poem, an ode to Dario and his shop, penned by another fan. Celebrities like singer Bruce Springsteen, actor Dustin Hoffman, the cast of *The English Patient*, and Sirio Maccioni, owner of New York's Le Cirque have all fallen under the spell of Dario, magician with a meat cleaver.

Alain Bonnefoit, French painter and part-time resident of Tuscany, stops by the shop to give Dario a painting of a nude woman, sparingly drawn in black, white, and red. Dario leaves his podium to greet the artist with a big hug and then, with arms

---

Going to Tuscany is like being in kindergarten—all you have to do is show up, and the simple pleasures find you. Your teacher bakes you brownies; you stumble upon a family-run *trattoria*. There is milk with the brownies right after nap-time; the owner's son brings you what he thinks you will like just by looking at you. You arrive at the airport and it is as if the whole country has been put on hospitality alert.

—Amanda Gary,
"Simple Pleasures"

upraised, he begins to quote from memory poetry written seven
hundred years ago by the medieval poet Dante. Then, the butcher
and the artist step into the meat locker for a private chat. A tourist
snaps their picture through the glass door.

Dario is famed for quoting whole passages from Dante's *Inferno*
as he carves up a boneless shank of veal and stuffs it with pecorino
cheese and rosemary or shaves off paper-thin slices of prosciutto or
salame using only the razor-sharp edge of a huge knife. Once, on
television, Italian MTV, Dario quoted an entire canto of the *Inferno*
while carving a massive *arista*, a circular crown of pork chops, including the loin, from a side of pork. The Gen-X host looked on
dumbfounded. Only in Italy would a butcher be showcased carving raw meat on television. Only in Italy would a Tuscan butcher
quote Dante from memory on MTV.

A fifth generation *macellaio*, whose family has owned the
butcher shop in Panzano for over 250 years, Dario was not destined to be a butcher. He says that his mother wanted him to work
in a bank and that she cried on the day his grandmother made him
his first butcher's apron—he was twelve. Six years later, while he
was attending college in Siena, family necessity dictated that he
come home to take over the butcher shop. Dario was not content,
however, to just follow the family tradition: he stamped it with his
own personality. Ten years ago, he renovated the shop to look like
a *macelleria* would in the 1800s with mammoth marble-topped
tables and antique oak butcher blocks. Iron butcher's hooks hang
from the ceiling holding whole prosciutto, long salami, ropes of
sausages, and bunches of fire-red hot peppers. The walls are decorated with antique butcher's tools and other artifacts.

Stepping into the shop may be like stepping into the past, but
it has a state-of-the-art sound system through which Dario's mood
of the moment is broadcasted. One Saturday disco music rocked
the place while Dario chopped cubes of pork for kebabs in time
with the beat. Two American "villa" ladies marched empty-handed
past me out the door. "I'm so disappointed," the older one said. "It's
been completely ruined. It used to be so picturesque—so authentic and Tuscan. I tell you, last year you would only hear opera or

maybe some jazz—never disco." The ladies should have waited: a half-hour later a quartet of musicians arrived and set up in the gallery space to play Sicilian folk tunes throughout the rest of the afternoon.

The experience of Dario's butcher shop on the weekends is how I imagine the village square used to be on market day—how it still is in parts of Tuscany: a place where friends and strangers meet to eat and discuss politics, food, life stories, or local gossip. It is a celebration of a culture and traditions that have endured in Tuscany for more than a millennium.

Ann Reavis thought she was taking a few months' vacation from her job as a trial lawyer when she went to Italy in 1998. She is still bemused by the fact that she never returned and continues to live in Florence. She has forsaken the law to become a tour guide and travel writer.

JOHN FLINN

* * *

Trekking Chianti

When it rains, two hikers
find more than shelter.

LIGHTNING FLICKERED ACROSS THE TUSCAN SKY. THUNDER crackled and boomed off medieval stone towers. As heavy drops splattered Volpaia's piazza, we dashed across rain-slicked cobble-stones to the sanctuary of the village's only restaurant.

What timing! All morning long we'd been walking with our backpacks through the Chianti hills, through vineyards full of plumping grapes and dark forests sheltering wild boar. This cozy little *trattoria* was the first real shelter we'd come to all day, and it had appeared at precisely the moment the gathering thunderstorm had let loose.

As the *signora* bustled out of the kitchen with platters of deli-cate, sage-scented ravioli braised with rosemary, bowls of hearty *ribollita,* and earthen pitchers of Chianti wine, I leaned my drip-ping backpack in the corner, listened to the downpour hissing on the cobblestones outside and thought: let it rain!

The genesis for this trip had come several months earlier, when a new guidebook had landed on my desk. In just seven succinct words its title managed to embrace two of my favorite places and two of my favorite endeavors: *Walking and Eating in Tuscany and Umbria.*

For years we'd been trying without success to plan an inn-to-inn walking trip through Tuscany. We had longed to saunter down the stony lanes of medieval hill towns, to picnic in the shade of gnarled olive trees, to sip the local wines with stubble-faced wine-makers, and to end each day with a four-course Tuscan feast, a hot shower, and a snuggly bed.

The adventure travel catalogs are full of such trips, but we had wanted to do it on our own. And we'd been stymied.

The problem, we realized, is that Tuscans are not recreational walkers. Their countryside is not crisscrossed by well-maintained, carefully signposted hiking paths in the manner of, say, England. And maps? The Italians put their exemplary skills to many tasks, but cartography, alas, does not seem to be among them.

But as I leafed through the guidebook it suddenly looked possible. The authors had cobbled together a series of walks making use of cypress-lined country lanes, rutted farm tracks, and half-overgrown forest paths—and, not incidentally, linking a series of tempting *trattorias* and *osterias*. The walk that caught my eye was a three-day along the spine of the gentle, vineyard-covered Chianti hills, which stretch through the storied heart of Tuscany between Florence and Siena.

And so it was one warm May morning that Jeri and I came to be darting around the crowded market square in the village of Greve, filling our backpacks with the makings of a fine picnic lunch.

The unofficial capital of Chianti, Greve is a prosperous little wine town that wouldn't look out of place in the Napa Valley. Its shop windows were filled with pricey kitchen knicknacks and designer sunglasses; its travel agency advertised flights to Ibiza and Sri Lanka.

But in the center of town, where the Saturday market was buzzing, Piazza Matteotti showed off a different Greve. Dressed in their finest, the townsfolk moved from stall to stall swapping gossip, thumping melons, slapping backs, sniffing wedges of cheese, tousling the heads of dogs, and scrutinizing tomatoes. They filled their shopping satchels with not just fruits and vegetables but also shoes, sweaters, kitchen utensils, soap, live chickens, even chain-saws. They didn't have a Wal-Mart in Greve, and this was how they made do.

Taking a deep breath, we plunged into the fray. At the fruit stall we bought a couple of Golden Delicious apples, at the cheese stall a small orb of provolone, at the *forno* a small loaf of crusty bread.

I pushed open the door to the salami shop and was hit by an aromatic blast that nearly sent me staggering backward. Inside, strings of thick, musty links dangled from rafter to rafter. The cured hocks of a huge boar hung in one corner, along with those of several smaller animals I couldn't identify. We bought a couple of small links, shouldered our backpacks, and set off into the Chianti hills. Our eventual destination was Vagliagli, three days and perhaps thirty miles to the south.

Our route followed a little cypress-lined country road that zigzagged uphill past a graveyard and the ivy-covered walls of several villas. Soon they were lined with terraced vineyards of grapes, the main component of Chianti wine. We began to see signs with the ubiquitous Gallo Nero—the black rooster, once the herald of the baronial alliance known as the Lega del Chianti and now the symbol of the Chianti Classico wine region.

"Vendito vino e olio," announced a hand-lettered sign at the Melazzano vineyard: wine and olive oil for sale. Tempting as it was to stop in and pick up a bottle of Chianti for lunch, I resisted. Painful experience has taught me there's no better way to ruin my motivation for an afternoon of walking.

It was springtime, and our little lane was surrounded by a riot of wildflowers—bright red poppies, pink dog rose, purple vetch, yellow broom, irises, and dandelions. D. H. Lawrence, who passed through in the 1920s, was similarly impressed: "It is queer," he wrote, "that a country so perfectly cultivated as Tuscany, where half the produce of five acres of land will have to support ten human mouths, still has so much room for wildflowers."

As we climbed higher above Greve the views began to open up. Gentle hills undulated in all directions, each covered with a patch-work quilt of vineyards and crowned with a fortified villa or hill town—a reminder that throughout medieval times this region was, more than anything, a theater of war. The golden, late-afternoon light blended with the ever-present Tuscan haze to paint the countryside like a Renaissance landscape.

Along the ridgetop we entered a cool, fragrant pine forest and a few minutes later, five hours after setting off from Greve, passed through an ancient stone gateway to reach our home for the night, Villa San Michele.

A monastery until ten years ago, San Michele now consists of a hostel-type inn, an *osteria,* and a 700-year-old chapel. In the candle-lit dining room, we sat down to a Tuscan feast of *crostini mista* (toasted bread with toppings); gnocchi with pesto; chicken with musky forest mushrooms; and salads of wild greens. It was simple peasant fare—*cucina povera,* food of the poor, it's called—and I can't believe Wolfgang Puck or Jeremiah Tower could top it at any price.

Best of all, we washed it down with a bottle of Terre di Melazzano, a Chianti Classico from the vineyard we'd walked through that morning. Chianti wine is the embodiment of Tuscany: It doesn't aspire to aristocracy; it's not meant to be sniffed, swirled, and held up to cross-examination. Rather, it's an earthy, unpretentious friend who makes a delightful—and delightfully in-expensive—dinner companion.

As we climbed the stairs to our room, the night was preternat-urally silent. We were finally beyond the whiny buzz of the Vespas, the mechanized mosquitoes of Italy. All we could hear was the breeze sighing through the pine trees. We slept well.

In the morning, as we were leaving, Jeri mentioned to the woman behind the counter that we hoped to reach Volpaia by lunchtime. Her face lit up.

"Ah," she said, struggling for words in English and finally giving up. She made a hugging motion and said, *"la signora—simpatica!"* I gathered we were in for a treat.

Midmorning, at the edge of a forest, we came to an old stone-hewn farmhouse that my map identified as Casa Lungagna. Outside, leaning on a gnarled cane, stood its owner, a weathered old man in a beret.

"Volpaia?" I asked.

In Italian he launched into a discussion of the routes, and through his gestures I made out that we could get there either on a well-tended wagon track or by an overgrown footpath that plunged into the forest. The guidebook said we should take the forest trail, so we thanked the man and set off. Before I entered the woods I turned to wave goodbye and saw him feeling his way slowly along the lane with his cane. It was, quite literally, a case of the blind leading the blind.

The forest was dark and a little spooky, our path overgrown with brambles and yellow broom. From the footprints in the mud next to a spring I could see these woods were far more popular with *cinghiale*—wild boar—than humans.

Our path passed by an abandoned stone farmhouse, called Dogole, which was rapidly being reclaimed by the forest. The roof had collapsed; a young oak pushed up through the floor and out a window. Since the early 1960s, when Italy's sharecropping system was dismantled, the *contadini*—peasant farmworkers—have been fleeing these farms for better paying jobs in the city. Few traces remained of the terraces they had patiently carved out of the hillsides over generations, and in a few more it will be hard to tell anyone had ever farmed here at all.

It had been warm and sunny when we had entered the forest, but when we emerged at the other side the skies were dark and gray and the temperature was falling rapidly. We raced the approaching storm to the fortified hamlet of Volpaia, reaching the shelter of La Bottega *trattoria* just as the downpour started.

And this is where the trajectory of our little adventure began to veer off course. The *signora*, rather than being *simpatica*, was clearly not happy to see us. I could hardly blame her: all the diners at the restaurant's outside tables had rushed inside, along with virtually every other Sunday day-tripper in Volpaia. Her little *trattoria* couldn't hold such a crowd; her overworked kitchen couldn't feed us. Pointing to the door, she ordered everyone without a reservation—including us—out into the rain.

I was zipping up my rain jacket and contemplating the soggy

walk to Radda, five miles distant, when some guardian angels came to our rescue. A group of Americans, the Feinberg family from San Diego, kindly offered us a ride.

On the outskirts of Radda they dropped us off at the *trattoria* Il Vigne, where we were midway between the antipasto and the *primo piatto* when the sun came out. Even though Radda was our intended destination for the night, we wanted to walk the stretch from Volpaia to Radda, reputedly one of the prettiest in Chianti. So when we finished our meal we hitched a ride back to Volpaia.

Young boys kicking a soccer ball against a ninth-century stone tower stopped to let us pass. Exiting the walled village through a vine-covered archway, we strolled down a lane lined with stately, missile-shaped cypress trees. Off to our right, atop one hill, stood the fortifications of a twelfth-century Romanesque church, Pieve di Santa Maria Novella. Directly ahead, another hill was crowned by the towers of Radda, the old capital of the Chianti League.

And just to our left was a farmhouse with a disturbingly familiar name. I pulled the sheet of paper from my backpack to make sure: Indeed, it was Pruneto—the *agriturismo* (farmhouse) where we had reservations for the night.

We had asked the woman at the local tourist office to book us a room in Radda. Apparently still not clear on the concept of hiking, she'd put us here, way out in the country, apparently miles from the nearest restaurant. Prunetto was perfectly charming, but it didn't serve meals. I fumed as I dropped my backpack in our bedroom. Not only would we have to share a PowerBar for dinner, but we'd have to make up the mileage with a long, long day of walking tomorrow.

But there was a note with our reservation sheet: the woman at the tourist office had made us dinner reservations at another farmhouse, Podere Terreno, twenty minutes' walk away.

The other guests were just sitting down at a long oaken table when we arrived. The owner, Roberto—who looked like a Tuscan Dick Van Patten—pulled out two chairs for us and filled our glasses with Chianti.

"It's the '97 from my vineyard here," Melosi said. "It's very young now, but I think one day it will be excellent. I hope you find it to your liking."

Melosi, who once worked at the Savoy in London, seemed more at home here in this sixteenth-century farmhouse of stone and oak. He and his wife, Marie-Sylvie Haniez, owned the surrounding 110 acres, including 7 acres of vineyards and 4 of olive trees.

As we sipped our wine, Melosi's wife began laying steaming platters of food down on the table. First came *paglia e fieno*—green and white pasta with fresh mint and pungent porcini mushrooms picked by Melosi on his property. The olive oil also came from his farm; it had been pressed at the mill up the road in Volpaia.

Next came *spezzatino*—a fragrant Tuscan beef stew with celery, carrots, red and white onions, bay leaves, juniper berries, and tomatoes. Except for the beef, Melosi had grown it all. A salad of *rucola* (arugula) and radicchio was flavored with fennel he'd picked just outside his door.

When my glass was empty Melosi refilled it with a 1993

We rolled into Radda on a cold March afternoon and were welcomed by our hosts at Podere Terreno. Despite their genuine warmth, I felt sheepish telling Madame that it was my wife's birthday and could she please prepare some kind of simple cake to come after dinner?

Dinner was outrageous, magnificent, and just for the seven of us—my wife, mother, aunt, three daughters and me—since we were the only guests that night. A fire in the grate warmed our backs as our host regaled us with tales of inn-keeping. Madame brought out the birthday dessert with an apology to all (and a small scowl in my direction, for so little notice): a gigantic stainless steel bowl of exquisite tiramisu, the likes of which we've never had. So much for throwing something together, I thought, painfully aware of the poverty of my own scrabblings in the kitchen.

—James O'Reilly, "On and Off the Autostrada"

Sangiovese-Cabernet—again, from his vineyard. Then he uncorked one of his 1994 Chianti Classicos and set the bottle down
between us.

Taking a break before dessert, Melosi stood up and offered to
show me around his farmhouse.

"Please—fill your glass," he said, "and bring it with you."

As we wandered past his crackling fireplace and down narrow
hallways, ducking beneath massive, rough-hewn oak beams, I asked
Melosi about the special relationship between the Tuscan people,
their landscape, and their food.

"For us, sharing food is more than eating," he told me. "It's an
excuse for gossip and love, a moment of pleasure and intimacy. It's
a way of expressing yourself to another person without any sec-
ondary motivation."

Melosi topped off my glass; he'd thoughtfully brought along the
bottle. Down a curving flight of stairs, his stone basement was dark
and musty. It seemed more like a cave, an organic part of the landscape. So, it seemed, did my host.

"When you cook you are pulling nature out of each ingredient," he explained. "You dissect the nature, get inside it like an
alchemist. You put it in the pot and the heat does the magic."

He took another sip of wine and tried to find a metaphor I'd
understand.

"Nature supplies everything; you just try to get the most out of
it," he said. "You're like a mechanic tuning up a Ferrari."

As I tottered back up the stairs toward dessert, I paused to fret
about the next day, about the miles we'd have to make up for having stopped here. I didn't fret long: The extra walking would be, I
decided, a trivial price to pay for one of the most memorable meals
of my life.

At the top of the stairs Melosi paused, held out his Chianti bottle, and arched an eyebrow.

"Please," I said, extending my empty glass.

John Flinn is the travel editor of the San Francisco Chronicle. *He lives in
the often-foggy coastal town of Pacifica, just south of San Francisco.*

MANFREDI PICCOLOMINI

⋆ ⋆ ⋆

Pomp and Intrigue at the Palio

One of the world's oldest—and oddest—horse races
make for an unforgettable spectacle.

IN THE GLITZ AND THEATRICS OF ITALIAN HIGH LIFE, AN INVITATION to the medieval city of Siena for the historic horse race called the Palio competes only with an invitation to opening night at La Scala in Milan. Actually, between the two, true sophisticates would immediately opt for the Palio, for it remains one of the few places where being seen is a clear sign of indisputable social status. Everybody knows that appropriate connections, and perhaps the right amount of money discreetly disbursed, can secure seats to La Scala's "sold-out" opening night. Not so for the Palio. No clout and no amount of money will yield an invitation that will enable a visitor to see the race as it should be seen—from the windows and balconies of one of the palaces, houses, or apartments over-looking Siena's Piazza del Campo, the charming, sloping central square where the race is run.

And certainly, unless you are already invited, there is no way to watch from the most advantageous spot on the square—the apart-ment of Don Giovanni Guiso, the Sardinian aristocrat who has been the social arbiter of Siena for thirty years. If you are lucky enough to join "Nanni"—as his inner circle calls him—and his friends, you not only will find yourself among members of royal families and such literary luminaries as Umberto Eco, you also will find yourself immediately over the starting line of the race, with an unmatched view of the Piazza del Campo, jammed with fifty thousand spectators, and the course that runs around its perimeter. For this privilege, at least in Italy, there is no price.

For nearly one thousand years, the Palio has been the most important ritual of Sienese life. To call it a horse race is somewhat like referring to the Pietà· as a mere stone carving. The event is a celebration of municipal pride that dates back to the Middle Ages, to the time when Siena was one of the leading cities in Italy, a pioneer in the cultural, political, artistic, and economic flowering that culminated in the Renaissance. The Palio is sometimes described as a long pageant of colorfully costumed participants through the city streets followed by a brief horse race, but it is, in fact, a collective ritual that lasts much longer than just two or three exciting days twice each year (the race is run on the second of July

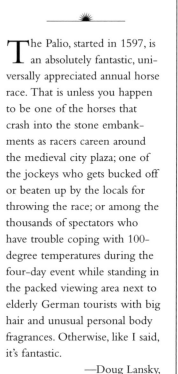

The Palio, started in 1597, is an absolutely fantastic, universally appreciated annual horse race. That is unless you happen to be one of the horses that crash into the stone embankments as racers careen around the medieval city plaza; one of the jockeys who gets bucked off or beaten up by the locals for throwing the race; or among the thousands of spectators who have trouble coping with 100-degree temperatures during the four-day event while standing in the packed viewing area next to elderly German tourists with big hair and unusual personal body fragrances. Otherwise, like I said, it's fantastic.

—Doug Lansky,
Last Trout in Venice

and the sixteenth of August, dates honoring the Virgin Mary, to whom the city has a long-standing devotion). Almost every day in the life of the native Sienese is occupied at least partly with some aspect of the race.

The contest is between *contrade*, the closest English equivalent of which is wards, or neighborhoods. Long before the Middle Ages, there were many *contrade* within the walls of the old city, responsible for military, political, and fiscal affairs. By the time of the Great Plague of 1348, they numbered forty-two. In 1729, in order to quell factional quarreling, the boundaries of each *contrada* were set, fixing the number at the present seventeen.

A *contrada* is more than just a loosely defined precinct. In fact, the territories are precisely delineated and—on festive occasions— marked by flags. Each *contrada* has its own seat, oratory, baptismal fountain, and society—a group that is now essentially recreational, but which is devoted to the traditions and history of its members. Each *contrada* also has its own leaders, and regularly collects voluntary donations from its residents (*contradaioli*) for such charities as housing the needy, summer activities for the young, and other worthy social purposes. It is only a slight exaggeration to claim that the *contrada* can provide many services of the modern welfare state. The Sienese people proudly claim that because of the *contrada* system, such modern plagues as drugs and crime that afflict other Italian cities have not hit them as hard. Almost an extended family, the *contrada* can tackle issues that would stump a government bureaucrat, without a lot of red tape—and with a good deal of warmth and love, at that.

As Alessandro Falassi notes in the magnificent book Palio, "The population of the *contrada* is made up of people who belong to it traditionally by birth, descent, or residence. According to the *jus soli* [right of territory], everyone born in the *rione* [district] is a member of the *contrada*." Over the years, this rule has become one of membership on the basis of residence. (Loyalties, though, never change. If a resident moves from one *contrada* to another, his allegiance remains with the *contrada* into which he was born.) In centuries past, membership in the right *contrada* was of paramount concern to Sienese families. Expectant mothers sometimes were hurried to a distant hospital so that the child would be born in the appropriate place. Nowadays, residents living in the newer wards outside the old city may join a *contrada* within—assuming they are accepted.

The names and emblems of the *contrade* are drawn from those of mythical animals, such as the dragon and the unicorn; of dangerous, menacing ones, such as the she-wolf and the panther; or, more simply, from domestic and ordinary ones, such as the goose, snail, and caterpillar. Each *contrada* also has its own colors—and even these are symbolic: white is for glory, red for strength and power, blue for peace, yellow for nobility. All of these elements are incorporated into the flags waved, and the scarves worn, by the *contradaioli.*

The seventeen *contrade*: Aguila (Eagle), Bruco (Caterpillar), Chiocciola (Snail), Civetta (Owl), Drago (Dragon), Giraffa (Giraffe), Istrice (Porcupine), Leocorno (Unicorn), Lupa (She-Wolf), Nicchio (Shell), Oca (Goose), Onda (Wave), Pantera (Panther), Selva (Forest), Tartuca (Turtle), Torre (Tower), and Valdimontone (Ram).

—JO'R & TAW

The great parade that takes place on the day of the Palio, however much it may look like a mere reenactment of a medieval event, is full of meaning. Dressed in beautiful and extremely elaborate costumes, the representatives of the seventeen *contrade* show off with pride the colors of their districts. The fine damask-and-velvet capes trimmed with ermine fur, the elaborate armor glittering in the afternoon sun and the multihued flags expertly waved by their bearers are all part of a ritual aimed at keeping the high honor of the *contrada.* Just getting dressed in the ancient costumes required a ceremony all its own, carefully attended by a volunteer staff of wardrobe keepers who throughout the year have the responsibility, and the honor, of taking care of the expensive costumes.

But despite the common desire to outdo the others with costumes or special flag-waving tricks, the *contrade* exhibit a collective pride as they come together first in the streets and then in the piazza. The enchanting riot of colors and sounds, especially in front of the *duomo,* or cathedral, where all the *contrade* congregate to pay homage to the archbishop, defies description. Red, green, yellow, and blue costumes compete for attention with the flags flying high against the cathedral's white and dark green marble façade. The sun glints off the silver armor and the drums play a fast marching beat. Later in the afternoon the parade triumphantly enters the Piazza del Campo, where more that fifty thousand people wave scarves in the colors of the various *contrade*, and makes a slow cortege around the square. The festivities and pageantry heighten the day's high emotional intensity, which continues to build as the last *contrada* in the parade makes its final presentation of flag-waving. Then, preceded by the explosion of a loud firecracker, the horses—bridled without a bit and ridden bareback by jockeys—make their entrance into the piazza and start moving slowly toward the starting line.

For centuries the people of Siena—and Palio connoisseurs, too—have been trying to understand what makes a winning formula for the race. Is it having the best horse? Or the best jockey? Or does one have to excel in the practice of rigging the contest and buying off the other racers? In fact, none of these factors, and no combination of them, is a guaranteed ticket to victory. Ten out of the seventeen *contrade* run an entry in each Palio (the seven that did not run that race during the previous year, plus three chosen by lottery), using horses that are brought in by an independent, citywide committee and assigned by the luck of the draw. And then, even if a *contrada* is lucky enough to get the fastest horse, the narrow racetrack, with its many sharp, sloping turns, is not exactly the best venue for it. If the horse runs very fast it can easily hit the mattresses appropriately placed at the turns and fall. The jockey is another variable. Never a native Sienese and strictly mercenary, the Palio jockey usually feels no allegiance to anyone and sells his services to the *contrada* willing to pay the most—which frequently is not the one that has employed him.

In an attempt to at least lessen the likelihood of underhanded activity on the part of the jockey, from the time he is hired he is closely observed, day and night, by at least one *contrada* member. Further, he is not allowed to speak to anyone or even to use the phone. Thus when the jockeys are finally freed of their bodyguards during the few minutes that precede the race, a lot of talking ensues as they are at last able to make their deals. Needless to say, these deals are often purely self-serving and do not coincide with the *contrada's* Palio strategy. Naturally the Sienese people hold the jockeys in distrust and say that they look honest only when, a few hours before the Palio, they take their horses into the *contrade's* churches to be blessed by the parish priest. In this very beautiful ceremony—made possible only by a special Papal waiver of the Church's strict rule against animals in churches—the people of the *contrada*, the

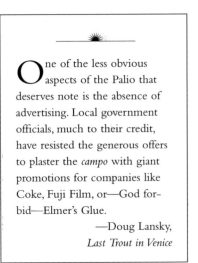

One of the less obvious aspects of the Palio that deserves note is the absence of advertising. Local government officials, much to their credit, have resisted the generous offers to plaster the *campo* with giant promotions for companies like Coke, Fuji Film, or—God forbid—Elmer's Glue.

—Doug Lansky,
Last Trout in Venice

jockey, and even the horse bow their heads to God and invoke His help in a race whose end is ultimately determined by fate and chance. Once the ceremony is over, mutual distrust again marks the relationship.

Winning the race, however, is not always the top priority of a *contrada*. In fact, one's honor is kept highest not by winning every year but by achieving a steady number of victories through the years. Like everything else in Siena, honor is a long-term proposition. If a *contrada* does not get a very good horse and its coffers are not overflowing with money, it may well use its horse in the race to work on its overall plans. It may, for example, sell its services to help another *contrada* win, or it may concentrate its efforts on preventing an enemy victory. Almost everything is allowed in the race, including whipping another jockey or muzzling another horse to keep it back, and such services are available, of course, for the appropriate amount of money. The few days that precede the Palio teem with behind-the-scenes negotiations and deals among

the *capitani* and *priori* (captains and leaders) of the *contrade*. Making
an adversary lose the race may cost every bit as much as buying fa-
vors to win it.

Yet even the most complex plans are often thwarted by unforeseen circumstances. A complex strategy may be fouled up even before the race starts if a *contrada* draws a disadvantageous position at
the starting line. Chance and fate play their parts and, some believe
philosophically, that the Palio is ultimately a metaphor for human
existence. There, too, rational planning runs against the will of
contrary fortune. In the whirlwind of the less than one-and-a-half
minutes of the race, anything can, and often does, happen. Upsets
are frequent, and no one can be assured of victory until the horse
has actually crossed the finish line after completing three fast runs
around the square. As the multicolored pack approaches the end,
the crowd in the square seems to explode and spill over onto the
track, where the entire gamut of human emotions is played out.
The joyous victors triumphantly kiss the horse and its jockey, then
rush, accompanied by their allies, to grab the Palio prize: a colorful cloth banner (known as a *palio* or *drappellone*) usually painted by
the leading Italian artist and from which the race originally derived its name (a *pallium* is a ceremonial cloth). The anguished
losers burst into cries and often take out their anger—whether
there is reason for it or not—on the jockey. Then entire night that
follows is for celebration, with the winners making the rounds of
the city, waving flags and singing.

But if the race is exciting—and there are few spectacles in
sport to match it—the festivities preceding it are just as memorable. Certainly this is true for Nanni's guests. As his guest, one
would have enjoyed, two days before the race, an "evening of
opera production" at his sixteenth-century villa just outside the
city. Nanni, who is a world traveler, writer, and art collector, also
collects antique miniature theaters. With a few expert friends,
Nanni manipulates small wooden marionettes to a tape recording
of the selected opera.

Then, the night before the Palio, Nanni and his guests join in
the large street fairs organized by the *contrade* to raise money and

bring good fortune. Long, narrow tables are set up in the winding streets of the old city, and entire neighborhoods sit down to enjoy the rich foods of Tuscany, often including game, and all accompanied by countless *fiaschi*—the rounded, straw-encased bottles of Chianti. The dinners last until the wee hours and make for a happy evening, as hopes run high for a victory.

The morning after the race, when the sun shines again on Siena's red roofs, the celebrations continue—and the plotting for the next race begins. In Siena, no one never says *"La festa é finita."* Even if Nanni's guests are already jetting to the four corners of the world, for the Sienese, *la festa* is perpetual.

Manfredi Piccolomini lives in New York City.

$\star \overset{\star}{} \star$

Taking the Cure

In which the whole family is restored.

"WHAT ABOUT A DISCOUNT FOR THE CHILDREN?" I ASKED. AS always, the hotel prices proved steeper than those listed in the guidebook. Yes, it was last year's book, and we did want a room with a bath, and it was high season. But I knew from experience that there was room to negotiate on the children's rate.

Riccardo, the manager, offered a 20 percent discount. The steamy swimming pool we had promised the kids throughout our Easter stay in Florence beckoned from the window. Here was the deal: if the kids could endure five days of early Renaissance artworks, we would spring for a weekend in Bagno Vignoni, a Tuscan village situated at the font of a thermal spring.

"Twenty percent? But look at them," I pleaded, shoving my skinny four- and six-year-old toward the desk, "they eat *nothing*." Riccardo sized them up. I buy their clothes with room to grow which does give them that waifish look. He offered 35 percent off full pension. Sold.

I was vague in reporting the actual cost to my husband. We are neither extravagant nor, on a professor's sabbatical salary, affluent, but we have for so many years gazed with curiosity at fancy European hotels, their pools and terraces obscured by trellises of wisteria, always choosing finally the more moderate establishment down the road. But now, for once, we were going with the pool and the wisteria. We owed it to the kids, we told ourselves. Hadn't they been saints throughout the endless galleries of the Uffizi?

The children had not been taken with the early Renaissance: too many frescoes too high up to see. "Let's go back to Rome," our four-year-old had suggested hopefully as we were deciding between the Bargello and the Church of Santa Croce. Rome is, in fact, home for the year and had never seemed more so to our son than when he was caught between a sculpture museum and a Florentine church. Only the hope of an enormous swimming pool could have buoyed our children through the endless web of Florence's dark medieval streets, its countless early Renaissance churches, and tedious fresco cycles. It can be a cruel fate to have an art historian for a father.

"Let's not worry about the cost," I told my husband. "We're here to enjoy ourselves." Yet somehow I sensed we weren't quite up to the standards of the other guests, especially as we lugged our assemblage of mismatched duffle bags, stuffed animals, and coloring books into the lobby. Moreover, it was hard to decide which were dirtier, the children's faces or their clothes. I'd packed all the wrong things: spring clothes for the weather I'd imagined. Easter came early this year and Florence was beset with sharp winds from the mountains. The kids ended up wearing the same sweatsuits day after day. It showed. Especially here in Italy where children are often nattier than their folks.

Bagno Vignoni, a popular escape since Roman times, is perhaps most closely associated with Saint Catherine of Siena. During the fourteenth century, while staying with her family at the baths, a young and already zealous Catherine saw an opportunity for self-immolation and plunged into the very font of the spring where the water temperature was close to boiling.

Other Tuscan thermal baths are known for their therapeutic powers. Chianciano Terme, one of the more elaborate, is the home of the "healthy liver." The waters of Montecatini Terme are said to do wonders for the intestines. Bagno Vignoni, however, is simply hot water, and I would happily forsake the health of my liver for a pool that doesn't smell.

Bagno Vignoni, in fact, offers little besides hot water: a few gift shops, a restaurant, yet in all directions roll the green hills of the Val d'Orcia, dotted with castles and lined with vineyards. Is it any wonder the Renaissance started here?

According to the prospectus, these waters could be bathed in, inhaled, used for irrigational purposes, or even drunk and were said to be *"efficace nei reumatismi, malattie cutaneem adenoidismo, asma e nelle affezioni ginecologiche,"* and certainly some of the customers looked as if they might well be suffering from some or all of these complaints, which made us unwilling to join them in the pool. So whenever we visited it, and it was a fascinating place, we steeled ourselves to drink a glass of the beverage, which was so horrible that we both felt that it must have been doing us good.
—Eric Newby,
A Small Place in Italy

It was half-past noon by the time we moved into our rooms. The children had never seen a swimming pool with islands and could hardly contain themselves. But lunch was served in less than an hour. There wasn't time to swim. So we unpacked, arranged stuffed animals, laid out bathing suits and towels, washed faces, and arrived in the dining room at the stroke of one.

The tables were set with batteries of knives, forks, and spoons. Lunch proceeded in typical Italian fashion with course followed by course, one better than the next. I noticed some of the guests, cigarettes in hands, declined certain courses—the cheese platter, the fruit bowl—with wags of the finger. But we ate everything, the kids astonishing me with their capacity to consume. Art may feed the soul, but not, apparently, the body. I looked about the restaurant hoping the manager was not among us and that he hadn't passed along to our waiter my claim that the two little gourmands sitting across from me "ate nothing."

By the time we left the table—first to enter, last to leave—the children had actually made use of all their silverware, if only to replace whatever fell to the floor. Stomachs satisfied, they raced over to inspect the pool outside the window. To their disbelief, what had shimmered and beckoned an hour and a half ago was now an empty shell of concrete. It was, we discovered, the afternoon of the weekly cleaning. This is one drawback to a spring-fed pool: more than hot water tumbles from the spring. Indeed, the calcium content is so high that each week workmen have to chip away at the sides of the pool where it deposits into a hard splintery surface.

My husband suggested that we check out the Signorelli frescoes at a nearby abbey. No, I interceded on behalf of the children, that would be cruel. Instead the two of us played a set of tennis and puttered about in the weight room while the children marshaled their toy ponies through the spacious lawn out back. Later that afternoon we let the children splash about in the ankle-deep tepid water as the pool refilled. They were jubilant.

We woke the next morning to find the water level back to normal but the skies overcast and the weather even colder and windier than it had been in Florence. We could pack it up and head back to Rome, but what would we tell the kids? We'd promised them a pool. So trying our best not to calculate what it was costing to look out the window at a cold gray pool, we roused the kids, dressed them—tired sweatsuits once again—and went downstairs for breakfast.

The children entered the breakfast room with eyes open wide: sweet rolls, cake, cereal, yogurt, squeezed juices. They tried everything—my skinny children who usually can't even finish a piece of bread for breakfast. And, as was to be expected, they both spilled their hot chocolate. The head waiter eyed the spills as he rushed past. Clean tablecloth: several thousand lire at least. Did he know about the discount?

We swam after breakfast—finally. The water was warm enough that the weather didn't matter and, if anything, the gray sky lent an austere beauty to the ruined castle in the distance. A cascade of naturally hot water poured into the pool, providing the shower of your dreams: hot, heavy, and endless. In a silent sort of modern dance, bathers sidled their backs, arms, legs, shoulders under the cascade, angling for the full impact of the water.

One older woman was particularly adept at positioning herself in the middle of the cascade and was completely mindless of the other bathers waiting their turn. No matter, our four-year-old was swimming for the first time. When one of the kids needed a potty break, the woman explained coldly that the bathrooms were only for hotel guests. But we are guests, I answered in my polite textbook Italian. Then you shouldn't track water across the marble floor, she snarled. Later that morning we saw her sitting behind the front desk. Riccardo's mother? Perhaps she found 35 percent excessive.

After our swim we drove to the hill town of Montalcino which, in addition to many wine shops, has a fine castle with ramparts completely intact. Our son enjoyed the arrow slits. We were astonished by the view. No landscape architect could have designed such vistas: a row of cypress tracing one horizon, a field of yellow flowers, a little woods nestled in the sharp cleavage of a hill.

We returned to our hotel in time for the traditional fish lunch—it was Friday. *Pasta al salmone*, followed by *merlozzo alla Livornese*. Whatever it was, it was fabulous. For the children we ordered *platessa*, two little fish which arrived lightly breaded, and topped with a lemon slice. Our waiter whisked them from his cart with such flourish that they flew right off the metal platter and dived onto the floor. Never missing a beat, he scooped them onto his cart, winked at the children, and disappeared into the kitchen, returning moments later with another pair fresh from the frying pan. I recalled the chocolate slicks at breakfast and felt relieved to note that our waiter was every bit as human as our kids.

For dessert we were served fresh doughnuts (*ciambelle*) that we dipped in glasses of chilled *vin santo*, a copper-colored Tuscan dessert wine. Who needed coffee?

That night at dinner, my daughter counted nine pieces of cutlery at her place. Moreover, she calculated that as a group we had eaten off twenty-three different plates.

After a dip the next day, we packed up teddy bears, ponies,

crayons, and wet bathing suits, and lugged them all down to the lobby. Riccardo presented me with the bill, pointing out the 35 percent reduction for the children. I told him how much we had enjoyed our stay. He gave me some post-cards of Tuscany, the same views we'd savored for the past few days, and said he hoped we would return. So did I.

Stomachs full, fingernails clean, the children were actually pleasant on the drive back to Rome. Bagno Vignoni, as I said, is not purported to possess any thera-peutic powers, yet we all felt healed, healed of the cold, healed of the Renaissance, healed of too many days on stone pavements, healed of a long Roman winter with too many sore throats and runny noses. It even felt good to return to our Ro-man apartment, where at last the sun decided to make an appearance.

As I lay in bed the next morning, formulating a strat-egy for the laundry and wondering what I would feed my omni-vores, especially given the fact that it was Sunday and all shops were closed, the kids entered the bedroom and announced that breakfast was ready. This came as a surprise because usually when they come in they ask, often with a whine, "When are we going to eat?"

A t the end of a long day of driving, we entered a cav-ernous and crowded restaurant with our three tired little girls and were seated at a table piled high with plates and bowls. We understood, of course, what those piles meant: hours and hours of eating, as though we were ducks being prepared for the indignity of being turned into *foie gras*. I looked across the table at the girls and saw a pair of huge blue eyes peeking—pleading—above the towering pile. I shrugged in shared dismay, and the gustation began. An eternity later, just when we thought it was safe to slink away, we were herded back to the table by an imperious hostess, who saw to it that we enjoyed a gigantic dessert.

—James O'Reilly, "On and Off the Autostrada"

Intrigued, I shuffled into the dining room to find boxes of cereal arranged buffet style and the table set with every knife, fork, and spoon in the apartment. So you see, children do learn from travel. Now all we need is a waiter and twenty-three plates.

Libby Lubin writes frequently for The New York Times *and travels regularly to Italy, often with her husband and two children, all of whom are splendid companions.*

STEPHEN S. HALL

⋆ ⋆ ⋆

If It's Tuesday, It Must Be Gnocchi

The author documents his "struggles" learning
to cook the Tuscan way.

WE ALL HAVE OUR FANTASIES, AND HERE IS MINE: I AM IN ITALY, OF course, and specifically in that part of Tuscany that lies between Florence and Siena and is known as "Il Chianti," where the formidably rumpled carpet of hills has discouraged trains—and therefore tourists—from venturing too deeply into this rugged but vine-friendly landscape. It is autumn, so as the car carrying myself and a few friends climbs from the Arno valley through the foothills, we switch back and forth in front of fields of sunflowers sadly past their prime, heads bowed and brown like a million penitent friars on a crusade to nowhere. Not as picturesque as in the postcards, to be sure, but then autumn is a tastier time in Tuscany, when porcini mushrooms reach the markets and each curve in the road reveals row upon purpled row of Sangiovese grapes, a reminder that the harvest for Chianti is only weeks away.

After climbing to nearly two thousand feet above sea level, the car turns off the highway and heads up a long and twisting driveway that runs the requisite gauntlet of cypress pines until a final turn opens upon a magical clearing where an eleventh-century abbey, its weathered gray belltower ageless against the green encroachment of an oak and pine forest, has been converted into a country estate. The sound of water trickling from a fountain greets the ears even before we enter the courtyard; a big, white sheepdog lazes on the pavement while two smaller dogs—"Babette" and a puppy named "Breadcrumb"—cavort underfoot. And then, walking toward us with the warmest and most familiar of smiles on her face, as if to say, "It's been too long since you were last here," comes Lorenza, the stately and elegant matriarch of the estate, who greets us as if we were family.

As if we were family....

And there, alas, is the flaw in an otherwise perfect magic carpet ride into the hills of Tuscany. Just about everything in the foregoing fantasy is true, except that we are not family, not even close. The grandmotherly woman waving us in is Lorenza de'Medici. Yeah, those Medici, and to hint at the distance that separates her family (known to historians as the "Pope's bankers") from my scruffy line of ancestors, suffice it to say that my mother's maiden name in Italian means "Albanian." But there is something that separates us even more than pedigree. Lorenza de'Medici is one of the finest and most famed cooks in Italy—erstwhile star of a PBS cooking show, on a first name basis with Julia and Wolfgang (not to mention her good friend Bernardo)—and we are mere dilettantes and dabblers, mere noses pressed to the kitchen window. Indeed, that is what has drawn me and ten other would-be tocque-heads to this former monastery. We're here to pray (and pay) for a miracle. We're here to learn how to cook.

For more than a dozen years now, Lorenza de'Medici and her husband Piero Stucchi Prinetti have flung open the doors of the family's stunning estate and winery, Badia a Coltibuono ("Abbey of the Good Harvest"), to well-heeled visitors who are willing to pay thousands of dollars for a week-long "Villa Table" experience. I say "experience" rather than "cooking school" deliberately, because this week is as much about learning how the landed gentry in Tuscany live and eat (*molto bene*, as long as you ask) as it is about learning how to knead dough. And part of the charm is that, for a few fleeting days, you unpack your bags, kick up your feet, and settle very comfortably into the illusion that you actually are friends of the family.

After a terrific welcoming meal (fried sage leaves, tomato-and-bread soup, veal slathered with porcini), we repaired to the refectory where, surrounded by beautiful sixth-century frescoes and warmed by generous after-dinner rounds of Badia's superb grappa, we began to get to know one another. The group included a young Chicago-area business executive and her partner; two sisters who had the lovely notion of treating their father, a North Carolina pediatrician, to a week in Italy; a woman from Montreal who works for a chain of television stations in Quebec; a lawyer from Los Angeles whose husband had given her a week at cooking school as a Valentine's Day present; a well-known television actress and her traveling companion, a Los Angeles insurance executive; and, as we would soon learn, a very strict vegetarian from Connecticut. Some of us knew a little about cooking, but on the hour-long ride up to Badia a Coltibuono, the minibus had become something of a confessional-on-wheels, as many people professed varying degrees of culinary ignorance.

It was clear we had come to the right place. There are many cooking schools in Italy, but it would be hard to imagine another where the culinary auguries are so pervasive and ancient. John Meis, our cultural guide and author of *A Taste Of Tuscany*, informed us, for example, that archaeologists believe the word "chianti" meant "water" to the ancient Etruscans who roamed these parts twenty-five centuries ago (and in pale but effortful imitation of the noble

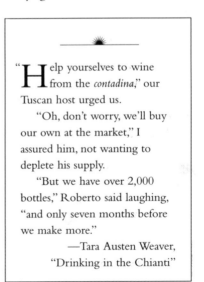

"Help yourselves to wine from the *contadina*," our Tuscan host urged us.

"Oh, don't worry, we'll buy our own at the market," I assured him, not wanting to deplete his supply.

"But we have over 2,000 bottles," Roberto said laughing, "and only seven months before we make more."

—Tara Austen Weaver,
"Drinking in the Chianti"

Etruscans, we were already doing our best to confuse the two). Not only has wine been made (and drunk) on this site almost continuously for a millennium, but the Benedictine monks who inhabited the abbey from the eleventh century until the early 1800s (when Napoleon rousted them out and put the property up for public auction) took as their spiritual leader San Lorenzo. This poor fellow had been browned and roasted as a martyr, and indeed the abbey's very apt coat of arms, overhead on the ceiling of the refectory, seemed to contain an object that looked like a barbecue accessory sold by Weber. Could it be a...grill? Yes, *la griglia*, Vanda Mugnaini of the Badia staff later pointed out. I got an even bigger surprise when I consulted the *Encyclopedia Britannica* to confirm this version of San Lorenzo's demise. "I am cooked on that side," he reportedly taunted his torturers. "Turn me over, and eat."

With such saintly inspiration, how could we be squeamish about learning how to cook?

Our grueling academic schedule began promptly at 9:30 each morning, when Lorenza poked her head into the dining room and said, "O.K., let's get started." After discussing the day's menu—usually six recipes, including bread, appetizer, first course, main course, side dish, and dessert—we would repair to the modest country kitchen (twice as large as many studio apartments in Manhattan, I regret to say from personal experience) and, for the most part, watch her make it. Every time a photogenic vegetable appeared on a cutting board, however, the cooking temporarily ground to a halt as class members took turns asking our celebrated mentor to stop and pose for a photograph ("Worse than Japanese," she finally muttered one day). Then, before you know it, lunchtime had rolled around, someone had uncorked one of the fine wines bottled on the estate, and we convened in the dining room to eat our morning lesson. If all lectures were so delicious, the world would be fat with knowledge.

Lorenza possessed a very warm, engaging smile, but like many grandmothers, she could be quite severe, especially in her thoughts about good cooking. She never came across as a diva vamping in the kitchen, however, but like a housewife who had become an exceptionally good cook, which is in fact pretty much her biography in a nutshell. After World War II, she told us, she wanted to be able to work while staying at home in Milan to raise her four children and ultimately started writing recipe books. Having reached her seventieth birthday and thirtieth cookbook, she remains a handsome woman and an even more attractive personality, dispensing strong opinions with a kind of casual, honest diffidence. One class member with a keen interest in dietary matters made the mistake one day of asking one too many questions about the gluten content of pasta. "Too much chemical talk!" Lorenza said abruptly, and that was that. Simplicity and pragmatism were the watchwords in her kitchen.

If nothing else, Lorenza annotated each recipe with engagingly demythologizing remarks. Her First Commandment of cooking was spoken in thunder the very first day: "We don't measure!" she cried, leaving a roomful of culinary Adams and Eves feeling naked without their measuring cups. And about the almost fetishistic American passion for fresh pasta, she expressed mere bemusement. "Fresh pasta is more American than Italian," she told us with a shrug. Indeed, pasta of any sort was until recently a rare sight on northern Italian tables. "In Italy, pasta used to be considered a vulgar thing," Lorenza explained. "We never, ever had pasta before the war. In the North we had rice and polenta. Pasta was from Rome down."

But as a concession to the New Vulgarians, she showed us how to make fresh pasta one day. With the help of her quick and nimble assistants, Hatidza and Romola (now if only they could be ordered through the Williams-Sonoma catalog), she rolled out long, narrow sheets of soft, elastic, yolk-golden dough, into which we took turns tucking a precooked filling of potatoes and onions. I won't say we were all thumbs, but the kitchen staff disappeared at one point to hunt up a sewing kit in order to procure the needles with which to puncture our hopelessly air-filled and thoroughly pot-unworthy ravioli. Romola, a stout, bright-eyed woman who has worked in the Coltibuono kitchen for thirty-two years and can convey a short ton of scorn with a twitch of an eyebrow, was fairly rolling on the floor with laughter as she manually aerated our ill-formed pillows of pasta. Someone in the group broke the news to Becky Williford and Margaret Crank, the daughters of a good-humored pediatrician named Bob Sheridan: "Your father just flunked ravioli."

Along the way we learned odd bits of kitchen trivia a la Lorenza: that most balsamic vinegars contain only caramelized sugar and that peas are the only vegetables good frozen. We learned that it takes one whole olive tree, up to forty-five pounds of olives, to produce one little liter bottle of olive oil and that the instructions on boxes of Italian pasta sold in the U.S. list longer cooking times than the same boxes in Italy, "because Americans like to overcook their pasta." We learned that Lorenza doesn't believe in serving salad with pasta or using fresh tomatoes in sauces. In the course of five days, we made olive bread and *schiacciata* (a kind of focaccia), a salt cod casserole, tomatoes stuffed with herbs, chicken *involtini*, spinach gnocchi, and desserts like *panna cotta* and apple torte, to name but a few of some thirty dishes we prepared. Well, if you want to be technical about it, we really

---

We stroll into the Signora's kitchen, and our discussion regarding dinner makes me realize that, in the Redini household, "mastery" is a concept that applies as much to the preparation of food as to the essence of being Tuscan. Nobody, according to the Signora, cooks like the Tuscans. In other provinces they merely *play* in the kitchen, she says. "And France! Well, what can I say about a cuisine that describes its ingredients in hushed, reverential whispers?"

"But is French cooking not just an advanced form of mastery?" I ask. Instantly I know I've said the wrong thing.

"If you are talking about the mastery of the few, then you are quite correct, *cara*. But if you are talking about mastery-at-large, mastery by an entire people— mastery that celebrates nature and family and exhilaration— then you can only talk about the cuisine of Tuscany."

—Anne Bianchi,
From the Tables of Tuscan Women

didn't make them. Aside from chopping a few vegetables and kneading a little dough, we kind of stood around and watched Lorenza make everything. Not that we didn't take our studies seriously, but no one had plans as far as I know to open a restaurant when they returned to the States. Indeed, I overheard one member of the group ask if the recipes were available in Spanish. They'd be easier, he explained, for his cook to follow back home.

I don't mean to convey that it was all work and no play, although many of us were so fatigued by the morning of cooking, and so charmed (as moth by flame) by the novelty of an unlimited supply of wine at lunch, that we followed the example of the monks who'd preceded us at Badia and retired to our rooms for an hour or two of deep, horizontal meditation. But then it was more study, study, study: at midafternoon each day, we would don our evening wear and pile aboard a little bus for some very elegant field trips into the nearby Tuscan countryside. John Meis, our able and very forbearing guide, provided a running commentary as juicy as some of the meals: how the caretaker of castle had run off with a young visitor, how much a foreign couple had paid for their house in that village. Each excursion would end with a meal in the home of "friends of Lorenza's." But what friends!

On Tuesday, it was a *palazzo* in Siena. Our host, Vittoria Nepi, was still stewing over the most recent Palio. I have always found it difficult to convey, in a sentence or two, the incredible richness of Siena's annual horse race, the Palio, which combines the pageantry and prestige of the Kentucky Derby with a kind of sanctioned medieval skullduggery. John Meis aptly referred to it as a "sublimated war game," and virtually any bit of duplicity—bribes, intrigues, dirty tricks, double-crossing jockeys—is an acknowledged part of the event. But that August running may have pushed the dirty tricks too far, even for the Sienese and certainly for the residents of the neighborhood Aquila, including Signora Nepi. Their horse entered the Palio as the pre-race favorite, but a rival "killer jockey" (rumored to have been paid $100,000) appeared to detain the Aquila jockey in an unusually long conversation while the rest of the field took off in a race that normally lasts but sixty seconds. As Nepi explained, "We have very few rules for the Palio—very few—but one of them is that you cannot grab the shirt of another jockey and hold them back!"

Later, over a meal of meatloaf and vegetables, Vittoria's young niece Fiamma admitted to some of us: "It is the dream of everyone who lives in Siena that we could hold the Palio and there would be no tourists, no outsiders, just us." I for one am grateful for such an inhospitable attitude; it is one of the reasons that the Palio remains one of the most genuine and thrilling spectacles in the world, which is why people plan a year ahead to witness it. (Indeed, each year one of the eight Coltibuono cooking classes is timed to coincide with the running of the Palio, so students can attend the race.)

The climax of our extramural wanderings, however, probably occurred on Thursday evening, when we mounted a friendly invasion of the imposing Castello di Brolio. After we cooled our heels at the portcullis (there's a turn of phrase I haven't had occasion to use much before), the electronic gate swung open, whereupon the current baron, Bettino Ricasoli, welcomed eleven pie-eyed North Americans into the castle keep of the Tuscan aristocracy. The Ricasoli, formerly the largest landowners in Chianti, have inhabited this property for almost one thousand years, and they remember remodelings that date back to 1478, when hordes of marauding Sienese arrived, unlike us, without an invitation to dinner. The baron and his wife Costanza ushered us into a high-ceilinged and, well, baronial banquet hall of such splendor, with coats of armor against the wall and stained glass windows, that they could have served Spam and moon pies and we would have begged for the recipe.

One of our number managed to overcome the collective awe long enough to offer a toast, and the baron, a short and slender man in his seventies who didn't quite fill his blue suit, replied with a grace and generosity as vanishing as the world of the Tuscan aristocracy itself. "Because you are Lorenza's friends," he said, "you are also our friends, even though we are meeting for the first time tonight." No cooking class may be considered complete without a lesson in hospitality, and the baron effortlessly offered us an advanced seminar. With a wink, he even wished us well in our "studies."

Ah, yes, our studies. I learned one of the most valuable lessons in cooking on graduation day, when Lorenza gave me a ride down to the nearby town of Montevarchi; she was looking for pearl onions for our grand finale evening meal, and I was looking for some exotic garden seeds to bring back to Brooklyn. Lorenza ducked into four stores in two different towns without finding the right kind of onions but emerged from the last shop with a triumphant smile. *"Ovuli!"* she cried, holding up a bag of wild, red-capped mushrooms whose season is so short-lived that it can be measured in days, if not hours. "These are fantastic," she said. The late summer rains in Tuscany had accelerated the season, and she snatched up this unexpected prize and to hell with the onion recipe. "What is in season is tasty," she had told us. "What is not in season is not tasty."

For our "last supper," I was pressed into duty chopping herbs, and after what was, in all modesty, a tour de force of menial labor, Lorenza glanced over and pronounced the effort an A+. Perversely, I lobbied for an Incomplete. "How can you grade us?" I cried. "We haven't even made anything!" I must have looked a little disappointed, because for one of the few times that entire week, Lorenza looked a little nonplussed. "You are making, you are making!" she replied.

In retrospect, I realize it would have been a dereliction of Italian culinary honor to entrust the fate of such an important valedictory repast to rank amateurs. So yes, in case you were wondering, we "made" a spectacular final meal. We prepared the mushrooms raw as an appetizer (sliced thin, drizzled with olive oil); *bruschetta*; a bread-and-cheese soup known as *passatelli*; roast pork with fennel, carrots, and raisins; lettuce rolls stuffed with bread crumbs, Parmesan, and smoked mozzarella; and a chocolate-mousse-like sweet with the engaging name of *Moro en camicia* ("Moor in a nightshirt"). We poured copious amounts of Badia a Coltibuono's stellar 1990 Chianti Classico Riserva and ate a wonderful meal, the secret ingredient of which—in addition to the expertly chopped herbs—was the group camaraderie that had developed over the previous week.

After the last of the night-shirted Moors melted in our mouths, the Badia staff held a little graduation ceremony. We cheered and applauded as each of us in turn received a diploma, an apron, and a congratulatory peck on the cheek from Lorenza, which in culinary arts has the prestige of a papal kiss. Then, all of us still in aprons, we serenaded Lorenza with a song of *nostra prodazione*, as they say in the gelato shops, and Richard Kagan, an accomplished pianist, provided background music that transformed the sixteenth-century refectory into something of a discothèque, Lorenza out-dancing us all. But the sight I'll treasure most of all that evening was a quiet, cheerfully teary moment shared by the Sheridan sisters and their father, Bob, their faces a frieze of both contentment and a little sadness, knowing that a marvelous experience was about to end.

As to the cooking, ineffability seemed to be a big part of the instruction. Early in the week, while Lorenza worked some bread dough, someone had asked how she could tell that the consistency of the dough was just right, and she replied, "We know." By the time I returned, after a week of eating rabbit and wild boar and downing some wines that even the Francophilic wine critic Robert Parker has termed "spectacular," I know a little more than I did before, and when dinner guests now ask how I can tell, when the focaccia is done or how I made the gnocchi so light, it's a pleasure to pause and, mustering as much casual diffidence as the master herself, say simply, "I just know."

Stephen S. Hall lives in Brooklyn, New York. He wrote this story for Forbes Magazine.

FRANCINE RUSSO

✦ ✦ ✦

On Elba

Napoleon didn't stay here long—perhaps it's time you took up residence.

VISITORS TO ITALY TEND TO LOVE TUSCANY, AND THEY ALSO LOVE Italy's islands. What could be better than a Tuscan island? Few Americans, it seems, even realize that such a thing exists. In fact there is an entire Tuscan archipelago, the jewel of which is Elba. The island is an hour's ferry ride from the smoggy industrial town of Piombino, which is just two to three hours by car or train from either Florence or Rome. I visited Elba last June, joining Mary and John, friends from the States, on a bicycling vacation. They made the arrangements for the car, the hotel, and the bicycles; I studied up on the sights and the history, which, of course, prominently features Napoleon.

Napoleon (I now know) told the island's French governor that he had picked Elba as his retreat when he was forced to abdicate the throne as Emperor of France, in 1814. Really he had no choice, but still he got a good deal: he became the island's ruler. And far from being a grim prison island, Elba, seventeen miles long and eleven miles wide, is a natural paradise of towering mountains, lush forests, sheer cliffs, and sweeping bays and beaches. It has been inhabited, coveted, plundered, and fought over since Paleolithic times, and is thickly layered with history—Etruscan and Roman ruins, ancient and medieval hill villages, walled Renaissance towns. Everywhere—on harbors, hills, and promontories—the island bristles with fortresses, ramparts, and towers.

Blame the mines. Very early on the island's folk discovered rich deposits of iron ore on Elba's eastern slopes and forged the stuff into crude implements. Soon outsiders, too, discovered iron—and some of the one hundred fifty or so other valuable minerals on this little plot of earth. Wielding swords, they came after it in ships. According to myth, Elba's glittering mountains attracted Jason and his Argonauts, who landed on the island in their search for the Golden Fleece. In real history, Greeks had moved in by the tenth century B.C. and were smelting the ore. Etruscans and then other Greeks shouldered them aside. The Romans took over next, mining the island and building luxurious villas overlooking the sea. From the twelfth century until the nineteenth a host of city-states and nations—Pisa, Genoa, Tuscany, Spain, France—traded the island back and forth, divvied it up, lost it, and reclaimed it. Under the peace treaty of Amiens it passed to France in 1802, reverting to the Grand Duchy of Tuscany after Napoleon's stewardship and becoming part of Italy after unification, in 1861.

As you approach Elba by ferry, you can see the red-rock mountains and barren gray moonscape of its iron-stripped eastern end. Round a bend though, and luxuriantly green mountains and lovely harbors come into view. Elba looks like three separate islands, and is in fact made up on three distinct geological zones, east to west. The ferry lands at Rio Marina, on the east coast, near the iron mountains.

We were staying at the Hotel Airone, an all-the-trimmings spa on the north coast, just outside Portoferraio, which, with about 12,000 residents, is the island's only town of any size. I had little interest in the hotel's acres of amenities (tennis courts, swimming pools, and so forth), but after our first day of cycling I did consider treating myself to a *"massaggio totale."* Alas, the masseuse was all booked, even so early in the season. I toyed with the idea of having a mud bath, but one look at the lake of brown muck on the manicured grounds dissuaded me. Also, the spa's brochure translated the substance—with, I think, unintended candor—as "slime."

I would have preferred an older grand hotel in the walled city to this spanking new resort on the outskirts. But as it turns out, there aren't any. Blame the mines. There was little need for tourist hotels while the metal refineries belched their persistent cloud of pollution over the island—an era that continued through World War II. It was thirty years before Elba's reputation as a dirty industrial site began to fade. In the seventies a few Italians, Florentines mostly, began to notice its beauty and took housekeeping cottages there for summer escapes. In 1996, the government, recognizing the new variety of gold mine, declared about half of the island a nature preserve—and new resorts, from the splendid to the utilitarian, began springing up in towns all along the coast.

There are some wealthy folks' villas near the beaches, and some very expensive-looking yachts in the harbors, but Elba remains a relaxed, unpretentious island, where Italians of all classes, and many Germans, vacation. Menus, newspapers, brochures—everything on Elba is in either Italian or German, although you might get a few halting words of English from hotel staff members. So unless you have at least a smattering of Italian or German (I had some of the former and less of the latter), you'd best do your research beforehand. As it happens, a simple map and a list of sights will get you everywhere you want to go.

I was eager to visit Napoleon's house, the Palazzina dei Mulini, in Portoferraio. The city starts atop a promontory and runs down to the sea, draping itself around its bay like two long embracing arms. Embracing and defending, this rocky outpost has been a stronghold for centuries. Cosimo de' Medici left the imprint that is most evident today. In the 1540s he commissioned three linked fortresses to protect the walled city against marauding pirates. The notorious Barbarossa—or Khair ed-Din, as he was called by his fellow Turks—had been a recent threat. Cosimo set his impregnable citadel on the ruins of fortifications built by the Romans, who had laid their stones over the remnants of an Etruscan outpost. Nestled between two of Cosimo's fortresses, the Stella fort and the Falcone fort, high above the town and harbor, is Napoleon's mansion. On display there are telling personal items: tiny satin slippers that belonged to Napoleon's sister, Pauline; an engraved announcement of the birth of the Emperor's son; and tender family portraits pointing out Napoleon's warm and fuzzy side as a doting father and a loving husband. "I am in a hermitage six hundred feet above sea level with a view of the entire Mediterranean, surrounded by a forest of chestnut trees," he wrote to his second wife, Marie Louise, in August of 1814. "I very much desire to see you and my son."

The Emperor had for company his court, his mother, and Pauline, but Marie Louise had ensconced herself and the three-year-old Napoleon II at the luxurious Viennese court of her father, Francis I, Emperor of Austria, and showed little interest in so much as visiting her husband in his mini-kingdom. "Mini" is the operative idea here, and though the gallery, reception rooms and library are decorated in the grand Empire style, all gilt and velvet draperies, the house resonates with Napoleon's diminished fortunes. Nonetheless, Napoleon held court here and drew many visitors from abroad, especially English ones. He also had a country house, the Villa de San Martino, which can be visited, but it is generally described as "modest," and apparently not even Napoleon went there much. He was too busy riding everywhere on horseback—supervising road building, modernizing agriculture, encouraging fishing, and, above all, sharpening his tiny army and navy into readiness for his escape.

In the formal gardens behind the house it seemed to me that I could imagine the exiled conqueror's brooding thoughts as he gazed over the balustrade where I now stood, toward the lighthouse of the Stella fort, the sparkling bay, and, across it, the green mountains of the Tuscan coast. Napoleon spent only ten months here before making his triumphal—if brief—return to France and power. No one thinks that St. Helena, in the South Atlantic, to which he was finally banished, is half as nice as Elba.

Though there are a number of little museums on Elba (for instance, an archaeological museum in Marciana Alta and a mining museum in Rio Marina), it's the villages themselves that are the most redolent of history. Besides, they're charming. Most days we would set out for one on our bicycles. Since the island is so small, bikes are a great way to see it; the drawback is that all those picturesque hill towns are...on top of hills. Unless you're a more stalwart rider than I am, you'll want a car, too. (You can rent one on the island or bring one over from the mainland on the ferry.)

One day Mary, John, and I bicycled into the mountains toward Mount Capanne, whose granite peak, at 3,300 feet, is the highest point on the island. Eventually we reached Poggio, a village of colorful stucco houses with flowers cascading over high garden walls. These rose along twisty passageways of stone steps—some mosaics of pebbles, others patterns of gray slabs. As I made my way to the age-darkened Chiesa di San Defendente, a small but impressive-looking early-sixteenth-century church, I saw very few people about. The church bells striking eleven, echoed off the walls. Poggio is the site of the Fonte di Napoleone, an ancient spring whose waters are served in seemingly every restaurant on the island. We filled our bottles with the delicious water pouring from the pipe jutting out of the mountain onto the road.

A little farther up the same road is Marciana Alta, a wine-growing center and one of Elba's oldest settlements. We ate at one of a row of outdoor cafés, on a tree-shaded terrace overlooking the sea. We picked a café that served unusual *panini* and *insalate* my salad was a tasty bowl of fresh-cooked peas wound through with strips of pancetta and mozzarella. After lunch the three of us wandered through a peach-colored stone archway labeled "Porta Medievale di Lorena" into a crumbling-walled town of many stairways and up to the ruins of a hulking twelfth-century Pisan fortress. The highest town commanding a view of the water, Marciana served the Pisans as a kind of early-warning system against pirate raiders.

Another day we went swimming just down the mountain at Marciana Marina, a bustling town that contains one of the island's fifty or so beaches. Pick your favorite: they come with fine golden sand, rough and rocky, buffered by jetties, walled off by sheer cliffs, and in quite a few other permutations. Last year an Italian group called the Enviornment League named Marciana Marina the best beach in Italy because of its pristine waters. We weren't crazy about walking on its small round stones, despite the canvas runner draped over them by the beach-chair-and-umbrella man. But swimming in the clear water was heaven. Splashing and lounging against the rocks in the water, we rested our heads on pillows of spongy marine life of kinds we'd never before seen—green mossy stuff and tiny, sliver-thin mushroom-shaped plants waving in the current.

The island is densely packed with settlements, and we saw a lot—the old fishing village of Porto Azzurro, with its Spanish-built fortresses; the ruins of an imperial Roman villa, its walls facing views of the bay in three directions; the busy workaday beach town of Procchio, where we bought peaches so sweet and juicy that we had to wade into the water to wash off their stickiness. We also missed a lot—Etruscan ruins, medieval chapels, and the mining towns of Capoliveri and Rio Marina. With its nearly unparalleled endowment of minerals, Elba attracts both scientists and amateur rock collectors. If you want to collect anything from amethysts and beryls to garnets and tourmalines, you can buy specimen cards in the shops to show you what you're looking for.

One sunny morning we donned life jackets, wedged ourselves into sea kayaks, and paddled as part of a group away from the sandy beach at Marina di Campo, a town on the south coast. We slid past deserted coves, rocky bays, and soaring cliffs, accompanied by Umberto, an Elban guide and kayak renter. We picnicked on a stony beach between sheer cliffs, floated on churning white water between giant rocks (the ultimate Jacuzzi), and glided into caves hollowed out by the sea to look up at fanciful stalactites. As we paddled back, Umberto kept up a steady stream of commentary. I struggled to lift my tired arms and to understand his Italian while he pointed things out: jagged shelves of rock created by volcanic action, little green succulents growing out of the cliffs. *"Finocchio di mare,"* he explained—whence comes a strong spice that's delicious with fish. When we reached a point where we could see no land but the Elban coast, he paused and pointed dramatically in three directions: *"Sicilia, Roma, Africa."* My Italian was up to this.

The sun was intense that day, as it tends to be in June. May and October are considered the ideal times to visit Elba, but even in November, and again in March and April, the temperature gets into the high sixties during the day. In the early spring Umberto leads people on serious trekking and mountain-biking expeditions in the very wild parts of the mountains. In fact, international mountain-biking competitions are held here annually in May and October.

We ate most of our dinners in Portoferraio, where the restaurants are all casual, the cuisine is Tuscan, and the fish is fantastic. One night we ate very well at Stella Marina, the local favorite—although travel writers, we were told, are more likely to tout the Trattoria La Barca. We tried that another night, and it, too, was terrific—you pick your own fish off the ice, pay by the pound, and order it the way you like it: grilled, baked, or fried. My favorite dishes on Elba were the *insalata de mare*, a mixture of fat, tender little sea creatures and chewy tentacled things, all shiny with olive oil, *pappardelle* with conch in the shell, and *ravioli al salmone*.

When our stay was almost over, we had dinner at the Osteria Libertaria, a small restaurant at the end of the main drag, overlooking Portoferraio's harbor. The grizzled, no-nonsense owner, impressive of beard and belly, sat the three of us out front with another diner, at a long table covered with a blue-and-white-checkered oilcloth. The other diner was Margaret, a retired bureaucrat from Bonn, who spoke English well but knew no Italian. Ordering was an adventure. When our phrase books were no help with the menu, I asked Margaret to translate the German on it into English. What was this *"Chiocciola pesto"*? or *"Schnecke"*? "Snake," she replied, tentatively. Surely not. Well, she pantomimed, it moved on the ground and had a shell. Turtle? No, no legs. After a while we gave it up. Suddenly Margaret exclaimed triumphantly, *"Escargot!"*

Well, I ordered them, and they looked like little garden snails to me—tiny shells whose smidgens of meat had to be extracted with a toothpick, a bit bland in a thin pesto sauce. But my main course, *orata*, a white fish, baked in paper with butter and pungent fresh thyme, was exquisite.

As we lingered over dinner, wishing we could remain on Elba longer, the sky grew dark and the lights came up around the harbor and glimmered on the water. Boats rocked gently at their moorings, and a round medieval tower sitting smack in the middle of the bay gleamed red and strange, its narrow slits trained toward generations of long-dead pirates. If they had known better, I like to think, they would have come as tourists.

Francine Russo is a theater critic for The Village Voice, *and writes about social issues for many national magazines.*

RICK MARIN

* * *

The Uffizi Can Wait,
the Prada Outlet Can't

Shopping can be as exhausting as culture.

THE JOURNEY WAS TWO AND A HALF HOURS BY CAR, THROUGH
Tuscany, from the Italian Riviera. The truffles at lunch were O.K.,
not great. But no one said religious pilgrimages were supposed to
be easy. The important thing was we were here, in Montevarchi,
outside Florence, finally setting foot upon holy ground.

The Prada outlet.

Not so long ago, only fashion's privileged insiders possessed the
treasure map to this king's—and queen's—ransom of deeply dis-
counted clothing and accessories. Now it has become as much a
tourist destination as the Uffizi Gallery and the Ponte Vecchio—if
not more so. The Prada outlet is not someplace you check out if
you happen to be going to Florence. It is a reason to go to
Florence. It is also the reason we never made it to Florence.

The outlet itself, called Space, is a low, unmarked warehouse
building. The perimeter is protected by high white walls and forbidding black gates. Very military installation and true to Prada's
martial aesthetic. Inside are the clean lines and radiant salesclerks
found in any Prada boutique. One difference: guards with guns.

Upon entering, our party of six peeled off in opposite directions, dogs on the hunt. My *principessa*—as Roberto Benigni might

123

call her—made for the shoes. I abandoned my seventy-five-year-old mother, who walks with a cane, in handbags. In the men's wear section, I began frantically fingering suit lapels and performing the tricky calculus of foreign sizings.

Only slightly more civilized than a New York sample sale, this was still no place for the ditherer. Shutting out the babel of affluent tourists—Japanese, German, Italian, the inevitable Texans—I put on my shopping face and attempted to focus. Price seemed irrelevant, so deeply marked down were these late-season leftovers. Suits that would be $1,800 on Madison Avenue were $500. And our potent American dollars were worth millions of weak lire.

Desperate to spend, I could find nothing. A couple of shirts I tried on didn't fit, and I'm not ready for a suit with velcro "buttons." I watched the *principessa's* father expertly hand off pants, sweaters, ties to bowing attendants. Stunned by my floundering, he thrust a pair of beige corduroy slacks into my hands, explaining that I must buy them not because I needed them, but because they cost only $70. His is a World Trade Organization approach to consumerism: If it's cheaper than it would be in New York, buy it. It's not a question.

I understood. The presence of the armed guards reinforced the value of the merchandise. Spending was not an option but my duty as a capitalist and trend victim. Not to do so would be as wrong as a pilgrim in the days of the Holy Roman Empire refusing to hand over his ducats for a relic or indulgence.

Fearing failure and ostracism, I selected a pair of gray flat-front pants ($80), a tie ($27), and a pair of women's gloves for a friend for Christmas ($65). According to the store's procedure, I handed the goods over to a salesclerk, flashing the small plastic ID I'd been given on the way in. These items were then stockpiled behind the registers until I was ready to cash out. Unfortunately, this moment did not occur until closing time, 6:30, when the cashiers were besieged by a frenzy of last-minute-impulse greed and duty-free form gridlock.

My purchases were deposited in white shopping bags that said "Space" in big black letters. I could see that I was expected to make a speedy exit. When I tried to retrieve my mother from the handbag section, a guard closed in on me and made it clear that re-entry with a shopping bag in hand was not permitted. I did not argue.

We walked to the car, bracing against the cold, me with my solitary bag—a paltry achievement next to the bundles the *principessa* was still ringing up—and my mother carrying the same department-store purse she came in with. "Conspicuous consumption," she summarized, not with disdain but amazement. She had thoroughly enjoyed the experience perhaps the only way a child of the Depression could: as a spectator rather than a participant.

It was too late for the Uffizi, so there was nothing left to do but load up the trunk and drive back the way we'd come, consoled by the knowledge that Florence would still be there the next time, and that the Medicis certainly would have worn Prada.

Rick Marin is a reporter in the Style Department of The New York Times *and author of the memoir,* Cad. *Born in Toronto, he now lives in New York.*

DAVID YEADON

★ ★ ★

Lucca, the Unsung City

Add this to your itinerary—you won't be sorry.

I WAS WEARY OF CROWDS. NORMALLY I AVOIDED THEM, BUT ONE cannot pass by Ravenna, Florence, and Siena without so much as a peep. The problem is my peep turned into a peer, and finally into over-long ponderings. I was museum-weary. My neck ached from gazing up at ornately frescoed domes. My eyes reeled from fine-etched forms and the subtle line. I was becoming a little too irri-table with short-changing waiters and drinks in outdoor cafés whose prices often meant the difference between a full dinner at night or a slice of pizza. I was ready for back roads again and the charms of lesser-known places.

And then came lovely Lucca. For some odd reason this en-chantingly compact and somewhat self-effacing city is often ig-nored by visitors to Italy. A place of sumptuous plazas, palaces, and Romanesque churches forty miles west of Florence and set against a backdrop of forested mountains in a quiet corner of Tuscany, it deserves far more attention and provides a welcome respite from the culture-congestion of Italy's better-known tourist centers.

Mention Lucca to any Italian and the associations will invari-ably be the same—"Ah! Opera, olive oil, and walls!" And you cer-tainly can't miss those amazing red walls—all two and a half miles of them. They completely surround the city—bulbous brick bastions topped by ancient tree-lined walks, set in parklands of meadows and streams. They are said to be the longest and finest in Europe, the kind of walls a city builds when it knows its centuries of strife and siege are almost over.

Lucca must have felt very secure in the sixteenth and seventeenth centuries, when these fine walls were completed. The long conflicts with Pisa were at an end (even Dante sniggered at the enduring rivalry between these two adjoining neighbors in *The Divine Comedy*); its position as a leader in the silk trade was established beyond question, and its bankers were among the most wealthy in Italy. Three of its most prominent non-Italian admirers in the nineteenth century were John Ruskin who eloquently sang its architectural praises, Henry James who described Lucca as "a charming mixture of antique character and modern inconsequence," and Hilaire Belloc who called it "the most fly-in-amber town in the world!" I'm still crafting my one-liner summary but it will certainly be complimentary and Belloc-like.

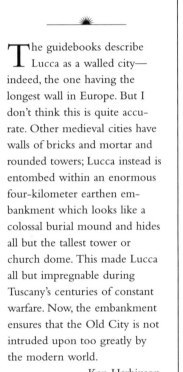

The guidebooks describe Lucca as a walled city—indeed, the one having the longest wall in Europe. But I don't think this is quite accurate. Other medieval cities have walls of bricks and mortar and rounded towers; Lucca instead is entombed within an enormous four-kilometer earthen embankment which looks like a colossal burial mound and hides all but the tallest tower or church dome. This made Lucca all but impregnable during Tuscany's centuries of constant warfare. Now, the embankment ensures that the Old City is not intruded upon too greatly by the modern world.

—Ken Harbinson, "Light and Music"

Today these magnificently gated walls are the scene of leisurely strolls, café-lounging in the shadow of Victor Emanuel II's statue, and one of the best vantage points for views over this church-filled city.

"We are an unusually religious people. We even have two of our own saints," one of the guides at the city tourist office told me. "And of course we are also the most enthusiastic music lovers in Italy. Lucca, after all, is the home of Puccini, Catalani, Boccherini, and, for a few years, Paganini. Everyone here knows his opera."

It's true. Lilting arias float out over the piazzas from sidewalk cafés, and the fall opera season, based around "our miniature La Scala" (the Teatro del Giglio), is usually booked solid a year in advance. The *concorso*, or operatic competition, held at the same time, appeal to the Lucchesi-*cognescenti* sense of artistic excellence. "Everyone in the audience is a judge," one of the competition organizers told me. "They follow every note and can tell very quickly which are the leading contestants. The real judges had better be good or there's trouble. People here take their music very seriously. You don't see many discos in Lucca—and you never will!"

"Lucca's just a city for old people," grumbled one spiked-haired teenager dripping with multitudinous ear and nose rings. With each arm he encircled a girl, both central casting contenders for the Munster family—long sticky strands of jet black hair, thick black eye shadow, black lipstick, and rivet-dotted black leather tunics that ended abruptly just below the panty-line. They all stared blankly at me, waiting for some kind of response.

"But you're all still here," was all I could think to say. Even that little smatter of logic seemed to leave them confused. "I mean…if it's so bad there's loads of other places you could live…" Their bleak, black stares unnerved me. I think I preferred the raucous miss-you-by-inches antics of the scooter-*yobos* or the ribald testosterone-charged grimaces and guffaws of Lucca's "*passeggiata* punks" whose constant barrage of sexual innuendos make the dolled-up, lanky-legged maidens of the town giggle and blush during their ritualistic evening strolls around the town.

"Well, nice to meet you," was all I could think to say as I edged away from the eerie trio. When they thought I was safely out of earshot, I heard one of them make a distinctly uncomplimentary remark—something concerning my geriatric attributes and the aged whiteness of my beard.

Now I'm rather sensitive about references to my beard (which is admittedly prematurely Santa Claus-like) so I turned, searching my memory for just the right offensive Italian riposte. Alas, none came to mind—at least nothing of sufficient vulgarity. So instead I gave one of those wonderful Italian slow and pronounced finger, arm, and ear gestures I'd observed in a bar in Venice which covered just about everything from their family heritage and physical appearance, to their mutual sexual impotency and utter intellectual inadequacy. That, I was pleased to note, seemed to translate eloquently and left them in stunned silence.

Then, just in case I'd launched a mini-vendetta, I sought the sanctuary of Lucca's amazing churches. I counted more than thirty within the walls—a panoply of architecture that made love to space, to the very air itself, except for one monstrous neoclassical edifice (and there are plans to build an even more prominent central dome here!)—the Sanctuary of St. Gemma, named for one of Lucca's two patron saints.

The remains of Lucca's second saint, Saint Zita (the protector of domestic maids), are displayed—all too visibly, some might say—in the Church of San Frediano, in the northern part of the walled city. I had just had breakfast and was unprepared for the glass coffin containing her richly adorned remains—her entire body in fact (much to the delight of reliquary enthusiasts) covered in dark brown, canvas-like skin.

An elderly British couple stood nearby, gazing at the saint's emaciated features illuminated by scores of prayer candles:

"Catholics do seem to love this kind of thing don't they dear?" whispered the wife.

"Disgusting," muttered the husband. "It's enough to make you cough up your cornflakes!"

"Oh Cecil…" she sniggered.

"Well…I mean…for God's sake!" hurrumped Cecil, his face a little greened.

"Well…I suppose it is really," the wife responded.

"What?"

"For God's sake."

"Must be a very different god from ours then is all I can say," he muttered and wandered off into the gloom.

My favorite church in Lucca, however, is definitely St. Michael's, originally established in 1070. Here I felt I'd arrived at the real heart of the city and gazed in amazement at this incredible Romanesque creation. Whereas the Duomo's façade has three tiers of galleried arches, this edifice boasts four even more extravagant layers of individualized pillars and exotic tracery above a sober base of tall blind arches, topped by a rather overbearing statue of Saint Michael. A delicate Madonna by Civitali, set in a halo of radiating golden shafts, stands at the southern corner of the façade, providing a fulcrum between the small piazza in front of the main doorway and the large space dominated by the campanile.

Purists point out, of course, that the size of the façade bears little relationship to the height of the nave behind it, and reject the whole work as "lacking in restraint." But surely that's the whole charm of such a building as this. Its creators enjoyed themselves mightily and were not afraid to show it. There were indeed once plans to heighten the rest of the church, and the façade was the first stage, but for whatever reasons the work was never undertaken. And it doesn't matter in the least. The Lucchesi love their unusual churches and glory in their eccentricity.

And eccentricity is indeed a significant word in Lucca. Some claim it is because of the town's domination by female rulers, beginning in the twelfth century with the Longobard Matilda and continuing when Lucca was presented by Napoleon in 1799 to his sister Elisa Baciocchi. Her enthusiasm for worthy public works knew no bounds. She supervised the design of the vast Piazza Napoleone, where her burly statue still gazes out at the passersby. She was also fascinated by city planning and is said to have enthusiastically promoted the arts, although cynical observers have suggested her prime interest was more in the artists themselves. One of the town brochures deals with the matter euphemistically: "Elisa took a distinctly personal interest in the careers of her selected artists, most of whom were young apprentices when they came to Lucca, and nurtured their creative endeavors with great ardor and enthusiasm."

A charming Italian gentleman who had casually appointed himself my personal guide for an hour or two was a little less circumspect: "The Bonapartes were a family of overweight, oversexed, overachievers. Even Madonna seems like a true madonna compared to that bunch...."

As Napoleon suffered setbacks in 1814, Elisa moved to Bologna, and a little later the city passed to Marie Louise of Bourbon for yet a third period of female rule. She is best remembered today for planting the beautiful double rows of horse-chestnuts along the top of the city walls—a favorite place for *passeggiata*.

Lucca's other eccentricities abound. The first morning after my arrival I suddenly thought I was in Venice. The Via del Fosso looked like a backwater off the Grand Canal, with its slowly flowing waters neatly contained by low walls. Peeling stucco mansions, ocher and terra cotta-colored, peered at one another across the water. The street has an uncommon silence, quite unlike the noisy Bar Giardino just round the corner on Via D. Fratta, its window brimming with the largest bottles of Italian wine I'd ever seen. One dark monster claimed on its dusty label to hold 100 liters of Chianti! Inside, the collection extended all the way down the back of the bar and across the far wall. The place was full of avid coffee drinkers chattering with one another at breakneck speed and flailing their arms with the eloquence of operatic prima donnas.

I dodged my way to the bar, hoping to meet Giardino and find out more about his unique collection of bottles. The barman told me he was on vacation and, in response to my questioning about the bottles, repeated over and over, "He's mad. He's crazy." Well—he's Luccese, yet not half as crazy as the man who mixed me a fiery local cocktail, the *"tista,"* out of crushed pine nuts and an alarming number of liquors in a small café nestled in the shadows of St. Michael's (which abruptly curtailed my wanderings that day as I wallowed back to my hotel prematurely in a woozy haze that lasted until the next morning). Or the well-dressed businessman, complete with briefcase and rakish Panama hat, who suddenly stopped in the center of the Piazza Bernardini and gave a fine rendition of a Puccini aria, raised both arms as if to receive a protracted ovation, and then resumed his walk nonchalantly. A few people stopped to listen and no one seemed at all surprised at the occurrence. At the edge of the square he knocked a huge door knocker (Lucca has a splendid range of "grotesque" door knockers) and was admitted into the formal confines of some important government office—but not before turning to face the piazza and giving a long, regal bow.

And then there were the lions—scores of them. Everywhere I walked I found lions, especially around the churches, carved in fine white marble and invariably eating serpents, dragons, or the occasional human. No one seems to know why the city has such a passion for lions, and no one seems to know either who decided that the red tower of the fourteenth-century Guinigi Palace should be topped by a splendid chestnut tree. It's yet another eccentric sight: but if you're really curious you can climb the steps of the tower to see exactly how it blends with the delightful roof garden.

Lucca's long history encompasses the glory days of the Roman Empire, when Julius Caesar regarded the city as his winter retreat (well away from the malarial marshes of Pisa) and met here in 56 B.C. with Pompey and Crassus to formalize the Empire's structure. The Roman stamp of city planning can still be found in the rigid central grid of cobbled streets, the great forum now a piazza adjoining St. Michael's, and the true Luccan climax—a Roman amphitheater. Actually it's not an amphitheater now, but rather one of Italy's most unusual urban spaces: an oval piazza, bounded by a continuous wall of shops and houses of different heights and entered through four dark tunnels. These buildings were added gradually as the old amphitheater walls, denuded of their protective marble, began to crumble. Sections are still visible on the exterior.

The morning I visited, the place was silent except for a group of young Italians sitting in the center, playing guitars and singing quiet folk songs that echoed off the curved walls. It's certainly one of Lucca's most delightful eccentricities. As was the elderly lady, tiny and almost bent double, who emerged from one of the tunnels bearing an enormous wicker basket of apples. She looked around furtively and then scurried around the piazza giving everyone in sight—including me—one of her delicious fruits. Even the singers paused in mid-chorus to receive her bounty. She was moving too fast to even accept thank-yous—and then she suddenly vanished again down another tunnel. The singers were laughing. I asked who she was and they shrugged—"she comes everyday at this time, always the same. Sometimes she brings oranges. Sometimes grapes…no one knows who she is…"

Above all Lucca is a city for casual walking—the ritual evening *passeggiata* tinged in occasional glitzy masquerade—pausing under the old clock tower along the traffic-free Via Fillungo, full of elegant shops; wandering through the alleys with cobblestones that gleam like polished silver and the tiny piazzas of the old town below the amphitheater; drinking a frothy cappuccino in the outdoor cafés under tall white campaniles; fishing about in the Saturday flea market stalls in Piazza San Giusto, and sampling the bold, unfussy food of Tuscany in the city's many restaurants.

Lucca becomes increasingly seductive the longer you stay, and I left here many days later than originally planned. "Life is too short for short visits," a happy wine-seller told me one evening. He was so right and you need these reminders occasionally. And Lucca, in its truly Italian manner, provides them generously.

David Yeadon is an award-winning author, illustrator, journalist, and photographer. He is the author of seven books, most recently, The Way of the Wanderer: Discover Your True Self through Travel. *He and his wife, Anne, divide their time between New York's Hudson Valley and Kyushu, Japan.*

PART THREE

GOING YOUR OWN WAY

PAUL SALSINI

* * *

Held Captive in a Room
by the View

The son and grandson of Tuscans returns home.

On the long flight to Rome I read *A Room With a View* one more time, disappointed again that E. M. Forster's characters abandon warm Tuscany too soon for cold England. Although my destination, Siena, was not Florence, I looked forward to something like the "beautiful hills and trees and marble churches opposite" that Lucy Honeychurch, the young Englishwoman, and her chaperone and cousin, Charlotte Bartlett, could see from their window in the fictional Bertolini hotel.

The last time I visited Siena, I stayed in a guesthouse run by nuns near the birthplace of Saint Catherine. It had a spectacular view of a skyline dominated by the brilliant white Duomo. I asked my travel agent if she could find something similar.

"I think I have something," she wrote in an e-mail a few days later. "It's a sixteenth-century stone tower, now a hotel. Eight rooms."

As the train (actually two trains, because there was a change in the village of Chiusi) sped north from Rome, the Italy that I remembered came into view. Clusters of houses gripping onto the hillsides. Fields of sunflowers. Rows of cypresses. After a business trip to Singapore in September, Siena was to be a retreat, a respite, a reward. The room would be just as invigorating as the museums, the churches, the shopping, and the public scene of that vast space, the Campo.

There was another reason. The brief visit was also meant to be a return to my roots. My father was born in a tiny hamlet in Tuscany; my mother's parents were from the same village. So both sides of my family were embedded on the same hillside—the local church held all the family records, the cemetery all of my ancestors. I could never understand why my grandfather and my father would, years apart, leave this lush country to follow their neighbors, move to northern Michigan, and work in dangerous copper mines. They never returned.

In three previous visits, I tried to solve this mystery, talking to cousins who would never dream of leaving. There were no jobs here at the time, they said. Everyone was moving to the United States. It was clear that my father and grandfather had not traveled much in Tuscany and almost certainly had never visited Siena. If they had, how could they leave?

Patrizia Landolfo, owner and manager, was sitting on the stoop when my taxi inched up to 7 Via di Fiera Vecchia and stopped outside the door that announced "Hotel Antica Torre." And an ancient tower it was. Despite my protests, Signora Landolfo, a tall, thin woman, grabbed my suitcase and led the way up the winding stone steps. As we climbed, the steps became progressively narrower and, it seemed, harder. I insisted on taking the suitcase for the last leg to the top floor.

Paintings have so accustomed me to seeing the Annunciation take place in the hills of Tuscany, I half expect to see flights of angels every time I sit here. (I would not be the first to wait in happy expectation: Citizens of the Republic of Florence believed their sacred city would be redeemed by armed angels descending from the skies.)

—Barbara Grizzuti Harrison,
Italian Days

Room 128 could have been in the Bertolini. Two arm lengths across and three down, it boasted a mammoth armoire, a bed with a white embroidered coverlet, a desk, two chairs, and a bed table. Whitewashed walls set off the slanted, beamed ceiling. The wooden floor gleamed, and the tiny tile bath was as modern as any in a Hilton. In a silver frame, a naked lady was being seduced by a centaur. I was expecting a Madonna, perhaps?

But the view, the view? Signora Landolfo pulled the shutters open.

There, just below and in row after row, were the red-brown tile roofs that distinguish this most medieval of Italian cities. Beyond, green fields. A church in the distance on one side, an old stone farmhouse on the other. A row of hills drenched in mist. A line of cypresses. Another row of hills. More mist. The pull to the horizon was as strong as a magnet.

When I edged down the stairs, clutching the railings that first night, I counted fifty-five. But something strange happened. Over the course of my visit, the number of steps decreased and grew softer.

By midafternoon the following day I had inspected the Maesta in the Palazzo Pubblico, the illuminated manuscripts in the Duomo, and the head of Saint Catherine in the church of San Domenico. I had staggered up the Via di Fontebranda, eaten chocolate gelato in the Campo, and seen far too many Pinocchios hanging in the shops. I was exhausted.

After climbing the twenty-four stairs to my room, I found a retreat. With the skies a dull gray, the tile roofs seemed cool and refreshing. The mist grew heavier at the horizon. Except for the antennae that sprouted from every roof, the scene had remained unchanged for 400 years. Wait: a workman emerged from a roof, dragging a television cable.

While serving black coffee and hard rolls in the tiny basement breakfast room the following morning, Signora Landolfo said that we were in the original part of the building. In the fourteenth century, this room was at street level and pottery was made here; the semicircular hole in the corner held water. The tower itself, she said, was built two centuries later, perhaps to serve as a lookout during Siena's wars with neighboring territories.

Lugging calendars and guidebooks and ceramic plates, I sprang up the twenty-four steps to my room when I returned at midday. I couldn't wait to see my view. Sunlight burned the tiles to a flaming red and brightened the distance. The mist had evaporated and the horizon extended farther. About fifty yards from my window was the only sign of life: on a rooftop deck covered with a glass canopy, amid the hanging laundry, a young man typed on a laptop.

Had I come thousands of miles to sit in a room and look out the window at rooftops and hills and sky? Shouldn't I be touring the museums, shopping, walking the streets? The guilt pangs lasted only a few minutes. I stayed.

That night, until a cool breeze forced me to close the shutters, I lay on crisp white sheets that smelled of bleach and tried to count the pinpoints of light in the black sky. With no fog and no smog, I could discover stars that I hadn't seen in years. Over there, was that Orion? Pegasus? Scorpius?

On my first visit to Siena I had an unexplainable feeling that I had lived there before. Everything looked so familiar. Now, staring at the night sky, I had the same feeling. Except for that naked lady on the wall, I felt at home again.

The first two mornings had been overcast when I opened the windows. On the third, and last, a sliver of light filtered into the room at 6:15. I gently opened the shutters. On the right, a huge red ball set the rooftops on fire. But in the distance the mist still shrouded the hills. For two hours, I watched the sun slowly rise, burn off the mist, and set Siena toward a new day. Dogs barked, motorbikes careened, and the sweet smell of fresh bread wafted through my window. Then I went down to breakfast.

Afterward, I ran up the dozen stairs to get my bag and a last view of my reward.

Paul Salsini is a journalist in Milwaukee, Wisconsin, where he spent his professional career as a reporter, editor, and staff development director at The Milwaukee Journal. *He has taught reporting and writing courses at Marquette University for many years and tries to visit Italy as often as possible.*

LUCY McCAULEY

* * *

Resisting Florence

The old phrase "carpe diem" *takes on
a new meaning for the author.*

SOMETIMES LIFE PRESENTS US WITH A TRULY PRIVILEGED MOMENT—
when things for an instant all fit together, and we are granted what
we wish for. Usually, we recognize these moments only after
they've passed. Rarely do they make themselves as unambiguous as
one that was made for me several years ago on a cool Florentine
afternoon, when an old Italian approached me and intoned: "Now
is an important moment."

It was my first trip to Italy, and I'd decided to travel in
December to avoid the tourist crush of the regular season. I'd in-
tentionally planned the trip alone as well, leaving myself free from
having to compromise about itineraries. My sole companion: the
gentle heft of a volume of E. M. Forster.

There's something about entering a city for the first time
through the pages of a book. The experience somehow becomes
magnified—each vista, every winding street, each sound and scent
overlaid with an extra mantel of significance. From reading *A
Room with a View*, I'd begun to know Florence long before I ever
set foot in Italy. So it was with that heightened sense of place that
I stepped out of my pension onto the Florentine streets for the
first time.

The winter light fell white and misty gray, like the light in a dream. I heeded the admonition of Eleanor Lavish, Forster's free-thinking romance novelist, to leave the Baedeker guide shut and the map behind and let the city take me where it would. As I moved through those cobbled, serpentine streets, trying not to find my way out of the labyrinth but rather to follow its subtle design, I began to understand what Camus meant when he called Florence "one of the only places in Europe where I understood that underneath my revolt, a consent was lying dormant." My only agenda: to find the Piazza della Signoria, where Forster's young heroine, Lucy Honeychurch, fainted into the arms of George Emerson, that odd and unconventional young man destined to become her husband.

The thirteenth-century piazza, the setting for public speeches and executions, contains the Loggia dei Lanzi, beneath which sculptures clamor together, with names as violent as their appearance: *The Rape of the Sabines*; *The Abduction of Polyxena*. And then there's Perseus, holding Medusa's severed head. A cluster of symbols that any self-respecting feminist would find telling—classic depictions of patriarchal attempts to control feminine power. The sight of these statues was the final sensory assault that would topple Lucy Honeychurch's delicate constitution after she'd witnessed a stabbing in the piazza. She swooned, and when she awoke, with George Emerson hovering above her, her life had changed forever, though for awhile she would deny it.

I couldn't have articulated it at the time, but I too wished to be changed forever by Florence. Not by meeting my George Emerson; rather, I sought to merge with another kind of lover, every bit as compelling: the city I'd read about, with all of its sensual delights and offenses. The taste and essence of Florence. Something that I imagined the Piazza della Signoria and the loggia of statues possessed.

But after a long first day wandering the streets of the city, I instead found myself pausing along the banks of the Arno River for a rest. I gazed at the jumbled perfection of the Ponte Vecchio, its nestled buildings in myriad sizes, shapes, and hues of gold that somehow created a harmonious medley. After a while, I pulled out a sketchpad and began to draw.

The old man was at my elbow before I realized he was near.

"Come, come," he said in heavily-accented English. Faded eyes peered at me from beneath a black cap. Absorbed in my sketch, I smiled politely and turned back to my drawing. It was then that I felt his hand on my shoulder, giving it an insistent shake.

"No, no, you must come! Perseo, Perseo," he persisted urgently: "Now is an important moment."

I looked at him. A snowy mustache, perfectly trimmed. White hair curling at each temple. A man who'd been handsome once, probably flirtatious in the way Italian men are famous for. Perhaps even now he was testing the powers of his charm.

"Perseo," he said again, his eyebrows raised in a plea. He pointed to the crowd that I hadn't noticed across the street—clustered inside the courtyard of what I now realized must be the Uffizi

Many years ago I was walking across the Ponte Santa Trinita in Florence with a young artisan, who asked me if I knew who had designed the palazzo we were approaching. I guessed a name. Yes, he said. But he died halfway through. Who continued? I did not know. And who designed the windows? And where does that particular bevel come from? And what is the name of the tool with which it is made? I could not answer.

"Ah," he said with a histrionic sigh, "you could never imagine the weight of all the geniuses who have worked in this city."

I was reminded of the nightmare which persecuted De Chirico when he lived in Florence, in which he felt himself gradually suffocated by the descending weight of a huge classical head.

—Matthew Spender, *Within Tuscany*

Museum (based on a quick glance at the guidebook back in my

pension). Just beyond that courtyard, I knew, stood the Piazza della Signoria and the loggia with its dramatic statues. My mapless wanderings had somehow brought me to my destination after all.

I am not proud of what I did next, or rather, didn't do. I wish I could say that I responded immediately to the way the old man's urgent tone had moved me. But I hesitated and kept sketching, while silently deciding what to do. I didn't want to appear naïve, like some too-eager tourist. What kind of fool goes dashing off across the street with a strange man? And what did he mean by "Perseo?"

I didn't recognize at the time the Italian name for Perseus—that mythic archetype of young-man-on-a-quest. The King of Seriphos, so the myth goes, sent Perseus to retrieve the head of Medusa, the only mortal of the three Gorgon sisters. Perseus knew that anyone who gazed on the Gorgons' nightmarish aspects—dragon-scale skin, hissing serpent hair—would be literally petrified. So when he found the sisters asleep, he used their reflection in his shield to single out Medusa and cut off her head. His gruesome task complete, Perseus flew away on his winged shoes.

The old man who'd approached me along the banks of the Arno wandered off, shaking his head, leaving me to ponder my behavior.

The paradox of traveling alone is that, though you do so in order to remain spontaneous, the fact that you're solo can also make you necessarily self-protective, a little wary even. Particularly if you're a single woman. A good and life-preserving instinct. Yet...

As I continued sketching, looking up periodically to study the Ponte Vecchio, the man's words echoed in my ears. In his gravelly voice I heard a lifetime of someone who'd laughed often and loudly, wept freely, whiled away nights with friends, smoking black tobacco on front door stoops. Exactly the kind of Italian, fused with life force, that Forster describes.

Suddenly, the drawing I'd been so busy with looked banal. I was curious about what had gotten the old guy so worked up. And, given his surely (I realized now) well-meant gesture, I felt foolish, regretting my wariness—my hypertuned, feminine radar, the sub-tle barriers I'd learned to place between myself and the world. I was no better off than Lucy Honeychurch, prim in her buttoned-up coat, observing the sites of Florence while rigidly resisting its sumptuous embrace.

I dropped the sketch unfinished into my bag and ran to the Uffizi square. In that moment I knew that rather than Forster's Lucy, I wished to be more like Medusa. Sensual, primal, and (her demise at the hand of Perseus aside) fearless. Willing to drop my armor, even without an arsenal of hissing snakes.

In the crowd, I looked for the man's black cap but couldn't pick it out in that sea of covered heads. The people all stood with necks craned, looking up, and I did too. It was then that I saw the greened-bronze statue of Perseus, his winged shoes lifting him heavenward. An enormous crane suspended the Renaissance sculpture in the air, inching it slowly toward a doorway in the Uffizi Museum.

A woman beside me said that Perseus was going in for restora-

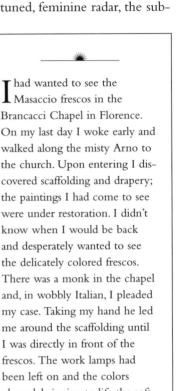

I had wanted to see the Masaccio frescos in the Brancacci Chapel in Florence. On my last day I woke early and walked along the misty Arno to the church. Upon entering I discovered scaffolding and drapery; the paintings I had come to see were under restoration. I didn't know when I would be back and desperately wanted to see the delicately colored frescos. There was a monk in the chapel and, in wobbly Italian, I pleaded my case. Taking my hand he led me around the scaffolding until I was directly in front of the frescos. The work lamps had been left on and the colors glowed, bringing to life the soft modeling of the master painter. I was struck breathless. Turning to my guide I found him grinning at me. In unison we said the same word, the only word we could have said: *"Bellisimo!"*

—Tara Austen Weaver,
"For the Love of Art"

tion and would be out of public view for perhaps a decade. No longer would Benvenuto Cellini's masterpiece stand among the other dramatic statues under the loggia of the Piazza della Signoria, where it had stood for centuries, inducing fainting spells in characters like Lucy Honeychurch. If the old man hadn't alerted me, I realized, I might have finished my sketch, moved on to the Ponte Vecchio—and missed seeing Perseus altogether that trip.

With each movement of the crane, the crowd alternately gasped at the threat of the sculpture crashing down or applauded at the sight of Perseus suspended in midair, both elegant and gruesome: his graceful torso, the curve of his thigh. A jagged sword in his right hand, his left holding high Medusa's severed head, haloed with snakes. For an hour I stood with the crowd, mesmerized by the sculpture's slow, pendulum-like swing. I thought how only Italians would do this, turn out by the hundreds to watch this transition in the life of an artwork. And suddenly I felt a kind of kinship with those around me—teenagers and mothers with babies and old men in black caps—all manner of Florentines turned out for the spectacle of Cellini's sculpture going in for rehab. All of us sharing a perspective on Perseus few had ever witnessed, perhaps not even his maker, from the bottom looking up.

At the same time, I was reminded of a more encompassing view of life that I'd almost forgotten—as something to take part in rather than to stand apart from. That was what had drawn me to Florence in the first place: Forster's portrait of the Italian spirit in all its exuberance. I had been willing to leave the guidebook behind, yet I'd almost let my reserved and cautious *internal* guide keep me from attending to a ripe, glorious moment.

Today when I come upon my half-finished sketch of the Ponte Vecchio, I think of that Italian man who approached me like a winged-shoe messenger. And I'll stop my perpetual motion and wonder if I'm not being reminded of something that even Forster's Lucy at last understood by the end of the novel: that happiness comes in moments. Only by allowing yourself to enter those moments and be present for them will you know their transformative power.

Lucy McCauley is the editor of Travelers' Tales Spain, Women in the Wild, *and co-editor of* A Woman's Path. *Her writing has appeared in such publications as the* Atlantic Monthly, Los Angeles Times, Harvard Review, *and* Salon.com. *A freelance writer, she divides her time between Cambridge, Massachusetts and Dallas, Texas.*

* * *

Tuscan Markets

*Temptation takes many guises, but seduction
is always the same.*

THERE WERE WEED-WHACKERS LEANING AGAINST PERFECT
rounds of pecorino cheese, Leonardo DiCaprio t-shirts hanging
over still-warm loaves of *focaccia*, rubber girdles like the ones my
grandmother used to wear surrounding sweet green plums. I stood
in front of a cardboard box filled with Nivea skin cream and
clutched my copy of *A Food Lover's Companion to Tuscany,* trying to
draw strength from its descriptions of homemade salami and baby
artichokes. I had come to this market in the small Tuscan town of
Panzano planning to worship at the shrine of *cucina italiana.* What
I'd found instead was desecration.

I averted my eyes from the cellophane packages of men's briefs,
the display of chain saws shining in the sun, remembering how I'd
prepared for this journey. Like a child preparing for her first communion, I'd spent hours memorizing the Italian words for tomato
(*pomodoro*), basil (*basilico*), and garlic (*aglio*)—the holy trinity of
Italian cooking. I'd repeated hallowed expressions over and over
like a catechism: *Come si fa questo piatto?* (How does one make this
dish?) and *E possibile prepare le salse prima?* (Is it possible to prepare
the sauce first?).

A gastronomical pilgrim, I'd come in search of a pure food.
Instead I'd discovered plastic ice cube trays and push-up bras lurk-

ing among the smooth-skinned apricots like the serpent in the Garden of Eden.

I surveyed Panzano's market square, looking for salvation. My three-year-old son, Alex, was leaning too far over into the town's goldfish pond. My husband was trying to photograph a couple of elderly Italian men who possessed six teeth between them. I went to stand before an altar of pale green and yellow lettuces.

A young Italian woman in a sarong skirt was arguing with the lettuce man. Each time she shook her head, the sun glinted on her nose ring, making it look as if she were shooting off sparks. I listened to her all-too-rapid Italian and understood that she was questioning the freshness of the escarole the lettuce man was shaking at her.

"Beh!" the woman exclaimed in the eloquent Italian explosion meant to connote disgust. She was unmoved by the lettuce man's desperate cries of, *"Si, signora. Fresca! Fresca!"* I watched her with awe, impressed by her ability to discern the crispness of a head of lettuce from six feet away.

The following day, we visited the market in San Casciano—a lovely town with warm yellow buildings and cobbled streets. San Casciano's market went on for blocks, the booths crammed with summer shifts, enormous cans of tuna packed in olive oil, and cassette tapes of Italian pop music played at ear-splitting volume.

My husband stopped at a stand displaying wire brushes, pink sponges, and bicycle horns. "We need these," he said, grabbing up two lemon-yellow citronella candles. Surely we would be allowed this one indulgence, I told myself, scratching a mosquito bite on my ankle with the sole of my other shoe. The night before, as we'd sat outside our rented house eating grilled sausages made from wild boar, ruthless Italian mosquitoes had devoured every inch of our exposed flesh.

In the next street, Alex dragged us over to a stall with a display of what looked like small red pumpkins. *"Che cosa questi?"* (What are these?), I asked the vendor, and he told me they were a kind of tomato that could only be grown in the soil near Florence. *"Acido"* (acidic), he said. *"Non e dolce."*

While Alex stacked up the Florentine tomatoes, the man explained how they should be served—sliced thin, salted, then dragged in olive oil. His hands flew as he demonstrated the proper way to soak up the olive oil, moving in the air above my head as if he were blessing me.

A few days later, we traveled to San Gimignano for the Friday market. In San Gimignano, everyone wanted us to taste. The roast chicken woman gave Alex an entire bag of fried potatoes. The salami man handed my husband a tall stack of fatty *salame toscano*. The cheese vendor, who had Paul Newman-blue eyes, bewitched me with a hunk of Parmigiano-Reggiano. Letting the cheese's sharp saltiness melt in my mouth, I was afraid of what the woman standing behind an entire octopus might offer us if we stopped by to pick up some calamari.

As we strolled through the market, I watched Italian housewives rub their fingers across the fabric of the summer dresses hanging in the stalls, testing the material the way they might test the flesh of a peach. At a booth filled with shoes, I saw them try on pumps and sneakers, placing their feet on the cardboard tops of shoeboxes to keep the soles clean. I found myself sorely tempted by a pair of sandals with gold buckles, but was able to resist thanks to Alex's desperate plea for a lollipop attached to a rubber monster finger.

The next day, we made a pilgrimage to the market in Castellina in Chianti to visit the stand of Duccio Fontani's Erbe Aromatiche. Heads bowed, we stood before Duccio like supplicants waiting for the communion wafer to be placed upon our tongues. He opened one of the small jars of organic herbs he dries and mixes, and held it in the air as if offering it up for divine sanction before passing it under our noses. Reverently I inhaled, and the scent of mustard, rosemary, and sage sent me into rapture. Duccio moved another small jar under my nostrils. Thyme, oregano, and garlic. It was a breath of heaven.

And then, just as I was bending my head to sniff a wickedly spicy mix of garlic and *pepperoncini*, I spied an alluring little leather bag in the next booth.

It was so pliant, so smooth, so cheap—I couldn't resist it. That leather bag was equivalent to the first bet for a compulsive gambler, the first belt of scotch for an alcoholic. A few days later, at the Wednesday market in Siena, I practically pushed aside a picturesque old man selling packets of zucchini seeds in order to get closer to a booth jammed with summer clothes. While my husband photographed the man and Alex mixed up his seeds, I succumbed to a clingy sleeveless shift (only 30,000 lira!). Then I allowed myself to be enticed by a couple of plastic ice cube trays, reasoning that our evening Campari-and-sodas really would be better with ice.

After that, I was unstoppable. The following Saturday, at the market in Greve, I barely stopped to pay homage to a beautiful *porchetta*, a whole roast pig stuffed with rosemary and garlic. Instead, I left Alex soaking himself in the public drinking fountain while I bargained for a pair of white linen curtains.

After the market the three of us sat in a café eating mortadella sandwiches and watching the vendors pack up. Across from us, in a stall overflowing with ravioli rolling pins and green-and-white pasta bowls, I spotted a sleek silver Bialetti coffee maker and sent my husband over to price it.

As I watched him go, I understood that my sin must certainly be greater than Eve's, for I had given in to temptations far more wicked than ripe produce. Yet as I ordered another glass of cool Vernaccia and waited to examine my shiny new coffee maker, I was unrepentant. Surely surrendering to temptation was the purest Italian experience.

Janis Cooke Newman is a writer who lives in Northern California with her husband and their son, Alex. She is the author of The Russian Word for Snow, *a memoir about Alex's adoption from Russia.*

* * *

Sinalunga

An English expatriate visits a place of ghosts.

I MET VITTORIA'S GREAT FRIEND CHIARA PARADISO IN THE library of an ornate *palazzo* in Siena, where the books were housed behind chicken wire nailed within baroque screens. She talked of her research. From time to time a waiter passed by, offering small stuffed edibles set upon a silver tray, and occasionally we raised our faces to the other guests.

It was not hard to sink back into the eighteenth century in such surroundings. Ceiling by Giulio Romano (school of), Sienese notaries passing through, their faces mild but slightly acidulous, like those of their bewigged ancestors in paintings on the wall.

Chiara told me of a room that she had discovered in her country house: by chance it had been kept sealed until her father had come across it in the 1950s. Manuscripts stacked against the wall, and in the corner a decayed spinet. The room in which a once-famous Sienese castrato called Il Senesino, Handel's favorite singer, had died.

Her shoulders were bare and her nose was sharp, and she was engaged in making lists of objects for a doctoral dissertation. It happens that I am fond of lists. Some of my finest moments, according to my admirers, have been spent in setting lists into chronological order. And she knew about paper, handwriting, and the use of watermarks in dating. It was a pleasure to listen to such passion, and after awhile I began to be curious about the material she described.

Soon afterwards she invited me out to the castle near Sinalunga. The appointment was at the unusual hour of two-thirty, "to permit a morning's work in the library," she said.

I forgot lunch. The day was hot and the last five miles climbing out of the valley, where the fields turned to woodland, grated on my soul. The oaks appeared curved over themselves like claws grappling with the surface of the earth, and the scraggy fields shorn of wheat cauterized the eyes. To soothe myself, I imagined them carved in wood, using thin hard shadows to emphasize the shapes.

At the end of a long dirt road, the castle rose, black as a woodcut against the shrieking sun. Two fingers of stone. Sighing, panting, I pulled up and looked up at the battlements with shaded eyes until I could discern the structure of the walls, in even layers like stacked bread. Underneath, a garden of roasted shrubs.

I was not expecting to bump into Vittoria when I arrived, and I was taken aback. I had somehow assumed she was on the island of Ponza for the summer.

"I was," she said firmly, "and now I am not."

Chiara sniggered.

"Why didn't you ring me when you got back?"

"But Matteo," she said, "I don't have to tell you everything about myself and my friends. With your permission…?"

Delighted, evidently. She linked arms with Chiara Paradiso. A small conspiracy against the token male.

We were walking among unpruned lemons in cracked pots set on small stands in a row, by a path of weedy gravel. Stunted box lined the path and rosemary took over the gaps in the garden wall.

"A long way," I murmured politely to Signora Paradiso, "to drive to Siena every morning."

"Oh, but I don't live here. I only come here in order to sell the house," said Chiara.

Another remark that begged a question. A huge wall reflected the heat back into the garden. They were definitely teasing me, enjoying my tense state. I looked up at twenty small windows, one open and a man's underpants hanging out.

Men run the country, but women run men. Italy is, in reality, a crypto-matriarchy.
    —Luigi Barzini, *The Italians*

"My father lives here," said Chiara, "but he tends to hide from visitors."

"Are we disturbing him? I could leave…"

"No no! It's just that he owes such a lot of money… We try to sell it every year, and many people come to look, but no one buys. You can imagine. When you think what it would cost to restore a place like this."

My head ached. The castle had bulbous turrets at each corner. From the armpits of the wonderfully unrestored roof sprung hairy grasses.

Chiara mentioned some Ghibelline ancestor, still further up the family tree than Il Senesino. I started talking about the thirteenth century, fast and squeakily.

"Of course, the valley between Florence and Arezzo was full of Ghibellines after the big towns had been taken over by the Guelfs. Somewhere near here a young man of '*la brigata Spendereccia*,' the Sienese wastrel that Dante mentions, must have died. Ambushed by the Aretines. I've always felt that he, with a name like that, was a relative of mine. After all, if you count a castrato among your forebears…."

"*Ma quanto sei 'struito,*" said Vittoria ironically—how filled to the brim I was with higher education. Except that the shortened adjective was usually applied to clever little boys on the front bench at school.

I was so willing to give them my historical interpolations, dazzle them with my views on Dante, the hooknosed bard of Florence. But they were immune to the charms of a hot amateur historian, and so I let them walk on a bit, among the sad statues and the withered trees of the garden.

I went to a well in the middle, where all the neglected paths met. Sat on its *pietra serena* rim, dropped a fragment into the hole. Pause. Thunk, the well was dry. Instantly the desiccated property acquired a desperate air.

Through a rusty gate closed with chain and padlock, the Val di Chiana was hazily visible, with a few flashing pearls on the autostrada in the middle. Far away, in the direction of Arezzo, the Mountains of the Moon, the most beautiful mountains in the world.

The garden was better smelled than looked at. I closed my eyes to its scruffiness and sniffed deeply for the wild body-smell of cypress, the twiggy smell of rosemary in summer, and the cool occasional whiff coming from the wood, smelling of nothing at all. The cicadas took up their themes within my head, and I dozed for a short while in the sun.

Sounds of a quarrel roused me. I got up, walked blinking through the bands of sunlight among the trees, skirted the castle on the right-hand side, and found the door of a brick baroque chapel leaning against the buttocks of a tower.

The voices came from inside. One deep, two chirrupy.

The chapel was in bad condition, its stucco reduced to fine rubble around the skirting, the altar casually propped with boards and an old curtain hooked across the door into the sacristy. The door frame was of carved chestnut, the door itself missing.

On the far side, Chiara and Vittoria were looking at a hole in the ground, rimmed with stone, and talking to a contrite *contadino*. Vittoria suddenly knelt on the ground and put her head inside.

Chiara said to the peasant, "I thought we had got rid of them all."

"*O Signora*, the ones which were buried in the garden have all been given back to the bishop, but truly I had forgotten about these."

"Forgotten! But these were the ones which had at all costs to be removed! The ones in the garden were fine, weren't doing any harm to anyone."

They were talking about dead monks.

"*Veramente, Signora,*" said the *contadino*, amused, "these ones are not likely to annoy anybody either, in the state they are in!"

I was beyond human company; I was even unamused by the idea, which strikes me now as very funny, that a sixteenth-century cemetery of dead monastics had to be evicted to make way for drains before a potential buyer would look at the place.

"Who knows," said Vittoria, her voice booming from beneath the earth, "there may be some saint down here."

"There was one in the chapel," said Chiara, "but we gave him to Baron Ricasoli."

"Why?" I asked.

She shrugged. "He was a Ricasoli as well as a saint."

I left them and entered the cool lower level of the castle through a small door, stumbling over the threshold.

It took me a while to get used to the darkness. At length I saw a staircase going upwards, behind a horse-drawn carriage which had been parked fifty years ago and left there ever since. The outside walls were so huge that the place felt cramped and claustrophobic.

On the first floor an imperial *salotto*, sitting room, optimistically promised a series of generations that would sit together over the years in patriarchal unity. Some of the ornate picture frames now held photographs from the 1950s, babes on the beach smiling at sand, incongruously facing an ugly oil painting of great-grandmother opposite. The frescos, done with glue, were peeling.

I went on upstairs uninvited. The voices from outside became inaudible. I had the feeling of ascending a fortress in the sky.

Up under the roof was a dark corridor not much used, with doors on either side. On the floor, a glove. I picked it up. It was of faded silk, with lace and seed pearls at the wrist. The hand was remarkably small.

I listened, but could hear nothing beyond the seething undertow of cicadas in the woods outside. I had no business to be up there. I opened the nearest door.

A thin crack in the shutters illuminated the spinet over by the window. The instrument was as healthy and inspiring as the shell of a lobster that has just been eaten—a rubbishy thing of ivory and red wire and discarded feelers.

I caught sight of a glass cabinet in the corner by the other window. I tried it, but it was locked. The top three shelves were filled with portfolios of old manuscript paper—it was hard to guess the date. The bottom shelf had some glass beads, a wooden crucifix, and some broadsheets in English. An eighteenth-century caricature of fat men in wigs was pinned at the back, its water-color faded to sepia. By it, a photo of a painting of the singer himself. Francesco Bernardi, all spit curls and plumptitude. Handel's great discovery, making a fine career for both of them for a while. A singing piglet, adored by the ladies because untouchable. What safer love-object could a gentlewoman have in London in the 1730s?

Did Il Senesino pine for his native Siena? No, there was no sentimentality in him. The Tuscans are immune to nostalgia, are born unsqueamish about the past; it is one of the nicest things about them. He quarreled with Handel about money, and went over the road to work with Nicola Porpora. Retired after ten years in London with fifteen thousand florins, a fortune in those days, and lived thereafter in Sinalunga with his spinet and Paolo Rolli, his friend. Leaving the lamenting ladies to rot in their sodden clime with him.

I left the room softly after closing the shutters. I felt I would just rest a moment, think a bit, avoid Vittoria in her conniving mood. So I sat uncomfortably on the tiles of the landing, neither in nor out, neither up nor down, and allowed the day's accumulated gloom to seep upwards through the fortress.

Thinking of Il Senesino led me to think about exile. Exile by force, exile by choice—*fuoriusciti*, such as the Ghibellines for whom this castle had originally been built.

I remembered that on a railway siding in upstate New York, my wife, Maro, had once shouted out, "Where are the Etruscan tombs?"

And when faces turned to her, apprehensively, she added more softly, "I refuse to live anywhere where there are no Etruscan tombs."

Madness in America is to be avoided, so the others on the platform turned away. Only I return to this image from time to time
with sympathy, as the various layers of exile unfold their petals to
me with the passing years. For her, the Etruscan tombs are tangi-
ble symbols for an air that has been thoroughly breathed, passed
through many lungs, and dirt that has been leavened in pleasure
and in pain by human bones. This is something she can brood
about as she scrabbles in earth with bare hands in the spring. Any
part of the world that has these qualities for her is livable. She carries her native land with her as she moves.

For Maro, in this suffering world each individual should listen
for a stronger pulse than that of some group supposedly mapped
out by race. The extended family, acquired friends, the haphazard
election of blood relationships. But beyond these gifts of luck, to
which one must be as loyal as possible, she recognizes no other unit
save the sum totality of man. You belong by chance, by love to a
group of fifteen, twenty people, or else you are of the world. And
so, down with ethnic minorities, with their insufferable demands.

High on the list of this mayhem of turbulent races, the English,
all the more an ethnic minority for not even being minimally
aware of the fact. And I of the tribe of the English, what voice can
I raise in their defense?

Brothers, there have been moments in a foreign land, in a coke-
sodden backyard in Szechwan, when I have smelled the Londonish
smell of my childhood (prior to the Clean Air Act of 1959) and
tears have rolled down my nose. Times when slumped in front of
the fire late at night, in the guts of a red settee purchased in the
Church Street market in 1966, that I have leafed through the
London A to Z and pined for London. Unable to focus as I fumble,
I have searched in the grounds of the gasworks on the map for the
Viking graves which, to me, are honorary Etruscan. With bitten
fingernail I have traced the passage of the Grand Union Canal
(Paddington Branch), blearily, from page to page.

My wife travels free. I travel with a bleeding piece of earth that
is forever Hampstead.

✳

Without thinking, I found that I had been staring at the lost pearly and lace glove on the floor. I rose, returned to the room of the long dead singer, and placed the glove on the keyboard of the spinet, groping for an empty chord.

It occurred to me that there might have been some conspiracy between the two distinguished research assistants, in having me see all this material. One never knows what is coincidence and what is not, does one? For some reason my good humor returned at this idea, partly brought by a cool wind that blew in at last over the hillside as the day waned.

And so I took the pair of them out to the nearby village for supper, where we drank wine and watched the sun sink below the sea, over above Viareggio as a bird might fly.

Sculptor Matthew Spender left his home in England for what was to be a brief visit to Tuscany. He and his wife now call Tuscany home. This piece was excerpted from his book, Within Tuscany, *a memoir weaving history, anecdote, and observation.*

RICHARD C. MORAIS

✦ ✦ ✦

Porca Miseria!

On the hunt for wild Tuscan boar.

GRAB YOUR BERETTA. 'TIS THE SEASON, IN TUSCANY, FOR FIRING 12-gauge slugs into 300-pound swine.

Beaters with baying hounds climb a steep, wooded slope, sweeping startled game before them up the mountainside. At the top, concealed behind a thicket, a line of twenty hunters waits, hoping they, at any minute, will see *cinghiale*—Tuscan wild boar. From my place in the line, I look up and see a perfect, Renaissance-blue sky. Through the trees: the ruins of a fairy-tale castle.

All at once we hear the sound of a dog's jingling collar bell close by; then, closer, what sounds to me like pounding hooves. A flash of fur, and suddenly an oversized fox—not a wild boar—bursts from the forest, stares wildly around, and bolts. My companion lowers his Beretta. Elsewhere, however, gunfire erupts, as a fellow hunter bags a fine young boar.

My obsession with *cinghiale* started last summer when, visiting Tuscany, I ate prosciutto made from these wild pigs. It melted in my mouth—a tender flesh with hardly any fat, its subtle flavor echoing the chestnuts and the acorns that these beasts eat, high in the Apennine woods. I enjoyed the taste so much I asked my waiter if I might not order fresh boar. He shrugged sadly: fresh boar, he said, could be had only during hunting season, from October to January.

So, this fall I returned to Tuscany with *cinghiale* on my mind. My wife and I stayed in Cortona, a medieval hillside town on the Tuscan-Umbrian border, probably best known to Americans as the summer home of Frances Mayes, author of *Under the Tuscan Sun* and *Bella Tuscany*. Thanks partly to the popularity of these books, tourists crowd Cortona in the summer.

In fall, though, it's a different story: the interlopers largely depart. The leaves of the chestnut trees turn a chocolate brown. Cortona reverts to a quiet town pursuing domestic pleasures. Locals scavenge the forest floor for porcini mushrooms; hunters go in quest of boar.

The sport is ancient. Medieval tapestries and illuminated manuscripts show our human, porcine, and canine predecessors going at it quite literally tooth and nail. In ancient times hunters used sharp pikes to spear boar. Then as now, however, the boar first had to be rousted from its hiding places deep within the woods. This was (and is) the dog's job. Illustrations from the Middle Ages show dogs dressed in armor—a single swipe from a 300-pound swine's tusks can be lethal. During modern

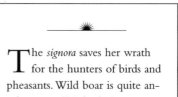

The *signora* saves her wrath for the hunters of birds and pheasants. Wild boar is quite another story. "Nobody is upset when a hunter shoots a boar. One needs only stand in a garden at sunset to feel the fear of those monstrous wild pigs with their long tusks and bristly snouts. Not only do they rob us of those wonderful truffles that grow at the base of our trees, but they have no manners. They charge into villages and trample our vegetables whenever a whiff of something becomes lodged in their nostrils; something aromatic enough to throw them completely off the course of their forest paths and into your tomatoes."

—Anne Bianchi,
From the Tables of Tuscan Women

hunts Italian vets stand ready on twenty-four-hour call to sew up unlucky (and unarmored) dogs.

Whereas boar hunting in the United States tends to be a rather straightforward affair fought with hunters stalking down a boar the same way they might stalk a deer, Tuscan hunts are "driven"— meaning beaters drive the boar toward a line of waiting hunters, the men standing motionless and fanned out thirty yards apart.

The rules are strict. You don't want to blast your neighbor, so shooters are assigned narrow fields of fire (between, say, 10 o'clock and 2 o'clock on the clock face). Even if tired out by waiting, experienced hunters neither talk nor smoke, since boar have extremely keen senses of smell and hearing.

Weapon of choice? A 12-gauge shotgun, loaded not with shot but with a single large, round slug, packed inside the shotgun shell. Berettas, manufactured locally, are the favorite make of gun.

Any top-rated Tuscan hotel can probably wangle an invitation to a hunt for you, and I made my hunting arrangements in advance with Ricardo and Silvia Baracchi, owners of Cortona's Il Falconiere hotel. To get a Tuscan license you must show a valid U.S. hunting license and comply with other rules that depend on whether it's private or public land on which you're hunting. Since purchasing the licenses usually involves time-consuming Italian red tape, you'd do well to ask your host to arrange the paperwork before you arrive.

Tuscany is for sybarites, with an onion roasted in hot ash and then dribbled with olive oil just one of the local treats. At our rustic inn, La Locanda del Molino, Silvia Baracchi's mother shows us her way with boar. Slabs of meat are marinated overnight in white wine and orange zest, then slapped on wood coals and grilled for twenty minutes. Mature *cinghiale* can taste, she says, "intensely bitter." Hence the long preparation to remove the gamy taste. After grilling the meat she layers it in a stewing pot, along with sage, onions, carrots, orange rind, bay leaf, juniper berries, and chili. She adds a splash of stock, and the whole thing cooks for three hours. It's tender—with a surprisingly strong taste of the orange zest—

but could almost be beef. Think I'd prefer roasted boar, gamy taste and all.

But first you've got to bag one. In Tuscany the hunts on which visitors are invited may be aristocratic or plebeian, depending on your hosts. My hunt was plebeian—and marvelously so.

On a cold Saturday morning a club of thirty-odd farmers, barmen and shopkeepers converged with a dozen hounds on the hills behind Cortona. Huddled around a birch fire, they grilled a breakfast of bacon and veal chops slapped between thick slices of bread. Earlier, scouts with walkie-talkies had studied boar tracks through the woods, locating a promising mountain slope for the morning's "drive." By custom, any *cinghiale* shot are divided equally—members typically take home two to three pounds of solid meat from each of the fifty boar the club kills each season. There are ten such clubs in the region.

Aristocratic hunts use the same hunting technique but display far more pomp: blaring trumpets, servants, a formal lunch. Ricardo Baracchi went to one of these the same day I flew home. He bagged five boar—a massacre! *Porca miseria,* as the Italian exclamation goes. This common outburst translates literally as "misery of pigs."

Richard C. Morais is a regular contributor to Forbes Magazine.

BARBARA GRIZZUTI HARRISON

* * *

The Hill Towns of Tuscany

Centuries of life and love have worn them smooth.

THE APENNINES—GREEN, GOLD, AND IN THE DISTANCE, BLUE—
curl around Tuscany like the bejeweled arm of a benevolent giant.
The sun makes a great business of setting behind these friendly
mountains, as if it were in perpetual and conscious competition
with Renaissance painters…or as if to extend an invitation to
enter the Renaissance painting, walk into the frame, and bathe in
the glories of art where art—this art that is so profound a part of
our received understanding of the world—was born.

Walt Whitman called the American landscape "the large *uncon-
scious* scenery of my native land." Here, in the sophisticated countryside of Tuscany—where the earth, once covered with dense
forests and blessed with what in the first century B.C. Varro called
"fat soil," has been cultivated since the time of the Etruscans, eight
centuries before Christ—nature possesses a unique intelligence:
when a soft gray cloud slips behind a velvet hill in the luminous
light of dusk, it seems to do so with will and volition. Nature allows us to think it has a conscious will of its own. But this humanized land of undulating hills and anointing light has been
formed and shaped by man.

It is civilized, it is old; and nothing here—trellised slopes of vineyards, waving fields of young green wheat, nodding fields of sunflowers gold as the gold of Midas's dreams, silver-gray olive trees, the bitter yellow broom that grows in solitary places, decorative exclamatory cypresses (like spiraling black fire)—is arbitrary. The patchwork and the cross-stitching of crops and flowers and trees that go every which way are orderly and logical, although it takes some time inside the picture frame to perceive this. No lines converge capriciously. The earth yields its bounty cyclically; man is bound to the procession of the seasons—and the astonishing (and calming) irregularity of the Tuscan landscape is a result of an ancient understanding of the needs of the land, its cycles, tides, and latent offerings. Man has imposed his will on nature here; but he has done so with nature's complicity and guidance. The joy of Tuscany is that—paintings, towns, land, and man—it is one continuous fabric: civilization.

If only we had a swimming pool, everything would be perfect. Even the fat bees are listless in the long grass and the purple clover. Lightning, a concentration and an incarnation of the summer heat, is stored waiting in rosy clouds.

We have rented a country villa—more properly speaking, a *contadinesco* (peasant) house, refurbished with sufficient grace—near the road that runs from Florence to Arezzo in the Valley of the Casentino, where the Arno rises. It is my sentimental conceit that the Arno is born in the tangled bushes behind our house. There several brown streams mingle; they look turgid and sluggish, but they are slappily and splashily (disproportionately) murmurous. They fill the simple house with music. And although the weather is beastly hot, at night I sleep under two blankets, as icy blasts come from the shallow river. At sunset, when fragrance is intensified, the smell of river water is married to the fragrance of peaches ripening on the kitchen table, and roses insinuate their sweet and cinnamony fragrance into this heady bouquet, and the green-soapy smell of pine, and, in August, the patchouli smell of newly mown hay.

(In Florence, at the fifteenth-century Pharmacy of Santa Maria

Novella, I will try to capture this fragrance—I will buy a bottle of *fieno* (hay) cologne, and one of rosewater; but it will evaporate immediately on my browning skin; and I will grow pale again.)

One night I awaken to a sky filled with milky radiance. The sky itself is blossoming; stretched above me is a tapestry of white and black flowers. Only gradually do my intoxicated senses understand that the elms and acacias outside my bedroom windows are patterning the moon-flooded sky. Thereafter the moon tugs at my senses every night and I awake and think: *White nights*; and fall simply asleep.

One of the nice things about nature in Tuscany is that it has houses in it—farmhouses and castles, too.

All walled cities are not alike. Some seem to wish to hold you in and others to keep you out. Perched, as Henry James said of Montepulciano, "brown and queer and crooked" on their hills, looking, from a distance, like "some big, battered, blistered, overladen, overmasted ship, swimming in a violet sea," the approach to them is often more serendipitous than, in the event, are the cities themselves. From a distance they look harmonious, complete (walls *resolve*); they offer the extravagant promise of safety, a freedom within fixed boundaries, snug protection from the alarm-

---

Even after years of traveling the world, I never knew until one sunset evening, driving down the white road (as dirt roads in Tuscany are called), that scenery could make me cry. I had stopped to admire the view across the valleys of the Orcia and Ombrone rivers, with their layers of velvet green hills studded with black cypresses against a pink-and-blue sky. That evening as I looked out across the valleys, I felt totally serene and in awe of the landscape. Its looks, its heritage, its ancestors and its history were all there for me to contemplate. Never before had scenery affected me so powerfully.

—Gary Topping, "To Live in Tuscany," *Town & Country*

ing and contradictory demands of everyday life; they appear to offer the architectural equivalent of that psychic unity that is our ideal.... They don't always deliver.

I tried hard to like Arezzo, the walled city nearest to us; in the end I conceded the last, laconic word to Aldous Huxley: "a boring sort of town," he called it, almost self-consciously devoid of effusion or prettiness.

"If I have any good in my brain," Michelangelo, born in nearby Caprese, said to Vasari, his fellow artist and chronicler of artists' lives, "it comes from being born in the pure air of your country of Arezzo." I can only think he was talking about the country*side* and not the commercial, wealthy city itself (its wealth deriving in large part from the design and manufacture of gold jewelry), an intimidatingly symmetrical city both frenetic and severe.

Arezzo, which has an enviable position on a promontory where three fertile valleys—the Valderno, the Casentino, and the Val di Chiana—makes it almost impossible for a tourist to find his way within its gates. Italians are not famous for giving directions: *tutte le direzione*—"all directions"—reads a road sign frequently encountered, which, as it defies linear logic, may go some way to explain why, when Italians say "right" (*a destra*) they invariably point to the left (*a sinestro*), and vice versa. In Arezzo, as the usually good-natured Kate Simon pointed out, no matter how diligently one labors up hills following the signs pointing to Arezzo's main square, Piazza Grande, one invariably finds oneself instead in the Passaggio del Prato, a big, tailored park wherein the Fascists, with their usual barbaric disdain for scale, saw fit to place a huge white memorial statue to the poet Petrarch, who was born in the old city. This medieval/Renaissance city Hawthorne called "modern" (he meant it was cold) and not "picturesque" (he meant it was withdrawn). Indeed, once I'd arrived at the Piazza Grande, I didn't quite understand I was there (nor did I especially, in this stony stoniness, care).

Gray rain turned the broody yellow houses and battlements and palaces a monochromatic gray: the city resembled nothing so much as a dignified prison. (It is said that flowers bloom, hidden from public view, in courtyards behind walls; I call that ungenerous.) Dante called the natives of Arezzo "snarling dogs," and I did sometimes wonder if the Aretines took positive pleasure in confounding foreigners. One long table at the monthly antiques fair was covered with a tarpaulin, and when I asked to see what was underneath, I was rewarded with a lascivious leer and a view of gynecological instruments old and new—it took me several moments to understand what they were, after which my stomach took a nasty turn.

Never mind. Arezzo has one great and abiding glory (one does not as a consequence love sober Arezzo, but one forgives it all): in the barnlike Church of San Francesco are the fifteenth-century Piero della Francesca frescoes, *Legend of the True Cross*, than which the Renaissance has nothing more sublime to offer. When one is in Piero's thrall, when one enters scene after scene of what H. V. Morton called "a brilliant, dignified world," one is tempted to believe that his is the gospel of the Renaissance, all other works a gloss upon it. We owe much of our understanding of perspective to Piero—but to say that is to utter a dry commonplace. There is nothing soppy, no fake emotion in Piero's paintings, no manipulative piety, and absolutely no sentimentality; there is only nobility and lucidity. In this dispassion and matter-of-factness there resides mystery. In this simplicity is not idealism but the ideal. This detachment is a form of magnanimity; one wonders if this—the thing being simply what the thing is—is the way God sees.

These soft-hued paintings are architectural—they prefigure cubism. And—although it is a mistake to confuse the work with the worker—they must surely have been the product of an integrated soul; they incline one to the aesthetic appreciation that color and form are not two separate elements of a work of art but one and the same. Keats said Euclid alone gazed upon beauty bare; not so—Piero did and showed us how. The folk legend of the True Cross, a naïve tale, is told gravely and with unchallengeable authority. And this is how it is, we think; *it could be no other way*. Looking at this radiant work we are at the still center of the

moving world. How beautifully Piero understood the magic of or-
dinariness, the holiness of everyday life.

Piero's birthplace is the sleepy arcaded town of Sansepolcro near
the border between Tuscany and Umbria, the main street of which
smells of perfume, owing not to any innate sweetness but to the
presence of a large Helena Rubinstein shop. In the modest little
Civic Museum of Sansepolcro is the painting Huxley called "the
greatest picture in the world"—Piero's *Resurrection*, a 6.5-by-7-
foot fresco in a marble frame. (Sometimes extravagant praise turns
one against a painting, as one feels one may not be up to it—in
which regard it is helpful to remember that Piero della Francesca,
fifty years ago, was rendered no homage at all.)

The Jesus of this *Resurrection*—risen from the sepulcher while
soldiers sleep in physical and emotional abandon—is God. There
is no other way to apprehend his watchful majesty and solidity. He
is of heaven and of earth. In this unforgettable picture, the article
of faith that instructs us to believe in a God who became man and
shared the human condition is vivified; it is superb visual propa-
ganda, an insistent, supremely quiet call to belief.

In this same room is Piero's polyptych, *La Madonna della
Misericordia*—the Madonna of Pity—a Mary very lovable, towering, and also sweet. Against a solid gold background the Mediatrix
stands, holding open her mantle, beneath which kneel sinners and
saints. Crowned queen of heaven, she is a simple girl; she looks
very much like her son—but then Piero's people, with their down-
turned lips and oval faces, all bear a family resemblance…one sees
their counterparts in Sansepolcro.

We make a pilgrimage (I have come to regard each journey to
see a Piero as a pilgrimage), driving past fields of poppies and
cornflowers and verbena, through an avenue of pines, to the pretty
cemetery of the medieval town of Monterchi. (Italian cemeteries
are invariably pretty, their dead in rows of drawers like filing cabi-
nets, floral offerings in silver vases, and beet jars.) Here, where life
and death mingles as naturally as fragrance and light mingle in the

spun air, is a small chapel standing all alone, in which is a sensual, inward-looking and weary Mary, one eyelid drooping, arrested in a moment of intense privacy almost terrifying (voyeuristic) to witness: one hand is on her hip, the other fingers her belly. She is guarded by twin angels, mirror images of each other (as Mary is the mirror image of every pregnant woman), who pull back the flaps of a tent to reveal her to us—a woman in the ninth month of her pregnancy, not an icon, but yearning, straining flesh. This is Piero's *Madonna del Parto*, before which village girls light wicks in olive oil and pray for a safe delivery. This fully pregnant Mary— pregnant to bursting—is both theater and protagonist of the greatest story ever told. One doesn't have to believe the story to believe the painting.

A young Asian man stands in the small chapel copying the Madonna.

Piero loved and honored women.

He died on the day Christopher Columbus landed in America.

Tuscany, honey-sweet and mystical and honeycombed with caves, has for centuries been the home of hermits. Until the thirteenth century, Sansepolcro belonged to the monks of Camaldoli, whose hermitage is in the heart of the Casentino fir forest, three thousand feet above meadows where Chiana cows and white oxen graze under acacia trees. It's a funny kind of place, composed of sanctity and of kitsch: twenty identical detached cottages, or cells, each with its private chapel and walled kitchen garden, house monks who live in voluntary silent isolation, meeting one another only rarely, for Mass, and, in fraternal tenderness, on feast days. Visitors are not allowed into the hermitage proper. (I entered the iron gates for a few moments to find myself in what looked remarkably like a Catskill Mountains resort crossed with a prototype for a utopia.) Holiday campers and hikers with heavy boots and hairy legs surround the settlement and lots of people visit the ancient Camaldoli pharmacy with its odd assortment of goods: "tears of the Abbot," an after-dinner *digestivo*; eucalyptus and acacia honey; chestnut, prune, strawberry, and blackberry jam; creams and unguents to enhance the beauty of the women the monks will never in their lifetime see; tisanes for insomnia, nerves, and liver—the liver, or *fegato*, being as important to Italians as neuroses and fitness are to us.

In the Camaldoli library there are dusty Oxfam posters, pictures of bloated brown babies (who'd buy them? Who'd display them?), repro Deco jewelry, and New Age books on sale to support Catholic missionaries. Lots of noise and lots of nuns and lots of junk and sugared fruit on sale at stands…. It all seems rather pagan and it is certainly incoherent; and with this noisy commerce and traffic outside, the cloistered hermitage seems like a theme park gone awry.

And yet: the vegetarian monks, ecologically minded, plant five thousand new trees each year…."Their relationship to the earth—their ancient mysterious mother—must have been the most intimate as well as the most interesting part of their lives," Edith Wharton wrote; what must they make of the doings outside their gates?

Inside the pharmacy there is a skeleton with this legend: *I am the true mirror, every other mirror distorts, in me you see what you truly are.*

La Verna is the most sacred of Tuscan shrines. Here, in these tortured outcroppings of rock, Saint Francis—to whom, in his mystical union with the physical world, the swallow became a sister, the wolf a brother, and clods of earth "lovers and lamps"—received the stigmata, the first person ever to receive in his body the visible wounds of the cross.

La Verna is romantic: a long white picture gallery, like a parenthesis, culminates with a window that looks off to a quintessentially Tuscan view: blue hills folding into blue hills; a numinous haze (gold dust)—the world is endless, sweet, and blue. In the Chapel of the Stigmata is a giant terra cotta by Andrea della Robbia of the Crucifixion in a frame of lemons (blue, yellows, bone white, sherbert green). The work of the fifteenth-century artist whose best ceramics are at La Verna cannot be called beautiful, but transcendentally pretty. Della Robbia was a virtuoso, which is not the same as a genius.

Romance yields to stronger stuff: here Saint Francis saw a rock rent in two while meditating on the Crucifixion. It is damp and cold in the silent, unpeopled cave, an icy womb. One experiences viscerally the mixed pleasure and pain of penetration (entry) and the anguish of birth (exit). One apprehends both the terror and the appeal of a hermit's meditative life, the thrill and the anguish of living on mortification and on air. One feels a reflexive urge to *kiss* something: the iron bed on which Saint Francis slept, the rough-hewn cross at which he worshiped. For, whatever happened here, *something* happened here. (I have felt this certainty twice before—once in the *scavi*, the underground necropolis of St. Peter's in Rome, where Peter is thought to be buried, and once in a temple in India, where I felt the presence of a god and heard the music of a flute.)

Si non credi, ammira! si sei sciocco, scrivi il tuo nome sul muro. "If you do not believe, admire! If you are crazy, write your name on the wall."... So reads a sign in the long white picture

---

We arrived at a Medici villa in Fiesole which was both an old folk's home and a hotel run by nuns. It was a good combination for a traveling family—the children were a pleasure, not a nuisance, to the aged residents, and the nuns and residents gave the hotel an air of grace and tranquility enjoyed by the guests.

I asked the nuns if there was a laundry on the premises, and they, with a smile, invited us to do our laundry with them. Down we went into the bowels of the villa to wash our clothes in stone sinks—hard work for softies used to the convenience of washing machines. Then they showed us the way to the "dryer": a garden with a view of all Florence spread far below. Slowly, and with the keenest delight, we hung our clothes out to dry in a shimmering spring light, certain of the presence of angels.

—James O'Reilly, "On and Off the Autostrada"

gallery.... And of course someone was crazy and did write: MARIO WAS HERE.

Something happened at La Verna, and something happened in the Val d'Orcia, at Castelluccio and at La Foce, too. Driving back from a visit to the thermal spa of Chianciano Terme (CHIANCIANO FOR A HAPPY LIVER, the signs say), we came upon the secular shrine of Castelluccio Bifolchi fortuitously, feeling the premonitory thrill of discovery before we saw, engraved in the courtyard of the castle, the sign: *"You who pass and see the peace of this valley pause and remember our deaths."... This castle is the gift of Marques Origo.* In this castle, and at her nearby villa, La Foce, Iris Origo spent a memorable part of her graceful, instructive life.

If she had written only two books—*The Merchant of Prato* and *San Bernardino of Siena*, classics that are indispensable to an understanding of medieval and Renaissance Tuscany—the reputation of this exquisitely modest woman would be secure. Her legacy to us is as enduring and as prodigal as Italy itself. As a girl, well-born of American and Anglo-Irish parents, she lived in the Villa Medici in Fiesole, a center of cultural life in Florence. In 1924 she married into an Italian noble family; she and her husband, Antonio, bought La Foce and its land:

> Besides the villa itself and the central farm-buildings
> around it, there were twenty-five outlying farms, some
> very inaccessible and all in a state of great disrepair....
> The olive trees were ill-pruned, the fields ill-ploughed
> or fallow, the cattle underfed.... In the half-ruined farms
> the roofs leaked, the stairs were worn away, many win-
> dows were boarded up or stuffed with rags, and the
> poverty-stricken families (often consisting of more than
> twenty souls) were huddled together in dark, airless little
> rooms. In one of these...we found, in the same bed, an
> old man dying and a woman giving birth to a child.

The Origos set themselves the heroic task of arresting the centuries-old soil erosion of thirty-five hundred acres of the Val d'Orcia, turning bare clay into wheat fields, rebuilding farms and bringing prosperity back to their inhabitants, restoring the greenness of mutilated woods.

In this beautiful aim, in the interval between the world wars, the Origos largely succeeded. But then Mussolini, and then civil war, came to the Val d'Orcia. During this terrible time, Iris Origo, at grave risk to her own life, concealed and sheltered partisans, escaped allied prisoners of war, Italian deserters, and Jews, and provided for her tenant farmers and for orphans of the storm, foxed the Fascists and the Germans, housed and schooled and gave medical attention to scores of refugee children—all (in the words she uses to explain the motives of a partisan) "from the simplest of all ties between one man and another; the tie that arises from the man who asks for what he needs, and the man who comes to his aid the best he can with no unnecessary emotion or pose." All over Italy, she wrote, this miracle was being performed: "For a short time all men returned to the most primitive tradition of ungrudging hospitality, uncalculated brotherhood."

During this time, when she and her husband were faced with the destruction of all they had created from clay, she kept a diary, limpid, sincere, "no unnecessary emotion or pose." One entry read: "Arrived in Rome, for the birth of my baby." Four days later, the new mother and her baby were in an air raid shelter, "the old dungeons...where Lucrezia Borgia was imprisoned—very deep and very damp"; and she made no ado of it. Toward the end of the war, she found herself very nearly without possessions; and this woman, from whose character had been scoured any hint of a sense of entitlement, wrote: "It is a very odd feeling to be entirely possessionless, but it seems curiously natural. One feels that one is, at last, sharing the common lot." That is not a consummation most people of her class would devoutly desire. She had gone through the eye of the needle.

In the Middle Ages it was believed that, God being light, sin made us opaque; if, according to this theology of light, man would eschew sin, his body would become radiant with light. I think of Iris Origo as being radiant with light. She gives us a new way to think of feudal overlords, in whose tradition she was acting. It is difficult for us to think of the Middle Ages as in any way benign (when I went to school, history was this: there were the Dark Ages, then a long tunnel, then the Renaissance), but it may be useful.

One night I went to the Castelluccio to hear a town-sponsored concert—Mozart, Boccherini, Dvorák—and I thought of the days when Iris Origo played with crying babies, making a game of disaster as bombs fell outside the courtyard. After the concert dinner was served in the garden that had belonged to Iris and Antonio Orgio; from the long green lawns, one could see the volcano of Mount Amiata, soft green fields between. Machine guns had once stood on these parapets, tanks rolled up and down these avenues of cypress trees, mines were planted, and partisans and the farmers who helped them were killed where now there are hollyhocks.

Brazen torches and soft candlelight illuminated the faces, the pretty dresses, the jewels of perfumed women. I thought of Iris Origo to whom not fifty years ago, a radio and a hairnet (the only lost possession she allowed herself to complain of) were so precious.

Thereafter, in southern Tuscany, I thought of her and of her goodness whenever my path took me where hers, in such terrible and ennobling circumstances, took her.

In the summer of 1944, after the liberation of Italy, the Origos were carried triumphantly up the nearly vertical roads of Montepulciano to the Piazza Grande on the shoulders of partisans. Had all feudal overlords been like the Origos the world today would be organized very differently.

Butterflies and buttercups. In the lavender light of dawn a will-ó-the-wisp swims up to my window to greet me—in Tuscany one finds oneself attributing volition even to dandelion fuzz, which Tuscans call "little Father Christmases." No other place could have given birth to Saint Francis.

We shop in the country village of Subbiano, whose history goes back to ancient Rome (subbiano = *sub Jano*). In the Monday morning market on the Avenue of the Martyrs of Liberation we buy everything from swordfish to hand-knit sweaters, suckling pig to Alessi glass-and-metal ware. The fishmonger, a pleasant man, gives us an extra ration of ice in which to preserve our *pesce spada*; he also cheats us. When, without animus, we call his attention to this, he says, smiling and unperturbed, "Of course, Italians have initiative." Then he gives us an extra half pound of swordfish.

In the café at Subbiano—which is exclusively a male domain except on market days—a little girl cries because her crayon has broken. Her mother says: "She is crying because of them," meaning us, "the foreigners." The mother speaks as if we were dumb and made of stone. She cannot imagine what we are doing here. The little girl offers us a part of her cookie to eat.

Near a tennis court in Subbiano there is a café where old men play cards and young men play cards, and often they exchange roles—the young are mentors to the old, the old are mentors to the young. The young are watchful of the old, but not condescending; old people here are not redundant. The old are tolerant of the young, and if they are envious of their blooded youth, their envy finds no overt expression. This café is near a hospital. The old men playing cards are young compared to the very old men and women who come here with their families, and with their nurse, a beautiful, vivacious girl (the leaven of the world). They play. They sprinkle one another with water. There is no scorn or fear of old flesh; if the young see their future written in these ravaged old bodies, they are not repelled by it. The very old people are spoon-fed gelato—and nobody loses dignity in the process. A baby coos and there is integration between those at the beginning of life and those at the end of life; and we are accepted too.

Barbara Grizzuti Harrison also contributed "In San Gimignano" in Part One. This piece is excerpted from her book, The Astonishing World.

LINDA WATANABE McFERRIN

✦ ✦ ✦

The Face of Love

Mythic figures and fantasy creatures
spring from real life.

"HOW CROWDED IT IS AT MIDNIGHT!" I EXCLAIMED, ADDRESSING the famous bronze Ghiberti doors at the baptistery of Santa Maria del Fiore on the night of our arrival in Florence. Standing on the steps of the baptistery, a structure that Florentines believe to have once been a Roman temple, I studied the details of those doors. Michelangelo called them the "Gates of Paradise."

Behind me, scattered about the piazza, scores of people chattered gaily and at length, heedless of the hour. The Piazza del Duomo was bright, ablaze with artificial light, the cathedral fine in its harlequin marble.

"Oh, you should see it during the day," came a voice from the crowd.

Surprised, I turned to see a handsome man emerge from the throng that milled around the baptistery. He wore a white linen suit. His dark hair was tied back in a ponytail that accentuated the square cut of his jaw. Flanked by his friends, he stood a bit forward from them, his Chianti-dark eyes dancing like a fabulous Tuscan cliché. Already hopelessly smitten with the graceful metropolis, I found the man's sudden appearance exhilarating. It was as if Florence had spoken to me.

"So this is the face of love," I thought, taking adolescent delight in the allegory.

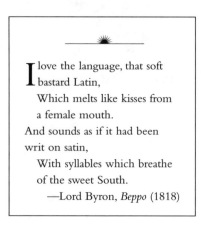

I love the language, that soft bastard Latin,
   Which melts like kisses from a female mouth.
And sounds as if it had been writ on satin,
   With syllables which breathe of the sweet South.
            —Lord Byron, *Beppo* (1818)

"*Ecce deus fortior me, qui veniens dominabitur michi.* Here is a god stronger than I who comes to rule over me."

These were the words of that famous Florentine of the thirteenth century, Dante Alighieri, when he first saw his muse, the nine-year-old Beatrice. A shy young man, he never found the courage to speak to her, but he pined for her for nine years (she died at eighteen), and inspired by this love, he wrote some of the western world's most elevating verse, including *The Divine Comedy*. Visiting Florence, the artistic heart of Italy and one-time home of creative luminaries like Dante, Leonardo da Vinci, Sandro Botticelli, and Michelangelo, I was ready to be swept away.

The stranger approached and, with arresting elegance, presented his card. Our fingers touched.

His name was Vittorio. He was Florentine. What did it matter that he owned a leather boutique a mere three blocks away and frequently strolled the busy streets with his cohorts in search of tourists like me? Vittorio transcended his surroundings. He was, I decided, a symbol of Florence. He would be my cupid, my divine beacon.

True to his symbolism, Vittorio was to appear again and again, an unofficial guide directing our little group through the city. On crowded corners, at an outdoor café—he was everywhere—always trailed by his entourage. He was supposedly at his leather shop by appointment only, but it was reported that he seemed to materialize miraculously for all drop-in visitors.

But more than Vittorio conspired to excite me into a kind of lyric delirium. My husband Lawrence and I were staying at the Porta Rosa, an ancient hotel in the city's historical center. Noted for its tremendous red doors, the figurative significance of its name provided more fuel for my imaginative vision of Florence as a city of romance. Red is, of course, the color of the impassioned heart. Doors symbolize entrance. In poetic parlance, the "Porta Rosa" thereby becomes "a place where the heart opens and love makes its entrance." Corny by today's standards, perhaps, but many a misty-eyed troubadour has managed to make his way into a boudoir through a well-planned metaphor.

The rooms of the Porta Rosa were enormous. They resembled ballrooms filled with antique furniture: creaky armoires (stuffed with stories, no doubt), lopsided beds, and showers that spilled water into the rooms and flooded the wide parquet floors. Changing quarters nightly, Lawrence and I found every room to be equally eccentric, albeit in different ways. Our first apartment was a turreted chamber, up a few skinny steps, that opened onto a cavernous third-floor salon. By some strange quirk of the architecture, we could hear every sound made in the much-used elevator—the laughter of guests, the arguments of the maids—and they, in turn, could hear every private rustling in our room.

The next night we opted for privacy, but there was no shower, and the burp of motorbikes flying over Florence's cobblestones was not to be stopped by the room's wooden shutters. Our next room was quiet, but its three small beds creaked like rickety carts (we tried them all) and a curious mildew smell was permanently lodged in the bathroom. In addition to the three odd beds—two of which we pushed together like the halves of a badly made locket—this room was appointed with two huge rectangular tables, many chairs, a tall chest of drawers, two walnut wardrobes, and plenty of room to waltz.

We enjoyed our game of musical rooms at the Porta Rosa. We liked the dusty carpets, the ringing halls, and the musty downstairs bar. In short, we adored our hotel. I forgot things there—a new

swimsuit and an old pair of sandals—both lost in the deepest
reaches of one of the immense armoires. They are probably still
there, hidden in some shadowy, rarely cleaned corner.

From this fanciful headquarters, we set out everyday to explore
the city, browsing the produce warehouse of the Mercato Centrale
with its stiff young zucchini—the squash blossoms still upon
them—and its smug pyramids of fat *porcini* mushrooms. We followed the crowds to the Academy to muse for hours upon
Michelangelo's towering *David*. We wandered through the Uffizi's
galleries where, dazzled by the Renaissance masters, we fell in love
with the sylphlike creatures that people their canvases. We savored
the sight of Botticelli's *Aphrodite* and the lovely ladies of his
Primavera. Arranged as they were in proximity, and intermingled
with his other work, it was impossible not to see that they all—the
women, the angels, everyone—had the same serene face, and that
this face, if we can trust the honesty of Botticelli's self-portrait, is
the same face as the artist's. So a roomful of Botticelli's really is,
quiet literally, a room *full* of Botticellis.

Among the many near-
perfect moments in that
town, I count one night at
the Osteria del Cinghiale
Bianco. Naturally, Lawrence
and I were directed there by
Vittorio. The *osteria* was on
the opposite side of the
River Arno, a short walk
under starlight over the
famed Ponte Vecchio. We
were told that the building in
which the Osteria del
Cinghiale Bianco was situated had been structurally unchanged
since the thirteenth century. The name of the restaurant, in
English, is the Inn of the White Boar. White being the color of
purity and the boar being a symbol of carnal lust, this *osteria* thus
represents the blessed fusion of these polarities; because in the

> **B**otticelli's real name was
> Sandro Filipepi. Botticelli,
> which means "little barrels," was
> a nickname given to his rotund
> older brother that later spread to
> the whole family.
> —Wenda O'Reilly, Ph.D,
> *The Renaissance Art Book*

absolute artistry of its dishes, it satisfies the craving of the most vicious of appetites, and with its fresh and surprisingly simple cuisine, it pleases even the most jaded of palates. It is a popular place. The white walls and white table linens were spotless. Candlelight and kitchen warmth cast a flattering flame on the faces and eyes of the guests.

We drank Chianti. Our Tuscan beans were *al dente*, cooked to such perfection that each bean seemed to have its own personality. The Tuscan bread, an acquired taste, had a chalkiness that suggested marble dust. I love that about the bread in Tuscany—I think I can taste the quarries in it. To our right was an elderly Israeli couple, to our left a British couple well into their seventies. We chatted like old friends, made reservations for dinner the next night, and rhapsodized over all we had seen in our travels around the world until the wine wound us into the more intimate influence of our own dinner partners. We fell into our worlds of twos.

After dinner, as Lawrence and I walked hand-in-hand over the Ponte Vecchio, I remembered a story we'd heard from a Florentine whom we'd met earlier in the day.

"During World War II, the Germans, fearing Allied pursuit, blew up all the bridges in Florence. This bridge, the Ponte Vecchio, they spared because it was here that the great poet Dante first beheld Beatrice."

I had not heard the story before. In fact, Dante was notorious for evading all mention of place, referring instead, in a purposefully vague way, to "a street which runs through the center of the city," or "a neighboring town" and to Florence, his home, as "the aforementioned city." I have not found the Ponte Vecchio mentioned in the *Vita Nuova* or *The Divine Comedy*, so I wondered about the anecdote's source. But I liked the spirit of the narrative, and I liked the allusion to Dante's first encounter with Beatrice.

The next day we walked again over the Ponte Vecchio and stopped to stand in the puddle of a small fountain, wedged between kiosks and old world-style stalls. A break in the row of shops that line either side of the famous bridge, as they have for centuries, afforded a gap through which to survey the wide sweep of the Arno. Small boats dotted the waters, a few children played in the high grass of the banks, and on either side of the river, Florence rose lofty and reserved, the well-balanced scale of its rooftops and walls reflected in shimmering symmetry on the Arno's Botticelli-like face.

Linda Watanabe McFerrin is a poet, columnist, travel writer, and novelist who has contributed to journals, newspapers, and magazines throughout the United States. She is the author of two poetry collections, the novel, Namako: Sea Cucumber, *and the short story collection,* The Hand of Buddha. *She is a winner of the Katherine Anne Porter Prize for Fiction.*

SOPHIA KOBACKER

* * *

The Snake at Her Back Door

It is good to live in harmony
with your neighbors.

THERE IS A SNAKE LIVING AT MY BACK DOOR. THE ANCIENT STONE slab at the doorstep just outside the kitchen, where I sit reading in the sun, is the path she slithers across to get to or from her rocky home, down behind the old green shutter. She's a beautiful snake, about five feet long, with lime green scales and black crosshatched diamonds on her back. Her belly is the color of lemons and her eyes are shiny black.

Two days ago, she peers up at my left arm as I sit on the step, blocking her passage home in the late afternoon sun. I jump up and frighten her into using a wide detour. She slithers around the broad granite slabs of the patio, through the rapidly growing grass sprouting up through the gravel beyond, over the low stone wall to the right, heavily shaded by trees and vines, and down the twenty foot drop to the chicken house below. There is no way to tell whether this is a local serpent or one that is just passing through and whether it's harmless or poisonous. I wonder in that moment if I should warn the Italian Nonna below (whose brother manages the padre's olive groves) that I've just seen a snake heading towards her chickens! I quickly find the Italian phrasebook and look up the words for snake and poisonous, *il serpente* and *il veleno*.

183

But in the back of my mind I hear the fearful Italian word *vipera* (adder) coming up for emergency use.

I hunt around for the silver-haired Nonna, whose head I've just seen recently, bobbing about at the clothesline below, scolding the chickens in her herb garden. She doesn't respond when I knock at her door, calling out *"Scusi, Signora!"* There's no sign of her, but I think she's hiding from me, the *straniera* (foreigner) who lives in the villa above hers. I suspect she's watching me silently from one of the upper windows, where the heavy wooden shutters are drawn to keep the afternoon sun from fading her holy pictures.

I speak to her old black cat with gummy eyes, who looks too lazy or sick to be worried about snakes. This half-blind cat, I realize now, must be the reason I keep hearing the mysterious sounds of smashing glass or pottery rising up from her patio below. I had thought the Signora might have a slight drinking problem.

I notice her small shrine to the Madonna, near the windowsill the cat is now stretched across. This shrine faces away from the villa, watching out over the fertile valley below. Half-burnt candles sit on a shelf in front of the white ceramic faces of the Holy Mother and Child. I sense whispered prayers in the air and feel I'm invading her sanctuary.

I continue searching for the old woman, feeling every bit the stranger I am, here amongst her meticulous private property, until I hear a vehicle pull up on the gravel driveway below. I reach the edge of the slope in time to see the Big Papa Signore jump out of the driver's seat. He's the padrone who owns this whole hillside of grapes and olives.

Two middle-aged women emerge from the other side of the large white van. They're dressed as though they've just been to church and look as if they could be sisters. I remember now that it is a holy day for the Pentecost. I call out *"Scuse Signore!* There is a *serpente* over there!"* (pointing up towards my place) "Is it a *vipera?*"

The big man looks up at me, with those wild blue eyes and snowy hair, as if I'm mad. I know I'm making a fool of myself in front of the well-dressed startled sisters, but I feel I owe it to my neighbor, the old Signora, (even if she won't open her door to me) to find out if the presence of this snake poses any real danger to the general community.

The Big Papa Signore finally understands what I'm talking about and asks me in Italian, "Where is the snake?" I mime for him (and to the sisters' great amusement) "At my back door!" by waving my hands in front of me, to mimic the opening and closing of French doors, and by pointing down towards the ground in front of me. He

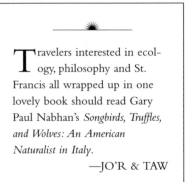

Travelers interested in ecology, philosophy and St. Francis all wrapped up in one lovely book should read Gary Paul Nabhan's *Songbirds, Truffles, and Wolves: An American Naturalist in Italy*.

—JO'R & TAW

understands this little performance and nods. The question has to be asked, in spite of my hopeless Italian grammar, "Is it *il veleno* (a poison)?" *"No 'il veleno'!"* he says with a wave of his hand and a big smile. As he turns to go, he cocks his head with a sly afterthought. He suggests, in Italian, that I close my back door. The sisters stand in a sympathetic huddle after witnessing all of this. They're now holding hands, shuddering at the thought that perhaps a snake might come through their own kitchen doors! One of them mutters a soft Ave Maria under her breath while the other lifts a finger to her lips. The padrone is greatly amused, however, and looks very pleased with himself, having just come to the aid of a helpless foreigner. Now, when he passes me on the road when I drive into the village, I see his great flash of white teeth and those crazy blue eyes as he waves and chuckles with the memory. That's the *straniera* with the snake at her back door!

This morning as I sit on the stone step in the misty early morning sun, the snake pokes her head through the gap above the hinge of the great green shutters astride the kitchen door. The snake's head is no more than six inches from my right arm, and the rest of her is coiled amongst the rocks. I register in a millisecond that this is not one of the many green or yellow lizards that feast on ants around the stone patio. It's that snake again!

I marvel at how quickly I leap forward, away from the snake, making no sound except for the hiss of the newspaper I've been sitting on (to insulate my bottom against the cold of the granite step, not yet warmed by the day's sun). I don't even spill my tea.

I'm standing in my pajamas thinking to myself, "There's a snake living at my back door!" It takes a few moments to absorb this new reality. I start thinking about how, day and night this past week, I've sat on that stone step, my bottom on that well-slithered path, reading in the sun, or watching the fireflies dance across the garden under the spring moon, just inches away from the snake's rocky den.

I'm the *straniera* with the snake at my back door; that's all. Now, when I open that door, I hiss, to give her fair warning.

Sophia Kobacker is an Australian-born writer and traveler. Her passion for ancient and indigenous cultures has drawn her into worlds as diverse as African and Peruvian shamanism, Afro-American voodoo, and Native American and Australian Aboriginal traditions. She lives by the sea in Santa Barbara, California, and loves its old-fashioned airport.

MIRANDA MOWBRAY

⋆ ⋆ ⋆

The Beautiful Machine of the World

Florence once seemed the center
of the human universe; perhaps it still is.

WHAT BEAUTY THERE IS IN THE MUSEUM OF THE HISTORY OF Science in Florence. The guidebooks tell me that I should be at the Uffizi or the Accademia, but in my opinion this is a museum of art too. The instruments are brassed, gilded, decorated, illustrated, and engraved with words and clear, elegant numbers. I am surrounded by celestial globes, armillary spheres, protractors, quadrants, clocks, night-navigators, compasses, set squares, theodolites, plumblines, graphometers, odometers, clinometers, thermoscopes, astrolabes—they're so lovely, those astrolabes with Arabic calligraphy—a dark portrait of a Renaissance scientist all in black except for his white ruff, the multiplication machine of Sir Samuel Morland (1679) made of rotatable discs encoded with engraved numbers, a pendulum clock by Galileo himself, all the instruments to measure and understand a world; what beauty.

I work for a company that makes descendents of Sir Samuel Morland's machine. Nowadays technological instruments are not works of art. I feel a momentary desperate desire to change the company's strategy.

But perhaps it is only possible to make instruments like these in times of scientific optimism. Today's science tells us that chaos is the natural order, and that it is useless to try to construct an instrument that measures more precisely than Planck's constant allows. We now know that science does not automatically tend toward the beautiful and the good, that the radiation that cures cancer can also make the bomb.

I remember standing here with my beloved many years ago, the first time I visited this museum. We paused shoulder to shoulder in the middle of the instruments, to imagine the universe spinning with us at its center. We were as egocentric as all young lovers. I even believed then that the force of attraction between us would be enough to hold the cosmos in its right orbit.

This time I am alone. I walk into the room housing the three-meter-high Great Universal Globe of Santucci, 1593. Next to it there is a sad notice in English: "Because of the precarious condition of the machine of the world, today it is not possible to make it rotate."

Oh, how I want to help it rotate again, the beautiful machine of the Renaissance universe, its globes circling and singing in harmony, art and science and metaphysics together. I murmur a prayer to love, the Love that Dante described as moving the Sun and the Other Stars: to the love that, once upon a time, made the world go round.

Miranda Mowbray is a soprano mathematician. Her hair is red. She likes mango ice cream, and lives in Bristol, England. Her writing also appears in Travelers' Tales Italy.

PART FOUR

IN THE SHADOWS

★ ★ ★

Stolen Beauty

*Possession, as they say, is nine-tenths
of the law—even if you're renting.*

SUN. A VILLA. TERRA COTTA ROOFS. PENCIL CYPRESSES.
Mozzarella di bufala. Extra-virgin olive oil. Ranks of grapevines. A
prospect of square-roofed towers. Is that it? Is that what all the fuss
is about?

You could say that Tuscany is full of other things. That it's
stuffed to the gills with expensive shoe shops, noble statuary, roadside wineries, open-air cinemas, and haunches of smoked ham
clothed in smoky dust.

You could point at the high incidence of Renaissance paintings,
plaster saints, zucchini, frescoes, nuns, tricolor pasta, Day-Glo
cyclists, olive trees, leaning towers, old women, equicidal horse
races, two-lane motorways, bridges, dogs, geranium mini-gardens,
Madonnas and Davids, baptisteries, and *tiramisu* ice cream—and
much of this would be true. But it still would not explain the big
attraction Tuscany exerts on the imagination of the British, from
Browning and the Sitwells to John Mortimer and the hapless
Blairs.

What takes them there is, alarmingly, the feeling that the place
is somehow theirs; as if they own the imaginative freehold.

"I felt, upon entering this world of refinement, as if I could have

taken up my abode in it forever," said William Beckford the Gothic
novelist, on first encountering Florence. Even more typically,
Matthew Arnold gazed at the Tuscan landscape and breathed, "It
was for this country that I was predestined."

In this (perfectly sophisticated) region of Italy, British people
can fantasize about a simple life that is, somehow, their heritage—
a life lived on the hillsides seen in Leonardo's paintings, eating simple food grown in the valley next door and lubricated by the fruit
of the adjacent olive grove. As we sit dining alfresco on the lawn
of our villa, grinding a ghost of black pepper over the *insalata
caprese* and murmuring together, we are as much self-constructed
figures in a landscape as are the apostles in Tintoretto's *Last Supper.*

We're not really peasants, of course. Good God, the very idea.
But we appreciate the idea of peasant simplicity. We note approv-
ingly that the weather-beaten chaps cutting ziggurat steps out of
this hillside are the same burly figures as the ones in the pages of
Boccaccio and the Bible scenes of Donatello. We've read the stuff
and we've seen the pictures, probably unlike the inhabitants of
these villages. We appreciate the landscape qua landscape, while
they merely live in the fields.

The spirit of E. M. Forster's characters, appreciating everything
about Tuscany except its life and soul, is shamefully detectable still
in our attitude to the place. We like to play at being aristocrats
here, the big-shot lords of the falling hillsides, surveying the magical valleys of Florence and Lucca with fond familiarity. And that's
why the classic British holiday in Tuscany has to involve a villa.

My traveling band of friends and children rented a villa—one
that lay down a nasty goat-track outside Malmantile, a small (and
mostly shut) village on the outskirts of Florence.

Just look at this house. It's enormous, fronted by a blank wall
of darkened brickwork and an entry vestibule the size of a tennis court. Inside, it's a cross between a luxurious monastery and
an austere Scots-baronial hall. Severely whitewashed, it's fur-
nished in dungeon chic: ancient mahogany cupboards, gloomy
old paintings, huge, blackened grates bristling with firedogs and
hung with chains. Three sofas form a grudging chill-out zone in

the front hall. A noble severity looks down its nose at you, disapprovingly.

Well of course, you think, surveying this amazing place, this is just so me. Like Matthew Arnold, you feel as though you were meant to be here. Give it twenty-four hours, and the stone-flagged floors are strewn with snorkels, towels, magazines, cameras, tennis rackets, tubes of baby sunscreen, Wasp-Eez, and Aloe Vera after-burn ointment.

Things take on a more human scale. The children are entranced by the warren of rooms—there's even an anchorite's cell, the size and shape of an economy Toblerone bar—and by the pool, the huge well in the garden, and the villa cat that clambers intrepidly up the fir trees at night in search of tiny birds in their nests.

The adults, meanwhile, are entranced by a single image: a white plastic table and eight chairs overlooking the olive groves (with globe lamps and lights in the trees for later), where we dish up sliced tomatoes, *taleggio* cheese, and prosciutto, and drizzle oil and chopped basil leaves over the salami and mozzarella, and crush nectarines and apricots and gorgeous, honeyed melon slices against our teeth, and drink far too much *orvieto* and *pinot bianco*; and it's a scene repeated day after day because nobody can think of anything better than it.

There are, however, reminders for the smug British visitor, with his lordly pretensions and recently acquired knowledge of Fra Filippo Lippi, that this land is not his land, not his gilded playground, after all. One is the hornets, which tend to make nests in your wall. "Just one *hornetto*" sing the children, hopefully. Italian hornets are enormous, like wasps on steroids. They hang around your kitchen window, buzzing malevolently, the size of small helicopters, airborne samurai bristling with weapons. I understand that they can be killed with a mighty blow from an espadrille, but I couldn't swear I tried it.

Another is the terrible bread; real Tuscan bread is unsalted and invariably as hard as a ship's biscuit; you have to drive for miles to buy some focaccia in a *supermercato*.

A third is the experience of driving on Tuscan hills. As you flog your rented Opel Cavalier up gradients of one in three and worse, finding at the top of a virtually sheer incline that there's an even worse one hairpinning round to the right; when you've been in second gear for twenty minutes, then first gear for ten minutes, and the wheels are slipping and sliding on the loose earth at the top of a mountain and the engine is groaning and straining like a behemoth in a torture chamber and you have no more gears to change into; when you're inching your way round a *molto pericoloso* unfenced corner on the outside edge of this Tuscan Matterhorn, swerving around just inches from a 900-foot drop to certain death on someone's terracotta roof, and a villager in a Fiat Panda passes you on the inside making hand-flapping "keep over" gestures—well, you have to concede that these mountainy chaps have learnt to be cool about their vertiginous backyard in a way you cannot share.

Even lordlings cannot lie in the pool all day, so you drive—to the walled town of San Gimignano with its fourteen towers (all that are left of the seventy skyscrapers that led to its nickname "the medieval Manhattan") where you walk through the streets for hours, noting the high incidence of tourist-crap shops but also the gaggle of old ladies with nut-brown arms and pink cardigans who sit in chairs watching the visitors, as if scrutinizing is a rule-free spectator sport; you drive some way down the 50-mile Chianti trail from Florence to Siena on the SS.222 that takes in the main Chianti wine towns of Panzano, Greve, and Castellina.

The towns are drenched in wine, with shops in every street, though you can also buy honey, lavender, cheese, oil, and, in San Polo in Robbiano, irises, which are grown there in the millions. And, eventually, you drive to Florence.

Florence is a daunting place in summer, so monumental, so crowded, its artworks so full of *déjà vu*, its colossal, perspective-baffling Duomo so ringed with queuing tourists, its outer roads so dismayingly wide, its central streets so crammed with shanty-market stalls run by importunate Senegalese dudes selling fake Prada purses, that your reaction swings between claustrophobia and exasperation.

Florence doesn't feel as if it's ever going to be yours. It's not a place for solitary communion with Great Art. It's a place for the masses to consume in droves and herds. The same heaving crowd that stands admiring the twisty sublimity of Giambologna's *The Rape of the Sabine Women* in the Piazza della Signoria can be found, five minutes later, watching a street artist draw a flattering likeness of a fat teenager from Laurel Canyon.

So many churches, so many shops, so much *bijouterie*, so much leather, such a population of statues and touch-it-for-luck monuments—*basta!* Your response is to find a quiet corner where you can ruminate in peace, such as the Piazza Santo Spirito on the south bank of the Arno.

In the square, where lots of trendy *ragazzi* are hanging out and talking urgently into mobile phones, you try the Caffe Ricchi, where they serve reviving portions of lasagne and *fagioli* salad. And there you find a perfect example of the creativity that Tuscany sometimes elicits from its visitors. All over the walls of the back room are pictures of the Santo Spirito church which dominates the square—but the church itself has been transformed. Instead of its real-life blank and boring façade (by Brunelleschi) it's been given a makeover by a hundred artists, so that the facade now boasts fat human arms, a vast eye, a nave of disappearing pillars, a grove of trees, and a jungle of writhing snakes.

Suddenly you feel close to the creative process, weighing up proportions and harmonies, seeing how it might have been possible to design this, to paint this, to imagine that.

Or else you find a little hideaway, when you're sick of being prodded by the fake Prada salesmen or mugged by young girls.

My best discovery was the perfume distillery in Via della Scala. Portentously entitled the Officina Profumo Farmaceutica di Santa Maria Novella, it's a gorgeous place. The floor is a diamond pattern of marble flags; globe lamps illumine the vaulted ceiling; soft classical music plays somewhere beneath the curvy sofa—you could be in a high-class brothel.

But this is a holy place. It's where perfume has been made by Dominican monks since the 1220s. Where they made a special

"Water for the Queen" for Catherine de Medici when she became Queen of France and the fragrance passed to Giovanni Feminis who manufactured it and called it after his adopted German home town: eau de Cologne. Now they make thirty-six different *eaux de cologne* in the original workshop.

All over the shop, the perfumes are arrayed in retorts and glass jars, their colors synesthetically full of aroma—whisky, lime, green Chartreuse, Grand Marnier, straw-yellow burgundy. The bottles are labeled—*essenza di muschio, estratto diviolette, acqua di millefiori;* but they offer curative potions too, especially Vinegar of the Seven Thieves, which is good for fainters. And their own-brand Liquore Mediceo is attractively got up to resemble a bottle of Jack Daniels. Seven hundred years, you think, 700 years of monkish concentration went into this. If I rub it on my wrist, can I detect the reek of the cloister?

Private epiphanies over lunch; the smell of history in the afternoon. These things may not be in the brochure, but they're guaranteed in Tuscany. No wonder we can't keep our arty, inspiration-hunting, colonizing hands off the place.

Journalist, broadcaster, and author John Walsh was born in London, educated at Oxford and Dublin universities, and is currently Assistant Editor of the Independent. *He is the author of* The Falling Angels, *writes for* The New Yorker, Harpers, Arena, Tattler *and* Playboy, *and is now working on a book about how movies influence your life. His recreations are, regrettably, the same as Brendan Behan's: drinking and talking.*

PHILLIP LOPATE

★ ★ ★

The Moody Traveler

He finds solace in honesty and an odd kind of contact.

TRAVELING ALONE HAS ITS PLUSES: YOU CAN GO WHERE YOU WANT when you want, and you are spared that runaway irritation which comes of suddenly spotting all the little flaws in your companion (who alone seems to be detaining you from perfect enjoyment) and the tension of having to keep that knowledge secret. However, the minus is that you will have no one to blame but yourself for the occasional rotten mood. The ecstasies and lone epiphanies of the morning museum eventually evaporate, and by late afternoon, after a mediocre, overpriced lunch has made you sluggish, you are ready to turn the big guns on yourself. To travel is to brood, and especially if you are your sole company. I would go so far as to recommend traveling alone as an excellent way of catching up with all the poor opinions of yourself that you may have had to suppress during the busy, camouflaging work year, when it is necessary to appear a self-approving, winning member of society.

I remember one such afternoon in beautiful Florence when the charm I derived from my personality was at a low point. I had mapped my agenda a visit to the nearby hill town of Fiesole. Though I could have taken the excursion bus near my hotel, I commanded myself to hike, ostensibly because it was good exercise, and because you see so much on foot, but in actuality, I realize now, to punish myself.

As I slogged uphill past "rows of cypresses and sumptuous villas" (Michelin guide), my mind was so filled with worthless thoughts that broke off and told me so little, that I had the impression not of a walk through a real landscape but of one continuous spiteful *déjà vu*. It was a playback of all those times I had walked enviously and stupidly through the world of rich houses where I didn't belong. Nothing less than owning a villa, *any* villa, on this Italian hill would satisfy me. Yet I saw so little of the actual residences I coveted, their gardens or marble sculptures or whatever I was supposed to look at, that even in my surly mood this envy struck me as comic. Envy for a landscape I took so little trouble to observe? Perhaps we only envy that which we look at superficially; and a deeper look would take care of our urge for possession? Nah. In any case, I kept walking.

I arrived at a flat village square cut into the hill, where tourist buses were parked in the afternoon heat. Fiesole. Was it sunny? Clouded over? I wasn't interested enough to notice. I headed for a café that seemed to exist on the trade of tourists waiting for their bus driver to return from

---

Warned of pickpockets on the Fiesole bus line, I noted the odd jostling of some young men as the crowd surged to the door of the bus which had just pulled up. I got on with my family, and the ride commenced. Standing in the aisles, no sooner had I begun to gaze out the window and daydream than I felt a hand in my pocket. I grabbed the attached wrist and said in English, no translation necessary, "Get your fucking hand out of my pocket!" The young men backpedaled and scurried to the exit. I remembered then my late uncle, a Franciscan priest, telling me he'd gotten so fed up with Italian pickpockets that he always carried empty decoy wallets upon his person.

—James O'Reilly, "On and Off the Autostrada"

who knows where and start his engine. I sat down at the nickel-plated soda fountain, with the momentarily satisfied sense of having stumbled on a "find." Not that the stopover was attractive, but it was at least an oasis of decrepitude: there were dusty cutout doll books and movie magazines, and a faded Italian novelization of Erich Segal's *Love Story*. I ordered a Campari, hoping for a mindless respite. Yet just as soon as I had drained it, a spasm of restlessness overcame me and I paid and walked out.

By now I was thoroughly fed up with my impatience. I was determined to slow down and practice "the discipline of seeing." It was a sometime conviction of mine that, wherever one found oneself, the world was rich enough to yield enjoyment if one but paid close attention to the details. Or, as John Cage once said, when something bores you, keep looking at it and after a while you will find it intriguing. Inside, however, I rebelled against this notion, which struck me as forced quietism—an aestheticizing trick to bring about the opposite of what one knows to be true. The day is boring, horrible? Very well, that's the card I've been dealt. Let's not pretend it's any better.

I was still arguing these two positions when I sat down on a bench overlooking what I knew most people would think a magnificent vista. All of the Arno Valley and Florence were stretched before us. The city fathers had wisely provided benches. Not only was this undeniably and obviously a magnificent vista, but it was an "officially recognized" magnificent vista, even more annoying. But then, what *had* escaped the tourist industry's exploitative eye in Italy? Where could one find any beauty in this country that was fresh and unframed?

This line of thinking soon struck me as foolish petulance. The truth is, I loved Italy, so what was I whining about?

I literally forced myself to concentrate on the Italian family a few benches over. The son was leaning semidangerously over the hilltop. That could be interesting. But then he sat down next to his father, who was cutting an orange rind circularly with a fruit knife. I wondered if this orange paring was an Old World custom. (Vapid anthropologizing to replace self-ennui.) The mother was taking thick sandwiches out of a plastic bag and handing them all around. They seemed a big, warm, friendly family—two daughters, one son, a father, a mother—speaking casually to each other, eating their picnic lunch, playing with the dog.

To fathom the secret of that Italian familial harmony, I watched them covertly for ten minutes, dividing my attention between their interactions and the landscape below, and I came to the conclusion that they weren't as warm as I had originally given them credit for. They simply ate a great deal. The more I watched them, the more it dawned on me that there was absolutely nothing exceptional about them. That in itself was unusual. Most families yield up fairly rich pathologies, but this one did not interest me in any conceivable way. My hypothesis about steady attention to detail was being contradicted.

At about this time an elderly Italian man, tall, angular, bald, toothless save for one top incisor, looking in his mid-seventies—about the age of my father, in fact—came up and asked with gestures if he could sit on my bench. This seemed a little odd, as there was another bench completely unoccupied, but who was I to deny a fellow man my company if he thought he could reap some nourishment therefrom? Had I not been complaining of the burden of my solitude? Perhaps this old guy would amuse me or turn into a *vivid anecdotal experience*, the goal of all tourists at loose ends.

"What is your name?" he asked me in halting English. I told

> In the year 1348 after the fruitful incarnation of the Son of God, that most beautiful of Italian cities, noble Florence, was attacked by deadly plague. It started in the East, either through the influence of the heavenly bodies or because God's just anger with our wicked deeds sent it as punishment to mortal men, and in a few years killed an innumerable quantity of people.
>
> —Giovanni Boccaccio,
> *The Decameron* (1348)

him. "And yours?" Nicola. He tried out his few English questions on me, and I answered him in my limited Italian. It was the sort of conversation one has on the road often, and which seems to exist in order to prove that the stiff dialogues of phrase books are, in fact, the height of naturalism. The old man began to talk about his work in a garage (I think he said he was a retired mechanic) and to complain that now he had nothing to do. He told me about his sons, his wife, his vineyard. These Italians, I reflected, are unquenchably sociable; they love to chatter. True, I had my doubts that this was going to lead to a vivid anecdotal experience, and was already feeling bored, since I understood only one out of every three sentences, but I congratulated myself on being such a good and patient listener. The man is obviously lonely, I thought; he reminds me of the aged pensioner in De Sica's *Umberto D*; perhaps I can reap from him some necessary lesson in humility and human dignity. Meanwhile, he was talking my ear off in Italian, and I was nodding and pursuing some interior reverie about how sad it is that society is so afraid of the old, how wrong that we back off squeamishly from them, and he had just gotten to the part where he told me his wife had died when he seized my hand in an iron grip.

At first I did nothing, pretending it was a sort of international brotherhood handshake; but then I tried to pull away and discovered that the old man was not letting go. I stared at his frayed white shirt, buttoned to the top, pulled taut by his chest; he was like a wooden plank, not a scrap of fat on him. I looked around for help to the picnicking family, but they had apparently wandered off without my noticing. Now he grinned in what seemed a possibly rather lecherous manner—at the same time trying to reassure me that he was not going to hurt me. He only wanted to hold my hand. So we sat there, my hand sweating in his. He had very large brown fingers, liver-spotted around the webs.

I began to speculate about his secret life, in and around his role as good family man and laborer, of chance pickups. I didn't even know if he was gay necessarily, or if he was so starved for human touch, the memory of young flesh, that it didn't matter which sex he accosted. How many tourists before me had he done this with? Were we all Americans? I wondered. If he did try any funny stuff, I thought I could hold him off. But all he seemed to be doing so far was holding my hand and smiling—every so often he would wriggle the wrist a little in the air and grin at me, as if we were both relaxing from a good arm-wrestle.

By this time other tourists had joined us on the hilltop (to my relief) and were consuming the landscape. I, too, looked down at the vista, since I had nothing better to do and was tired of trying to figure out the old man's game. Now the shifting pattern of light over the valley—a dusky evening light that brought out the muted pinks, the muddy browns, the raked greens of cultivated country-side and, in the distance, Florence, all salmon and white walls— seemed to me extremely fetching. For the first time all day, I was able to enjoy the physical world around me. Were I given to look-ing on the bright side, or religious allegories, or megalomania, I might say that the old man was an angel sent down by God to handcuff me to one spot and force me to attend to the earth with pleasure.

I suppose part of what kept me from retrieving my hand was the flattering knowledge that someone at least desired me, needed me at that moment, in this place through which I had taken it upon myself to travel alone. For the longest while, neither of us said anything. Then he got up, gave me a courtly bow, muttered *"Grazie"* in a hoarse, dry voice, and strode off. Watching his bald brown head and stiff back recede, I laughed disbelievingly at what had just happened. The weirdness of it had driven away my black mood, and I kept laughing all the way home on the tourist bus. For those who do not like happy endings, my apologies.

Recipient of Guggenheim and National Endowment for the Arts fellow-ships, Phillip Lopate's writing has appeared in Best American Essays, The Paris Review, *and Pushcart Prize annuals. He is the author of* The Rug Merchant, Confessions of Summer, Bachelorhood, Against Joie de Vivre, *and* Portrait of My Body, *from which this story was excerpted.*

ALESSANDRA STANLEY

⋆ ⋆ ⋆

Salute for a Soldier

Memories of war reach into a new century.

ALBERT BURKE, EIGHTY, SILENTLY STROLLED AROUND THE ruins of a medieval fortress in the village where dozens of black servicemen were killed on December 26, 1944, and broke down. "I felt I owed it to the fellows to come back," he sobbed as two other frail veterans held him up. "But I don't think I want to come back here anymore."

The place that stirred him so deeply is Sommocolonia, a poignant footnote in both World War II military history and the still uncompleted story of America's black war veterans. Among Mr. Burke's comrades killed here was a lieutenant named John Fox, who died shortly after ordering his own men to fire on his position because it was about to be overrun by advancing Austrian and German soldiers. A hero of the black 92nd Infantry Division in a segregated United States military, Lieutenant Fox was awarded a Medal of Honor only in 1997.

Mr. Burke, Otis Zachary, eighty-three, and Richard Hogg, eighty, toured Sommocolonia, their first visit to the battle zone in almost fifty-six years, seeking to close the most vivid chapter of their lives. And the anguish they relived was echoed among the Italian war survivors who welcomed their return.

203

The black veterans and their Italian hosts have more than war memories in common. Just as Mr. Burke and his comrades and relatives cannot shed their bitterness over the United States' long refusal to recognize the combat records of black servicemen fully, many Italian veterans cannot forgive their own countrymen who fought against them more than fifty years ago.

Sommocolonia, a dying mountain village of fewer than fifty inhabitants that overlooks Barga in Tuscany, wants to forge out of its ruins some sort of peace memorial to honor Lieutenant Fox and all those who died: black soldiers, village civilians, Italian partisans, and Italian and German troops. But that still hazy plan has resurrected old rancors.

"Peace is always won through liberation from oppression, and you cannot put together oppressors and liberators," said Moreno Salvatori, sixty-seven, who withdrew from the "Fortress of Peace" committee in protest. His father was taken prisoner by the Germans during the war and died in captivity. "It's a mixing of memories that I cannot share."

Perhaps the only thing that everyone agrees on is that Lieutenant Fox was a hero whom all sides must hurry to honor here before those few left who remember his heroism die.

It was that sense of urgency that led Solace Wales, an American writer who has commuted between Marin County, California, and Sommocolonia since 1972, to invite "Buffalo Soldiers," the name first given to black servicemen in the 1860s, back to Sommocolonia for a memorial ceremony, even before the town had agreed on what kind of monument to build.

Ms. Wales, who began twenty years ago to research the history of Lieutenant Fox and the other black soldiers who fought around Sommocolonia, is a little like Frances Mayes, author of *Under the Tuscan Sun*, only in addition to fixing up her sixteenth-century villa and garden, Ms. Wales wanted to restore Sommocolonia's place in history. "Somebody had to tell the story," she said. "It had been in the shadows too long."

Unrooting the story of Lieutenant Fox was not difficult here, where survivors warmly recall the black soldiers. They were part of the Allied forces seeking to keep Axis troops behind the so-called Gothic Line, which in 1944 stretched from the Ligurian Sea to the Adriatic.

The surprise German attack was part of a somewhat desperate attempt to push through Allied lines and take the port of Livorno. An Austrian unit captured Sommocolonia and Barga on December 26, but proved too weak to hold its gains. By January 1, the Allies had more or less re-established their original positions. Some military historians credit Lieutenant Fox with buying time as the Americans retreated so that other men could be saved.

On the Piazza Martiri della Resistenza, a memorial in a wooded park at the top of Sommocolonia, seven stone slabs commemorate slain Italian resistance fighters. Next to them another memorial reads, in Italian, "John Fox. Lt. American Army. 26.12.44" It was erected in 1979, three years before the United States Army, under pressure from black veterans associations, awarded Lieutenant Fox the Distinguished Service Cross.

"They were wonderful, so nice to us," said Irma Biondi, now seventy-seven. "My little brothers followed them like shadows."

"We had never seen so much food," she added, remembering the chicken, rabbits, chocolate, and cheese that the more than sixty black servicemen stationed here gave out on Christmas Day, 1944.

She also vividly recalled the sound of the stomping boots of Austrian soldiers under German command who began storming the town that night. "We fled out into the streets, passing over the bodies of dead Americans and Germans," she said.

At least seven civilians died that day. German war records show that forty-three members of the Austrian Fourth Mountain Division died in the fighting. United States Army records are sketchier, but historians say about forty black American soldiers died here.

"We still have fellows who should be recognized now," said Mr. Burke, president of the 92nd Infantry Division World War II Association, a Buffalo Soldiers veterans association, talking about lingering discrimination against all black veterans.

Reminiscing earlier at their hotel in Barga, the three men joked as they recalled petty injustices inflicted by their senior officers, who were white. But when Mr. Zachary, still cocky at eighty-three, reached the tower, he too was overcome. After trying to console Mr. Burke, he collapsed himself.

"Burke," he keened, "I see him in the tower, I see John."

Arlene Fox, the widow of Lieutenant Fox, arrived to stay with Ms. Wales in Sommocolonia, accompanied by her sister-in-law, her daughter, and two grandchildren. But she did not go with her husband's comrades on their first tour of the crumbling fortress. "I have a lot of unresolved feelings about being here," she explained. "Its so beautiful, and people have been so kind, and that helps. But it is not easy."

That was what Antonio Nardini, seventy-nine, said, only he was talking about dealing with his own experience as a soldier in Mussolini's army. Mr. Nardini, who volunteered in 1939, was taken prisoner by Italian partisans in 1945, and said he was rescued from execution by the Americans.

"Before 1943, Italy had 40 million Fascists," he said, citing the year Mussolini was overthrown and Italy switched sides. "Afterward," he said sarcastically, "there were 40 million anti-Fascists. Except one: me."

Several former partisans said that it was time to get over wartime enmities and to honor all the dead, including the Fascists and Germans. Mr. Nardini, who is president of the Barga chapter of the Lucca Historical Society, agreed. He, like most other former Fascists, mourns his fallen comrades in private ceremonies.

"There is a lot of demagoguery about the resistance," he said. "But there is no debate about Fox."

"His gesture may have been futile," he said, noting that the Germans took the town anyway. "But he acted like a real soldier."

In tiny Sommocolonia, the desire for a monument is not just about Lieutenant Fox, or even the war. It is about surviving post-war demographic shifts that have turned a once vibrant village into an almost deserted retirement home.

"We need something alive, for the town, not a museum for the dead," said Dario Giannini, who coordinated the weekend activities.

"The bombs didn't just destroy the fortress, they killed the hope of the entire village."

Alessandra Stanley lives with her family in Rome and works in the Rome office of The New York Times.

PART FIVE

THE LAST WORD

JOY SCHALEBEN LEWIS

⋆ ⋆ ⋆

Legacy of Love

*The author finds a touchstone in the place
her mother was born.*

"*CIAO*, CECILIA," SHOUTED MY MOTHER AS WE LOOKED DOWN
across the steep vineyard. "*Dove stai?* (Where are you?)" she cried.

A door from a lone hut nearly lost in the great green vines
opened. A humped figure dressed in black waved. Her dress was
muddy, her shoes torn. At 90, this frail woman still worked among
the grapes of Massa Marittima, the Tuscan hill town where my
mother was born. She hobbled towards us, leaning deftly into her
cane.

"*Bella, cara, tesora,*" said this strange bundle of crumpled black
reaching up to caress my face. She was calling me "beautiful, dear,
treasure." I bent down to kiss my great aunt. Once, more than half
a century ago, she had held my mother's little-girl hand in the
piazza. Now, her hand clasped mine.

In the days that would follow, many more hands would clutch
mine and lovingly stroke my face. My mother had finally lured me
to Italy to meet the relatives. At the time, I was twenty-three and
not particularly keen about vacationing with my mother in the old
country. But, when she insisted on paying my way, I couldn't resist.
And I was, at least, faintly curious about her place of birth.

My mother, the fifth of seven children, was christened Ida Pia Eleka Arnella Elena Androvandi. Honestly, she does have all those names. As a child, I used to impress my friends by rattling off her name-litany as a tongue twister. But that was all I'd concede was different about my mom. I preferred her to be 100 percent American, not Italo-American, as she would identify herself.

I never could understand why she was, well—so darned Italian. You know, kissing everyone and making such a big fuss about the family. As for all those people back in Italy with odd names—they were her relatives, not mine.

And then, her childhood had been so poor: not enough to eat, living in two small rooms, no running water, no electricity, owning only two dresses and no other outfits when my grandmother took her brood to a new life in America.

They had settled in southern Illinois in 1923, where my grandfather had been working in a coal mine for several years. In the New World, my mother, at age nine, had enough to eat but not much more. Throughout her girlhood, she never even had one doll, ever!—a fact she told me every time she reminisced about her childhood.

I, in contrast, had a new doll every Christmas. My growing up was a carefree and secure existence with two younger sisters and a brother in a well-off Milwaukee suburb.

"Joy-a, get into the car." After only one day in Italy, Mother had taken to pronouncing my name Italian style. "We're going to drive Cecilia back to Massa Marittima and then meet your Aunt Anita." She was in her element. At last she was opening the doors of her childhood to me. Clearly, Mother was in command.

For one thing, she knew the language. I didn't. What's more, people in Massa Marittima treated her like visiting royalty, hugging and kissing her, calling her name as she walked the cobbled streets, bringing her gifts of welcome. She'd been back several times and had become a kind of town heroine. And just because I was her daughter, I, too, was instantly beloved.

I was impressed.

I was also astonished by the beauty of Massa Marittima, a walled, medieval stone city teeming with arches, alleyways, stepped passages, red-tiled roofs, green shutters, and wrought iron balconies rimmed with flower pots. Below, olive groves, vineyards, and wheat fields reached ten miles to the sea. On an exceptionally clear day, I could see all the way to the resort town of Follonica and even beyond to the island of Elba where Napoleon had been exiled.

Massa, as locals call their hometown of 10,000, was immaculate, just like my mother's house in America. And its people—many had her same handsome features: fine bones, narrow hips, straight noses, blue eyes, smooth light-olive skin. And the women, petite like her, were "dressed to kill," as mother says, and does. That meant looking "*molto bella*," especially when promenading arm-in-arm in the piazza at dusk.

Massa Marittima, acclaimed for centuries for its artisans and nearby silver and copper mines, is sectioned like a three-layered cake. At the bottom is the "Borgo" (little village). At the top is the "Cittanova" (new city), where my mother was born. In between is "Cittavecchio" (old city). "All eyes notice you here," Mother warned, frowning at my Bermudas and tennis shoes as we strolled into the main square.

How proudly she showed me the nooks and crannies of her memories—the big stone basins at the foot of the hill where she washed clothes as a small girl, the huge clock tower with its sweeping view of the valley, the frescoes in the mighty Romanesque Cathedral, and her favorite place to play—the so-called "500 Steps," a steep, wide passageway leading to the Cittanova.

And then, of course, there were all the *parenti*—relatives. Each morning over cappuccino in the piazza we'd review who was who.

"Let's see," I mused, "the old woman in the hospital, with the broken hip is Maria—another great aunt. Narisco is the man with the little farm who gave rabbits to GI's during World War II; he's your cousin and therefore my second cousin."

"No, no," she interrupted. "In Italy, you don't have second or third cousins—just cousins."

Before long, the names of my mother's relatives no longer sounded so foreign: Mazzini, Liana, Sergio, Caesare, Bruno, Fulvia, Nuncia, and a whole string of others were now my family too. I liked having an Italo-American mamma. In Massa Marittima, she was bequeathing me my inheritance.

One day, my mother announced she had something special to show me—the tiny two-room apartment where she had lived with her four cousins and two brothers. It was on the fourth floor of a run-down building at the end of Via Bogetto, an area where the poor miners lived when my grandfather was a young man.

"We're lucky," she said. "The rooms aren't occupied. They're going to be renovated." Excitedly, she opened the door and said, "This is where I took my very first breath."

I entered cautiously, not anxious to confront what I thought were bleak memories. There they were: the walls and floors of my mother's childhood—as dark and dreary as I had imagined. And here was the hearth where she'd severely burned her elbow, the tiny back window where my grandmother sat wet-nursing other women's babies to earn a few lire.

I couldn't wait to get out, to leave this molding old building that testified to my mother's dismal start.

Yet, my mother lingered cheerfully, recalling instead games she had played with her "toys"—pebbles from the street—and the good minestrone her mother cooked and how all her sisters and brothers giggled together on one mattress. Finally, outside again in the bright, fresh air that was Massa, she sighed happily. "It's fine to return to the past, but I live for today," she said simply.

"*Andiamo!*" Let's go.

My mother, like me, still makes almost annual pilgrimages back to Massa. She remains a happy woman, full of life and Italian embraces. In fact I've only seen her cry once.

It happened precisely a few years ago, on Mother's Day, when I gave her a present I'd bought in Italy. When she saw what was in the box, she was flabbergasted. Tenderly, she lifted the gift and clutched it to her breast. "*Bella, bella,*" she murmured over and over.

At last my mother had a doll.

Joy Schaleben Lewis may reside in Milwaukee, but her temperament and spirit belong to Massa Marittima, the splendiferous town where everyone calls her "Gioia, figlia della Ida" (daughter of Ida).

Index of Contributors

Index

Acknowledgments

It has been a pleasure to work with Tara Weaver on this project. I appreciate her dedication and energy in the research and editing of this book. I would also like to thank my family and friends for their usual forbearance while I put a book together. Thanks also to Larry Habegger, Sean O'Reilly, Tim O'Reilly, Susan Brady, Natanya Pearlman, Kathy Meengs, Krista Holmstrom, Christine Nielsen, Cynthia Lamb, Michele Wetherbee, and Judy Johnson for their support and contributions to the book.

—James O'Reilly

A huge and hearty *grazie* to James O'Reilly for inviting me along on this Tuscan journey, and to the entire Travelers' Tales gang—Larry Habegger, Susan Brady, Wenda O'Reilly, Lisa Bach, Natanya Pearlman, Jennifer Leo, Kathy Meengs, Krista Holmstrom, Christine Nielsen, Sean O'Reilly, Deborah Greco, Michele Wetherbee, Cynthia Lamb, and Raj Khadka—for making it a joy to come to work every day; and to Tina Stromsted for playing fairy Godmother to my career and connecting me to such wonderful people.

Molto grazie to my mother for her love, support, and encouragement in everything I do; and to my brother David for reminding me to laugh, especially at myself.

Mille grazie to my wonderful friends—Shonquis Moreno, Violeta Richards, Amy Robinson Bellomo, Paul McCann, Matt & Mireya Morales Quirie, Darrin Weyers, Amy Stafford, Frank Brosnan, the Fitch Family and the entire Camp gang—for brightening my life and propping me up when need be; and to my friends in foreign and far-flung places: Karen Patrois Clement, Yasir Samir, Diane Wyllie, Heidi Ellis, Marci Aitken and my Japanese friends and family, for always being happy to receive my phone calls, whatever the hour. Finally, to Tina and Roberto Zecca for making me feel like I too had a home in Tuscany.

—Tara Austen Weaver

Additional Credits (arranged alphabetically by title)

About the Editors

James O'Reilly, president and co-publisher of Travelers' Tales, wrote mystery serials before becoming a travel writer in the early 1980s. He's visited more than forty countries, along the way meditating with monks in Tibet, participating in West African voodoo rituals, and hanging out the laundry with nuns in Florence. He travels extensively with his wife Wenda and their three daughters. They live in Palo Alto, California when they're not in Leavenworth, Washington.

Born to traveler parents, Tara Austen Weaver crossed her first international border at five weeks of age. She has since lived in San Francisco, London, Vienna, high in the mountains of central Japan, and on a small island off the coast of western Canada. She first traveled to Italy as an art history student and lost her heart to Tuscany while sipping Chianti on the terrace of a friend's villa at sunset, the music of Monteverdi playing in the background. She has traveled to thirty counties and been published in both the U.S. and Asia, most recently in *Pilgrimage: Adventures of the Spirit*. When not dreaming of future travel, she works, plays, and writes near the beach, on the foggy side of San Francisco.

TRAVELERS' TALES

The Soul of Travel

Footsteps Series

THE SWORD OF HEAVEN
A Five Continent Odyssey to Save the World
By Mikkel Aaland
ISBN 1-885-211-44-9
$24.00 (cloth)

"Few books capture the soul of the road like *The Sword of Heaven*, a sharp-edged, beautifully rendered memoir that will inspire anyone." —Phil Cousineau, author of *The Art of Pilgrimage*

TAKE ME WITH YOU
A Round-the-World Journey to Invite a Stranger Home
By Brad Newsham
ISBN 1-885-211-51-1
$24.00 (cloth)

"Newsham is an ideal guide. His journey, at heart, is into humanity." —Pico Iyer, author of *Video Night in Kathmandu*

LAST TROUT IN VENICE
The Far-Flung Escapades of an Accidental Adventurer
By Doug Lansky
ISBN 1-885-211-63-5
$14.95

"Traveling with Doug Lansky might result in a considerably shortened life expectancy…but what a way to go. —Tony Wheeler, Lonely Planet Publications

ONE YEAR OFF
Leaving It All Behind for a Round-the-World Journey with Our Children
By David Elliot Cohen
ISBN 1-885-211-65-1
$14.95

A once-in-a-lifetime adventure generously shared.

KITE STRINGS OF THE SOUTHERN CROSS
A Woman's Travel Odyssey
By Laurie Gough
ISBN 1-885-211-54-6
$14.95

— ⋆⋆⋆ —

ForeWord Silver Medal Winner — Travel Book of the Year

STORM
A Motorcycle Journey of Love, Endurance, and Transformation
By Allen Noren
ISBN 1-885-211-45-7
$24.00 (cloth)

— ⋆⋆⋆ —

ForeWord Gold Medal Winner — Travel Book of the Year

THE WAY OF THE WANDERER
Discover Your True Self Through Travel
By David Yeadon
ISBN 1-885-211-60-0
$14.95

Experience transformation through travel with this delightful, illustrated collection by award-winning author David Yeadon.

THE FIRE NEVER DIES
One Man's Raucous Romp Down the Road of Food, Passion, and Adventure
By Richard Sterling
ISBN 1-885-211-70-8
$14.95

"Sterling's writing is like spit-fire, foursquare and jazzy with crackle.…"
—*Kirkus Reviews*

Travelers' Tales Classics

THE ROYAL ROAD TO ROMANCE
By Richard Halliburton
ISBN 1-885-211-53-8
$14.95

"Laughing at hardships, dreaming of beauty, ardent for adventure, Halliburton has managed to sing into the pages of this glorious book his own exultant spirit of youth and freedom."
— *Chicago Post*

THE RIVERS RAN EAST
By Leonard Clark
ISBN 1-885-211-66-X
$16.95

Clark is the original Indiana Jones, relaying a breathtaking account of his search for the legendary El Dorado gold in the Amazon.

GREECE
True Stories of Life on the Road
Edited by Larry Habegger, Sean O'Reilly & Brian Alexander
ISBN 1-885-211-52-X
$17.95

"This is the stuff memories can be duplicated from."
— *Foreign Service Journal*

FRANCE
True Stories of Life on the Road
Edited by James O'Reilly, Larry Habegger & Sean O'Reilly
ISBN 1-885-211-02-3
$17.95

The French passion for life bursts forth from every page, featuring stories by Peter Mayle, M.F.K. Fisher, Ina Caro, Jan Morris, Jon Krakauer and many more.

UNBEATEN TRACKS IN JAPAN
By Isabella L. Bird
ISBN 1-885-211-57-0
$14.95

Isabella Bird was one of the most adventurous women travelers of the 19th century with journeys to Tibet, Canada, Korea, Turkey, Hawaii, and Japan. A fascinating read for anyone interested in women's travel, spirituality, and Asian culture.

Europe

TUSCANY
True Stories
Edited by James O'Reilly, & Tara Austen Weaver
ISBN 1-885-211-68-6
$16.95

Journey into the heart of one of the most beloved regions on earth, the rolling hills and ancient cities of Tuscany.

IRELAND
True Stories of Life on the Emerald Isle
Edited by James O'Reilly, Larry Habegger & Sean O'Reilly
ISBN 1-885-211-46-5
$17.95

— ★ ★ ★ —

ForeWord Bronze Medal Winner
— *Travel Book of the Year*

PARIS
True Stories of Life on the Road
Edited by James O'Reilly, Larry Habegger & Sean O'Reilly
ISBN 1-885-211-10-4
$17.95

"If Paris is the main dish, here is a rich and fascinating assortment of hors d'oeuvres."
— Peter Mayle, author of *A Year in Provence*

ITALY (Updated)
True Stories of
Life on the Road
Edited by Anne Calcagno
Introduction by Jan Morris
ISBN 1-885-211-72-4
$18.95

— ★ ★ ★ —
ForeWord Silver
Medal Winner—
Travel Book of the Year

SPAIN
True Stories of
Life on the Road
Edited by Lucy McCauley
ISBN 1-885-211-07-4
$17.95
"A superb, eclectic collec-
tion that reeks wonderfully
of gazpacho and paella, and
resonates with sounds of
heel-clicking and flamenco singing."
—Barnaby Conrad, author of *Matador*

Asia/Pacific

AUSTRALIA
True Stories of
Life Down Under
Edited by Larry Habegger
ISBN 1-885-211-40-6
$17.95
Explore Australia with
authors Paul Theroux,
Robyn Davidson, Bruce
Chatwin, Pico Iyer, Tim
Cahill, and many more.

JAPAN
True Stories of
Life on the Road
Edited by Donald W.
George & Amy
Greimann Carlson
ISBN 1-885-211-04-X
$17.95
"Readers of this entertain-
ing anthology will be better
equipped to plot a rewarding course through
the marvelously bewildering, bewitching
cultural landscape of Japan." —*Time* (Asia)

INDIA
True Stories of
Life on the Road
Edited by James O'Reilly
& Larry Habegger
ISBN 1-885-211-01-5
$17.95
"The Travelers' Tales series
should become required
reading for anyone visiting
a foreign country." —*St. Petersburg Times*

NEPAL
True Stories of
Life on the Road
Edited by Rajendra
S. Khadka
ISBN 1-885-211-14-7
$17.95
"If there's one thing tradi-
tional guidebooks lack, it's
the really juicy travel infor-
mation, the personal stories about back
alleys and brief encounters. This series fills
this gap." —*Diversion*

THAILAND
True Stories of
Life on the Road
Edited by James O'Reilly
& Larry Habegger
ISBN 1-885-211-05-8
$17.95

— ★ ★ ★ —
Winner of the Lowell
Thomas Award for Best
Travel Book—Society of
American Travel Writers

HONG KONG
True Stories of
Life on the Road
Edited by James O'Reilly,
Larry Habegger &
Sean O'Reilly
ISBN 1-885-211-03-1
$17.95
"Travelers' Tales Hong Kong
will delight the senses and
heighten the sensibilities, whether you are
an armchair traveler or an old China hand."
—*Profiles*

The Americas

AMERICA
True Stories of
Life on the Road
Edited by Fred Setterberg
ISBN 1-885-211-28-7
$19.95
"Look no further.
This book is America."
—David Yeadon, author
of *Lost Worlds*

HAWAI'I
True Stories of
the Island Spirit
Edited by Rick &
Marcie Carroll
ISBN 1-885-211-35-X
$17.95
"Travelers' Tales aims to
convey the excitement of
voyaging through exotic
territory with a vivacity that guidebooks can
only hint at."—*Millenium Whole Earth Catalog*

GRAND CANYON
True Stories of Life
Below the Rim
Edited by Sean O'Reilly,
James O'Reilly &
Larry Habegger
ISBN 1-885-211-34-1
$17.95
"As entertaining and
informative for the arm-
chair traveler as it is for veteran river-rats and
canyoneers." — *The Bloomsbury Review*

SAN FRANCISCO
True Stories of
Life on the Road
Edited by James O'Reilly,
Larry Habegger &
Sean O'Reilly
ISBN 1-885-211-08-2
$17.95
"Like spying on
the natives."
　　　　　　—*San Francisco Chronicle*

AMERICAN
SOUTHWEST
True Stories
Edited by Sean O'Reilly
and James O'Reilly
ISBN 1-885-211-58-9
$17.95
Put on your boots, saddle
up, and explore the
American Southwest with
Terry Tempest Williams, Edward Abbey,
Barbara Kingsolver, Alex Shoumatoff,
and more.

MEXICO (Updated)
True Stories
Edited by James O'Reilly
& Larry Habegger
ISBN 1-885-211-59-7
$17.95

— ★ ★ —
One of the Year's Best
Travel Books on Mexico
—The New York
Times

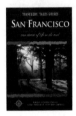

BRAZIL
True Stories of
Life on the Road
Edited by Annette Haddad
& Scott Doggett
Introduction by Alex
Shoumatoff
ISBN 1-885-211-11-2
$17.95

— ★ ★ —
Benjamin Franklin
Silver Award Winner

CUBA
True Stories
Edited by Tom Miller
ISBN 1-885-211-62-7
$17.95
A collection that sheds light
on the dazzling mixture
that is Cuba, in
all its fervent, heartstopping
complexity.

Women's Travel

A WOMAN'S PASSION FOR TRAVEL
More True Stories from A Woman's World
Edited by Marybeth Bond
& Pamela Michael
ISBN 1-885-211-36-8
$17.95

"A diverse and gripping series of stories!" —Arlene Blum, author of *Annapurna: A Woman's Place*

A WOMAN'S WORLD
True Stories of Life on the Road
Edited by Marybeth Bond
Introduction by
Dervla Murphy
ISBN 1-885-211-06-6
$17.95

— ★ ★ ★ —

Winner of the Lowell Thomas Award for Best Travel Book —
Society of American Travel Writers

WOMEN IN THE WILD
True Stories of Adventure and Connection
Edited by Lucy McCauley
ISBN 1-885-211-21-X
$17.95

"A spiritual, moving, and totally female book to take you around the world and back." —*Mademoiselle*

A MOTHER'S WORLD
Journeys of the Heart
Edited by Marybeth Bond
& Pamela Michael
ISBN 1-885-211-26-0
$14.95

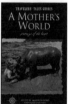

"These stories remind us that motherhood is one of the great unifying forces in the world" —*San Francisco Examiner*

Spiritual Travel

A WOMAN'S PATH
Women's Best Spiritual Travel Writing
Edited by Lucy McCauley,
Amy G. Carlson &
Jennifer Leo
ISBN 1-885-211-48-1
$16.95

"A sensitive exploration of women's lives that have been unexpectedly and spiritually touched by travel experiences.... Highly recommended."
—*Library Journal*

THE ULTIMATE JOURNEY
Inspiring Stories of Living and Dying
James O'Reilly, Sean
O'Reilly & Richard Sterling
ISBN 1-885-211-38-4
$17.95

"A glorious collection of writings about the ultimate adventure. A book to keep by one's bedside—and close to one's heart." —Philip Zaleski, editor, *The Best Spiritual Writing series*

THE ROAD WITHIN:
True Stories of Transformation and the Soul
Edited by Sean O'Reilly,
James O'Reilly &
Tim O'Reilly
ISBN 1-885-211-19-8
$17.95

— ★ ★ ★ —

Best Spiritual Book —Independent
Publisher's Book Award

PILGRIMAGE
Adventures of the Spirit
Edited by Sean O'Reilly
& James O'Reilly
Introduction by
Phil Cousineau
ISBN 1-885-211-56-2
$16.95

— ★ ★ ★ —

ForeWord Silver Medal Winner
— Travel Book of the Year

Adventure

TESTOSTERONE PLANET
True Stories from a Man's World
Edited by Sean O'Reilly, Larry Habegger & James O'Reilly
ISBN 1-885-211-43-0
$17.95
Thrills and laughter with

some of today's best writers: Sebastian Junger, Tim Cahill, Bill Bryson, Jon Krakauer, and Frank McCourt.

DANGER!
True Stories of Trouble and Survival
Edited by James O'Reilly, Larry Habegger & Sean O'Reilly
ISBN 1-885-211-32-5
$17.95
"Exciting…for those who enjoy living on the edge or

prefer to read the survival stories of others, this is a good pick." —*Library Journal*

Travel Humor

NOT SO FUNNY WHEN IT HAPPENED
The Best of Travel Humor and Misadventure
Edited by Tim Cahill
ISBN 1-885-211-55-4
$12.95
Laugh with Bill Bryson, Dave Barry, Anne Lamott, Adair Lara, Doug Lansky, and many more.

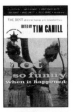

THERE'S NO TOILET PAPER…ON THE ROAD LESS TRAVELED
The Best of Travel Humor and Misadventure
Edited by Doug Lansky
ISBN 1-885-211-27-9
$12.95

— ★ ★ ★ —
Humor Book of the Year
—Independent
Publisher's Book Award

— ★ ★ ★ —
ForeWord Gold Medal Winner— Humor Book of the Year

Food

THE ADVENTURE OF FOOD
True Stories of Eating Everything
Edited by Richard Sterling
ISBN 1-885-211-37-6
$17.95
"These stories are bound to whet appetites for more than food."
—*Publishers Weekly*

FOOD
A Taste of the Road
Edited by Richard Sterling
Introduction by Margo True
ISBN 1-885-211-09-0
$17.95

— ★ ★ ★ —
Silver Medal Winner of the Lowell Thomas Award for Best Travel Book— Society of American Travel Writers

HER FORK IN THE ROAD
Women Celebrate Food and Travel
Edited by Lisa Bach
ISBN 1-885-211-71-6
$16.95
A savory sampling of stories by some of the best writers in and out of the food and travel fields.

Special Interest

365 TRAVEL
A Daily Book of Journeys, Meditations, and Adventures
Edited by Lisa Bach
ISBN 1-885-211-67-8
$14.95

An illuminating collection of travel wisdom and adventures that reminds us all of the lessons we learn while on the road.

THE GIFT OF RIVERS
True Stories of Life on the Water
Edited by Pamela Michael
Introduction by Robert Hass
ISBN 1-885-211-42-2
$14.95

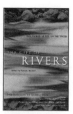

"*The Gift of Rivers* is a soulful compendium of wonderful stories that illuminate, educate, inspire, and delight. One cannot read this compelling anthology without coming away in awe of the strong hold rivers exert on human imagination and history."
—David Brower, Chairman of Earth Island Institute

FAMILY TRAVEL
The Farther You Go, the Closer You Get
Edited by Laura Manske
ISBN 1-885-211-33-3
$17.95

"This is family travel at its finest." —*Working Mother*

LOVE & ROMANCE
True Stories of Passion on the Road
Edited by Judith Babcock Wylie
ISBN 1-885-211-18-X
$17.95

"A wonderful book to read by a crackling fire."
—*Romantic Traveling*

THE GIFT OF BIRDS
True Encounters with Avian Spirits
Edited by Larry Habegger & Amy G. Carlson
ISBN 1-885-211-41-4
$17.95

"These are all wonderful, entertaining stories offering a *bird's-eye view!* of our avian friends."
—*Booklist*

A DOG'S WORLD
True Stories of Man's Best Friend on the Road
Edited by Christine Hunsicker
ISBN 1-885-211-23-6
$12.95

This extraordinary collection includes stories by John Steinbeck, Helen Thayer, James Herriot, Pico Iyer, and many others. A must for any dog and travel lover.

THE GIFT OF TRAVEL
The Best of Travelers' Tales
Edited by Larry Habegger, James O'Reilly & Sean O'Reilly
ISBN 1-885-211-25-2
$14.95

"Like gourmet chefs in a French market, the editors of Travelers' Tales pick, sift, and prod their way through the weighty shelves of contemporary travel writing, creaming off the very best."
—William Dalrymple, author of *City of Djinns*

Travel Advice

SHITTING PRETTY
How to Stay Clean and Healthy While Traveling
By Dr. Jane Wilson-Howarth
ISBN 1-885-211-47-3
$12.95

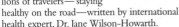

A light-hearted book about a serious subject for millions of travelers— staying healthy on the road—written by international health expert, Dr. Jane Wilson-Howarth.

THE FEARLESS SHOPPER
How to Get the Best Deals on the Planet
By Kathy Borrus
ISBN 1-885-211-39-2
$14.95

"Anyone who reads *The Fearless Shopper* will come away a smarter, more responsible shopper and a more curious, culturally attuned traveler."
—Jo Mancuso, *The Shopologist*

THE PENNY PINCHER'S PASSPORT TO LUXURY TRAVEL
The Art of Cultivating Preferred Customer Status
By Joel L. Widzer
ISBN 1-885-211-31-7
$12.95

World travel expert Joel Widzer shares his proven techniques on how to travel first class at discount prices, even if you're not a frequent flyer.

SAFETY AND SECURITY FOR WOMEN WHO TRAVEL
By Sheila Swan & Peter Laufer
ISBN 1-885-211-29-5
$12.95

A must for every woman traveler!

THE FEARLESS DINER
Travel Tips and Wisdom for Eating around the World
By Richard Sterling
ISBN 1-885-211-22-8
$7.95

Combines practical advice on foodstuffs, habits, & etiquette, with hilarious accounts of others' eating adventures.

GUTSY WOMEN
More Travel Tips and Wisdom for the Road
By Marybeth Bond
ISBN 1-885-211-61-9
$12.95

Second Edition—Packed with funny, instructive, and inspiring advice for women heading out to see the world.

GUTSY MAMAS:
Travel Tips and Wisdom for Mothers on the Road
By Marybeth Bond
ISBN 1-885-211-20-1
$7.95

A delightful guide for mothers traveling with their children—or without them!